© IAN FRAZIER

Dr. Jan Pol has been a practicing vet for almost forty years and has run his own practice in rural Weidman, Michigan, since 1981. Dr. Pol has been married to his wife, Diane, since 1967. The couple has two daughters, Kathy and Diane Jr.; one son, Charles; as well as two horses, three dogs, five cats, five peacocks, two doves, about twenty-five chickens, and who knows how many fish.

David Fisher is the author or coauthor of eighteen *New York Times* bestsellers and lives in New York.

Never
Turn Your Back on an Angus Cow

MY LIFE AS A COUNTRY VET

DR. JAN POL

with David Fisher

GOTHAM BOOKS

GOTHAM BOOKS
An imprint of Penguin Random House LLC
375 Hudson Street
New York, New York 10014

Previously published as a Gotham Books hardcover

The Library of Congress has catalogued the hardcover edition
of this book as follows:

Pol, Jan, 1942– author.
Never turn your back on an Angus cow : my life as a country vet /
Dr. Jan Pol with David Fisher.
ISBN 978-1-59240-897-9 (hardback) 978-1-59240-912-9 (paperback)
I. Fisher, David, 1946 April 16 - author. II. Title.
[DNLM: 1. Veterinarians—Michigan—Autobiography. 2. Veterinarians—
Netherlands—Autobiography. WZ 100]
SF613.B76
636.089092—dc23
[B] 2014014746

Printed in the United States of America

First trade paperback printing, August 2015

1 3 5 7 9 10 8 6 4 2

Set in Sabon · Designed by Elke Sigal

I dedicate this book to my whole family,
far and wide, who always stood by me or behind me
and pushed me so that I would finish my work.

CONTENTS

Everywhere King Piyadasi made two kinds of medicine available, medicine for people and medicine for animals. Where there were no healing herbs for people and animals, he ordered that they be bought and planted.

Egyptian *Papyrus of Kahun* (1900 BCE)

ONE

Open Your Mouth and Say Moo

Why I Became a Vet

When I was in veterinary school in the Netherlands in the 1960s, a farmer brought a cow to our clinic. "My cow is not eating," he told us, "and she is not making manure." We were all very confident students. We could diagnose everything and fix anything. So we examined this cow and discovered she had a fever, her stomach was not working, and she clearly was in some pain. All of those symptoms pointed toward hardware, meaning that the cow had swallowed a piece of metal, and then when her stomach contracted, that metal went through the wall of the stomach, causing the pain. This is very common; cows are indiscriminate eaters. A cow will eat anything you put in front of her, and too often there are little pieces of metal lying around the farmyard.

We had a brand-new X-ray machine at the college. Our

professors were proud of this because it allowed us to see what was going on inside the animal. This X-ray capability was going to change veterinary medicine; it was going to make us all smarter and better animal doctors. After we diagnosed this cow with hardware, we sent her to the new X-ray department. The X-ray came back negative. "No metal in this cow," we were told. "Look again," our professors told us. "She does not have hardware."

So then we examined this cow again. Same thing: elevated temperature, stomach's not working, pain. Diagnosis: hardware. We sent her back to the X-ray department and got the same result: "There is no metal in this cow." So the professors put her in the stable to see what would happen. And what happened was that she died. So then they sent this cow to pathology: There was the stomach, the heart, the lungs, on a table. And they said to us, "Take a look at this." And that cow had hardware.

Except that it wasn't metal, which was why that expensive X-ray machine didn't pick it up. It was a broom bristle six inches long. That cow had swallowed it and it had punctured the stomach wall and was going into the heart, and it had killed the cow. If we had listened to what that cow was telling us—*Hey, I got some hardware inside my stomach*—we would have done surgery, opened up the stomach, taken out the broom bristle, closed up the stomach, and given her some antibiotics, and she would have been fine.

So I learned how to be a hands-on veterinarian, an old-style vet. I use all the wonderful machines we have and I pay attention to what the animal's owner tells me, but mostly I look at the animal; I put my hands on the animal and I listen to what that animal is telling me. I have been practicing animal medicine for nearly a half century; I've treated just about every type of creature you can imagine, from a white mouse to a twenty-six-hundred-pound horse, and I've discovered that the longer I have been in practice, the smarter the animals have gotten!

I have spent my whole life being with animals, as a vet and as an owner. Until they start inventing new animals, I think I can say there isn't a type of animal I haven't looked in the eyes and wondered how it was feeling. My wife, Diane, and I once estimated that I've handled more than a half-million patients, without one of them ever complaining about me! In 2009 my son, Charles, who had moved to Hollywood to be in the entertainment industry, thought that people might be interested in a television reality show about a farm vet. I asked him who he thought would be interested in watching an old man who speaks with a funny accent putting his hand up the back end of a cow.

"You'd be surprised," he said.

"Yes, I would," I agreed.

"Everybody likes animals," he explained. "Every day in the practice is very different," he said. "You're dealing with life and death all the time and doing it with patients who can't tell you where it hurts. And unlike most city vets, you also have to consider the economic impact on the farmer's business. Besides," he added, "you're a character."

I didn't know if your son calling you a character was a compliment. But when he also pointed out that we would be telling the story of American farmers in the Midwest, that got me intrigued. I come from a farming family, I know how difficult that life can be, and I know that is a story very much worth telling. So I agreed to let his camera crew follow our staff for a few days, still wondering if anyone was going to watch.

It turned out Diane and I raised a smart son.

When I opened my practice outside the small town of Weidman, Michigan—which is about twelve miles from the larger and better known Mount Pleasant—in 1981, it was about 80 percent large animals, farm animals, and about 20 percent pets. It was mostly family dairy farms when we started, with several pig farmers. We took care of all their animals. But those family farms are mostly gone now; instead, we have the big concerns that supply to the chain stores, and they have their own vets. The workhorses are mostly gone too, and there are no more pig farmers. I remember that not too long after Diane and I moved to Mount Pleasant, I got a call from a farmer named Don Hatfield. Don and his brother had just taken over their uncle's dairy farm in Mecosta County, and they needed help with a calving. "We're having trouble getting the calf out of the cow," he said in his wonderfully deep voice I got to know so well. When we started talking, Don admitted he didn't know much about dairying because his uncle, who had recently died, had taken care of the cows. So I spent quite a bit of time with at the farm, helping them out, teaching them how to care for their livestock. Don's family had been on the land a long time; that barn was just about one hundred years old. He was a wonderful man whose real passion was the history of this part of central Michigan. He interviewed all the old-timers and then compiled thick books telling the story of this area. Don did okay on the farm for a long time; then he more or less retired and sold the cows. When Don quit the barn I went over there and picked up some things I found lying around that I still have, like porcelain mineral cups for the cows. "Take whatever you want," Don told me. I still hear that beautiful grumble of his voice in my head.

The next thing I knew, the farm was sold to a potato farmer, who dug a big hole and pushed the beautiful old stone house and the barn into it and covered them up. I drove by the place once and stopped to take a good look, and I couldn't even tell where the house and barn had been. All that was left standing was the electrical pole with a transformer. I just sat there for a little while staring sadly at that field and remembering the people who had once been there. A hundred years of farming history pushed into a hole.

Now my practice is about 60 percent small animals. There are basically three classes of animals: farm animals, work animals, and pets. There is obviously a big difference between them; the relationship between the farmer and his animals is based on economics. These animals are the farmer's livelihood. The relationship between pet owners and their animals is based on love. That difference doesn't matter at all to me; I treat all animals with the same concern.

I love animals; believe me, I don't remember a day of my life that I haven't loved animals. My whole family has always been comfortable with all kinds of animals. My mother used to tell us a story about her grandfather, who was said to be able to hypnotize animals. In his town in the Netherlands there was a butcher who had a big, mean German shepherd– Saint Bernard cross. My great-grandfather and the butcher met on the road, and the butcher warned him, "Watch out. He's a mean dog."

"No, he's not," my great-grandfather said.

"Oh yeah? Well, this dog will take you."

"Then go ahead and turn him loose," my great-grandfather challenged him. The butcher released the dog from his leash. My great-grandfather and that dog looked at each other. Neither one of them moved. Then the dog sat down. My great-grandfather took a step forward; the dog moved backward. And that dog was never very much of a guard dog after that.

Many people who have watched our show on the Nat Geo Wild channel know that I grew up on my father's forty-acre dairy farm in the Nazi-occupied Netherlands during World War II. We lived way out in the country, in an area that was called Wateren, and we had no electricity or running water. Wateren wasn't even a town; it was just a road with some houses on it. It was so far from everybody else that the daily newspaper came to our house a day late; it had to be delivered by the mail carrier. My dad hated that because he wanted to be on top of the news, but there was nothing we could do about it. We didn't even have a radio until 1950.

We lived in a big house, big enough for our whole family and all our livestock to be under one roof—all the livestock except the pigs. Many farmhouses in that region were built that way. There was a hallway that led directly from our living area into the cow stable, so if you had to check on a cow at night you didn't have to get dressed; you just put on your slippers and walked into the barn. We didn't have indoor plumbing, so we used to take our baths in one of the big wooden tubs in the stable behind the cows because that was always the warmest place in the house. The cows kept it warm!

Behind the cow barn was the big area where we stored the hay and wheat as well as the farm machinery in the winter, and a stable for our three horses. All of this was under one big roof. Outside was the little shed for the pigs. We couldn't keep them inside because they smelled too bad. When you grow up living with animals, you learn how to respect them.

During the war people would ride their bicycles out to our farm to get away from the city or simply to get something to eat or milk to drink. The winter of 1944 was known as the Hunger Winter because the Germans cut off most of the food supplies to punish people for supporting the Resistance. My parents never turned away one person.

I was the youngest of six children, and we all were expected to do chores every day. We had all the farm animals—we had about twenty cows, which we milked by hand; we had horses and chickens, turkeys, geese—but my protector was a Saint Bernard that would not let anybody he didn't know come too close to me. We always had big dogs, still do. I learned from my father that if a farmer doesn't have respect for an animal, that animal will not work for him. He used to tell us, "If you don't treat an animal right, that animal won't treat you right either."

My love of the animals almost got my family in terrible trouble one day. During the war we were not allowed to own anything; everything belonged to the occupier. All the production was for the benefit of the occupier. These weren't TV Nazis; they were the real thing. These people were very dangerous. They would come and inspect your farm, and if you got caught hiding anything, the best thing that would happen is they would take you to prison for a few years. Well, before I could talk, I called all cows "boo." Don't know where that came from, but to me all cows were "boo." Even with all the danger, my father would sometimes hide a calf or some of the food we grew so we would have at least a little milk and food for ourselves. One day the inspector came to see all our cows. I was just a toddler holding on to my mother's hand. As we walked around, I pointed to each of the cows and said, "Boo." But then I pointed to a closed door, the door that led to the place we were hiding that calf, and said, "Boo." My older sister tells me that everybody got very scared for a few seconds; nobody took a breath. "Boo," I said again, still pointing at the door. If that inspector opened the door, it was going to be a very bad time for us, but the inspector ignored me and kept walking. From then on I wasn't allowed anywhere near that German inspector when he came to our farm.

In those times it wasn't just livestock that we hid. For a time we sheltered a young Jewish boy who was somewhere between my age and my next oldest brother, who was seven years older than me. There was also a Jewish family hiding in a little shed, which wasn't much more than a deer-blind, in our woods. All the local people brought them food and the Nazis never found out about them.

My sister Henny tells me that my first pet was a crippled chicken. It was a chicken that had been stepped on and probably had a broken leg, so it limped or hopped. In Dutch, that's a *kreupel kipi,* crippled chicken, but the best I could pronounce it was *urpa bipi.* My sister says that my chicken stood by the door waiting for me to come outside. And I sat there with my chicken for hours, just petting it. So even then, I guess, I wanted to look after the hurt ones.

In the Netherlands at that time farmers didn't rely too much on the veterinarian. There were not many vets in the Netherlands then because, in fact, there wasn't that much they could do that farmers couldn't do by themselves. Farmers had to be self-reliant; if they weren't, they wouldn't be farming very long. If you had a cow, then you got a calf. If you had a horse, you got a foal. If you have a sheep, it gives lambs. If there was a problem, you'd better be able to fix it yourself. Only when you couldn't fix it, or your neighbor couldn't fix it, would you call the vet.

The nearest vet to us was Dr. Van der Eyck, who lived more than eight kilometers away. We didn't have a telephone, so if there was a problem, one of us had to get on our bike and ride as fast as we could to his house; when we got there we rang the doorbell and hoped he was home. There were times he was at the farm before we even got back.

The most famous vet in the Netherlands was a fictional character named Dr. Jan Vlimmen. There were several novels written about him, and there was even a movie made. But one story sums up very well the way the Dutch people thought about vets. Late one night Dr. Vlimmen's bell rang. When he answered, a man was standing there. "How much would it cost to make a farm call at this hour?" he asked.

After finding out how far away this farm was, Dr. Vlimmen told him, "That will be ten guilders."

"Good," the man said. "I will ride along with you to show you the way."

· 9 ·

So off they went. When they reached the farm, Dr. Vlimmen looked around but did not see any animals in distress. "So where is this sick cow?" he asked.

"Oh," the man admitted, "I don't really have a sick cow. It's just that you were cheaper than a taxi!"

I decided I wanted to be a vet when I was twelve years old. I can still remember the day. It wasn't because I thought I could make a successful career out of being a vet; believe me, I never even thought about the business part of it. In fact, on our very first day in school they warned us that there were very few opportunities for vets in the Netherlands and that most of us would never practice. I didn't worry about that; I became a vet because it was the only thing I ever wanted to do.

My life changed forever the day Dr. Van der Eyck drove into our yard. "Come with me," he said. I was tall and very thin, but that morning the most important thing was that I had very long arms.

As long as I can remember, I have been helping animals giving birth. There are some animals that take care of their young as soon as they are born, but not pigs. Sometimes animals are born with the afterbirth over their faces, and if it's not cleared away pretty quick, they die. A cow will lick its offspring to help it breathe, but a sow doesn't do that. The little piglets come out, and they'd better find their own way to mama's belly and start nursing, because the mom is not going to do anything to help. A lot of the piglets don't survive; that's one reason pigs have so many of them in each litter. When I was as young as six years old, my job on our farm was to sit behind the pig waiting for her babies to come out, and when they were born I cleaned them up until they were breathing on their own. I was handling newborn piglets all the time. Yes, it was slippery and there was some blood in there, but it was not dirty. It was the miracle of life in my hands; it was a very natural process. This was my job; I never even thought about it.

Dr. Van der Eyck was a typical large-animal vet; he was a big, strong man, with thick, muscled arms. We had to go to my brother's farm, he said. My brother had married and had his own farm about a half mile away. He'd bought some gilts, young female pigs that have not had their first litter, and one of them was about to give birth. The problem was that this gilt was having great difficulty because her pelvis was too small. That isn't uncommon in animals, and usually the farmer or vet will reach inside the animal and help. Dr. Van der Eyck's hands and arms were way too big to go through the pig's pelvis and grab a little one, though. So he soaped up my arm and told me exactly what I had to do.

I lay down in the straw behind the gilt and slid my hand inside its pelvis all the way up to my armpit. I reached deep inside the sow and began pulling out her piglets. In pigs it doesn't make any difference if the piglets come out headfirst or butt first. Some of them I couldn't pull all the way through, but I got them to a place where Dr. Van der Eyck could reach them. One by one they came out. And I had helped them. Oh, that feeling was fantastic. It was so much fun, and from that time I knew that I wanted to work with animals for the rest of my life.

Vets are specialists, and we specialize in every aspect of animal health and well-being. People have a special doctor they see for every part of their body; we have eye, ear, and nose specialists; heart specialists; orthopedic doctors; hand and foot doctors; and even dentists. The vet is all of those things for an animal. In fact, almost the only thing we don't do for animals is psychoanalyze them.

So we had to learn how to treat the whole animal. Utrecht University's School of Veterinary Medicine is the only vet school in the Netherlands. It's a six- or seven-year course that emphasizes what are known as large animals, basically farm animals. Pigs and goats, for example, are considered large animals. The emphasis in all of our courses was on keeping livestock healthy and productive so farmers could make money. The school was very difficult. In the Netherlands, if you graduated high school you were entitled to go to college. We paid only room and board; there was no tuition. But because of that system they made the school very, very hard to weed out people.

On my first day there were three hundred new vet students sitting more than one to a seat in a classroom built for one hundred people. By the second year more than half of them were gone. Of the dozen friends I started with, only two of us made it into a regular animal practice. The others went into teaching or into research, became slaughterhouse directors, or worked in other places, but only the two of us became practicing vets.

People had come to the school for different reasons. Some of them were there because their fathers had been vets, so they became vets. There were students there who didn't even like animals very much, and we even had a few students who were allergic to them. You could see by the way they handled animals that they were indifferent; to them it was a job. Not for me. For me, it was a calling.

The veterinary school was spread out over several long blocks in the city, with stables on both sides of the road where they kept the animals we worked on. We had departments of Surgery and Internal Diseases, we had Obstetrics and Technology and Anatomy and even a museum, where they displayed all the abnormal animals. The small-animal clinic was outside this area. We had only five minutes between classes, and the school was so big it was impossible to walk from one place to another, so as soon as a class ended we all hopped on our bikes and raced to the next classroom. The classrooms were mostly amphitheaters with our seats arranged in a semicircle looking down at the podium.

Our first two years were exactly the same as premed and predental; we wore jackets and ties to class every day, and we learned all the parts of the body. Many body parts are universal; they may not look exactly the same in two different animals, or even between people and animals, but they perform similar functions. We started by learning the bones. They had piles of bones in the lab and we just grabbed bones and with the help of a professor and our books we learned the names of every hole and point and surface of every bone—in Latin. It was all memorization, and oh, it was boring. We had to learn every single bone. Those first two years we never even touched a live animal.

We also dissected animals, large animals and small animals, front quarters and rear quarters; they even had a freeze-dried cow cut in half lengthwise and crosswise so we could see how everything was working. Today an artist does that same thing and puts it in plastic and then sells it to a museum for millions of dollars. We didn't know we were looking at art.

But what I learned from that is that bodies are put together so fantastically, it is beautiful to learn how it all works.

The second year was the hardest for me because we studied organic chemistry. I managed to stumble through it, but after that we got separated from the medical and the dental students and started studying veterinary medicine, which is when it became fun for me.

At one time, I remember, we needed a microscope for microbiology and I couldn't borrow one. I wrote to my father and told him it cost 600 guilders, which was about $175. You bet that was expensive for a Dutch dairy farmer. So my father sold a cow to pay for my microscope. I used that microscope for years, and I still have it. I wouldn't sell that, ever.

Our third year, most of our classes focused on animal care. We still had to learn about plants and spore technology; we had to be able to recognize what we were looking at under that 600-guilder microscopes and know what it meant and what to do about it. But mostly it was theory and textbooks.

It was in our fourth year that we began actually working with live animals. At Utrecht our teachers taught respect for animals; animals were creatures of God and it was our job to take care of them. But they were clear that these were animals, not human beings, and we shouldn't mistake them or treat them as equal to humans. It was never, *Oh, poor baby this*. No, a cow had a calf, not a baby. Dogs had puppies, not babies. A horse had a foal, not a baby. But, oh my gosh, if you ever mistreated an animal, you would be branded with that forever. The animals were not there to be hit or abused; they weren't there for us to take out our anger. As I learned in my career, sometimes for your own safety it becomes necessary to show an animal who's the boss; but that was rare and never, ever abusive. We learned to take care of them to the best of our ability, while never forgetting that they were animals.

And we learned that we weren't there to save every animal. On the farm every animal is worth money and the farmer has to make a living off that animal. And to do that the farmer has to take care of it. If you don't take care of the cow, it won't produce milk; if you don't take care of the horse, it won't pull for you or ride for you. We were taught all the time that on the farm the animals have to fill certain needs, so the farmer who doesn't take care of them will be out of business.

We didn't spend too much time in that school studying small animals—dogs and cats and even smaller. But in my practice I've learned there is a financial balance that needs to be considered where pets are concerned too. I am sorry to admit that there are a few small-animal vets who will shame people into spending money for tests and treatments they don't want or can't afford, when the outcome—sometimes it's a sad outcome—can't be changed.

Having grown up on a farm, I was more comfortable being around live animals than many of my fellow students. I knew that when I was examining an animal, for example, the most important thing for me to do was to let that animal know where I was at all times. Animals will defend themselves when they are threatened, and they are threatened by anything un-usual or unexpected. For that reason I learned that as I moved around an animal I should keep talking in a calm voice or touching the animal as much as possible to make sure that it knows that I'm not a danger. My brother told me a story about an animal trainer who worked in a circus. This man always kept a colorful bandanna tied around his waist underneath his shirt. When a new horse came to the circus, he would walk by its pen and throw the bandanna in there with the horse. The horse would find it, smell it, and probably play with it a little bit. A short time later the trainer would walk up and he would have the same smell as the bandanna. The horse would say, *Hey, I know this guy. I don't associate anything bad or dangerous with him. C'mon in, everything is fine.*

And just as important, I learned that the one thing a vet should never do, under any circumstances, is turn his or her back on an animal. I remember one time we had an animal trainer come in to do a demonstration of this for us. In those days they were still catching wild animals to sell to zoos. He had three tigers in a six-by-six, ten-foot-long traveling cage. He walked in front of that cage and those tigers backed up; they were practically on top of one another to get away from him. He was about fifteen feet away from them. "Now," he told us, "watch this."

He turned his back on them. He hadn't even finished completing his turn when all three of them hit the front of that cage so hard the cage moved. If that door had popped open, I don't know where I would have run. But it was a message not one of us ever forgot: You turn your back on these animals and they will get you. Every matador knows that—and so does every farmer or rancher. Most of the large animals I have dealt with are bigger and stronger than any person—but they don't know it. These aren't pets; a cow is not a sweet, docile animal. It is an animal that can kill a person without even intending to, without even knowing it. When I'm examining an animal, I'm always in a place where I can very quickly jump over a gate or a fence or get behind some other kind of barrier. And there have been times in my career when an animal has helped me get over a fence.

But for many people their careers as vets begin the day they stick their hands inside an animal's butt for the first time. The concept of it probably makes people much more uncomfortable than actually doing it. Mostly it's very warm inside a cow; the temperature is about 102 degrees. On a very cold day in a drafty barn, it will keep you warm. It's not uncomfortable at all. And the cow doesn't seem to mind.

One time the Nat Geo Wild TV crew was filming me doing pregnancy tests, and when I finished I asked if any of them wanted to try it. A few hands went up, but they went up pretty slowly. And everybody looked around to see who else had his or her hand up. I told them, for many people, putting your hand up a cow's butt is a once-in-a-lifetime experience. And when they went back to their homes and people asked them what they were doing, they would be able to tell them very nicely, well, there was this cow . . .

In class when they taught us how to do a rectal exam, some of my classmates were pretty nervous. I'd done it for the first time when I was twelve, but many of my fellow students had never done it. In the Netherlands, vets didn't use plastic gloves; they would take off their shirts and go in bare-handed. When you were done your arm was green; believe me, we came home dirty. Thank goodness by the time we graduated they let us use gloves.

Our instructor would give the cow a tranquilizer and

stand on the animal's right side. "Okay," he told us, "get your shirt off and reach in there." Some students were pretty tentative, but that cow didn't feel a thing. She was just standing there chewing her cud. Once your hand was inside, the instructor would guide it to all the different organs, through a hole in the cow's side. The instructor wanted us to know what everything felt like in a healthy animal so we would recognize problems: "This is what the uterus feels like. Now follow it to the end; here's an ovary."

If you were right-handed, you were taught to use your left hand, so your more coordinated hand was free to give a shot to the animal if necessary or make a note or do whatever else had to be done. I always close my eyes when I do a pregnancy test so I can see with my fingers. My fingers tell me exactly what is going on in there. Many years later I tore some muscles in my left arm when a cow pulled away from me, so for three or four weeks I couldn't work with my left hand. One day I was doing a pregnancy check with my right hand and the farmer started laughing. "What's so funny?" I asked him. And he told me my left hand was moving whichever way I wanted my right hand to move, as if it was telling my right hand what to do. After many years of doing the same thing thousands of times with one hand, my brain was trying to adjust to doing it with my other hand.

Most times cows give birth without too much difficulty. Farmers usually take care of normal deliveries because it would be much too expensive if they had to call a vet for every birth in the herd. So vets get called only when there is a problem, which means that most of the time we deal with difficult births. We studied all types of problems in school: Often the calf or the foal was positioned wrong and couldn't fit through the pelvis, or it had died already and was rotting inside. We had to learn how to manipulate it so it could be delivered or, when it was necessary, cut the dead foal or calf up into pieces so we could get it out.

The farmers who lived near the vet school knew that if a cow was delivering and had any problems, they could call the school and a vet would come right out with two or three students. For the school it was a teaching opportunity; for the farmer it was a way of getting good professional treatment at a very low cost, as well as getting some good entertainment. The farmers knew that we students didn't know what we were doing, and they would stand on the side, watching, with big smiles on their faces. The more we struggled, the more they enjoyed it. I remember one of the first times I went out on one of these lessons, the cow was trying to deliver but the calf wasn't moving. Our professor reached in there first. Okay, he knew what was going on. He told one of my classmates, "Get in there. What do you feel?"

It was a uterine twist, a condition in which the whole uterus is twisted around like a plastic bag. We had all read about it, we had watched the lecture, but this was the first time any of us had to actually tried to fix it. We approached the problem with all the confidence of students: The best way to deal with that is to lay the cow on its side, hold on to the uterus, and roll the cow over. You're actually untwisting the problem. Sometimes, though, it's possible to shift the calf inside the cow.

"Okay," our teacher said to the first student, "get it out." That student began shifting his body, moving around, but nothing was happening. The sweat started coming down his face. A minute went by, two minutes. "Okay, get out of there. Next."

The next student stepped up. "You feel the twist?" Yes. "Get it out." Two minutes, he started sweating. "Okay, get out. Next." When my turn came, I felt pretty confident I could do this. I remembered my lessons: If the twist is to the left, then you have to flip the uterus to the right in order to get the twist out. I took my shirt off and reached in; the twist was to the left, I decided. I thought this through and started applying gentle pressure. But that thing didn't move. I had to push a little harder. That thing still didn't move. Now I was getting more determined and a little anxious. I pushed harder. I was determined to be the student who solved the problem. Now I was really starting to sweat. "Okay," the teacher said, "two minutes. Get out."

The farmers were shaking their heads. This was a great show for them.

The teacher reached inside the cow again, but this time he did a little of this, a little of that, and within a few seconds took his hands out and stepped back. "Okay. Now feel. Is it straight?" We all reached in. The uterus was straight. We had no idea how he had done that until he explained, "If it doesn't go one way, try the other way." We had all thought the twist was to the left, so we were trying to twist to the right. If we had twisted to the left, it would have easily been straightened. It was a good lesson for all of us, and a good laugh for the farmers.

Eventually we all learned how to work inside an animal. Before those days, cowhides had been pretty valuable, especially calves' skin, so we were even taught how to cut the hide off a dead calf while it was still inside, before we had to cut the calf into pieces to remove it from the cow. Now we use an instrument that is known as the Utrecht fetotome, which is basically two handles held together by a piece of thin wire, which is used to cut apart a dead animal trapped inside the uterus. We never do a C-section for a dead calf, because it would kill the cow; instead we work inside the cow and cut the calf apart to save the cow.

One night, I remember, a cow came in with a calf that was way too big to fit through the pelvis. The vet in charge right then had just graduated ahead of us, so we all knew him very well. I was with three other students. Somebody had been working on this animal trying to get the calf out, but the cow was all swollen inside. We started cutting and got part of the calf out; then we got a hook on the calf's pelvis and pulled, but the cow's swelling was so bad, we couldn't pull the calf out.

If we couldn't get the remains of that calf out, that cow was going to die.

The new veterinarian was just as scared as we were. We tried everything we had learned without being able to get it out. I was the tallest, so I said, "Let me try one more time." I lay out flat on the ground behind the cow. Two people were standing by my feet so I could push hard against them. I stretched as far as I possibly could inside that cow—I was inside up to my shoulder—and I just grabbed the calf and pulled it into a better position. Two of us cut the pelvis in half, and we got it out. That was the first cow I saved. We treated the cow for infection, and the cow got up and a few days later went back to the farm. I can remember that feeling of satisfaction so well. That was the first time I felt like I was a real vet.

Our final year in school we did rounds, learning how to diagnose problems—and learning that sometimes those problems were with the owner as well as the animal. You could call it barnside manner. I remember when I was working in the small animal clinic a lady came in with her boxer. Usually I don't remember what the client looked like; instead I remember the animal. But this was a very big lady and she was bringing in a very big dog. They were a perfect pair. This dog was so fat that it had no defined neck. She couldn't even keep a collar on it. The lady complained that her dog must be sick because it wasn't eating. When an animal stops eating, it often is a sign of a significant problem. Our professor carefully examined the dog and found nothing wrong. It didn't have a high temperature, he found no unusual bumps, its color was good; everything seemed normal. None of us had anything to suggest: Why would an apparently healthy dog suddenly stop eating? It was a mystery for all the students. And then the professor made his diagnosis: The dog wasn't eating because it wasn't hungry. She had fed it so much that the dog finally said, *Look, lady, I can't eat anymore. I'm not sick; I'm full!*

That was probably the one diagnosis we hadn't considered. The dog was being killed by love. The answer was standing on two feet only a few feet away from us. What we had to do was learn how to look for the most obvious cause. The woman had forgotten the most important lesson: This was a dog; this was not a person. In this case the cure was a simple one: Stop overfeeding your dog.

In our last year we had to spend six weeks working in a slaughterhouse to learn how to properly inspect meat. All the veterinarians in the Netherlands had to be qualified meat inspectors because we had a lot of slaughterhouses and not enough vets to certify that the meat was safe. Being in a slaughterhouse is not something anybody looks forward to, but it was an important part of our education. We each had a big butcher knife that we used to inspect lymph nodes. As hard as it is for some people to accept, large animals are commodities; many of them are raised to be slaughtered, and the job of the vet is to make sure that meat is safe for human consumption. It isn't a task anybody can enjoy, but it is a necessary part of the job of a large-animal vet. In my practice farmers sometimes butchered their own animals, and if they had any doubts they called me to come and make sure the meat was safe to eat. I'd walk up to the carcass and stick my nose in it. Most people would say, "Ugh, that stinks." But fresh meat has a certain smell. Many people may not like that smell, but I learned in the slaughterhouse what normal meat smells like. If it smelled good, it probably was good to eat. Then I'd look at the lymph nodes and make my determination. My motto was, If I don't want to eat it, I'm going to tell you it's no good to eat.

The slaughterhouse was in Utrecht. Each day they slaughtered a different animal: one day cows, the next day horses, the next day pigs. Different people worked on different animals; people who worked on pigs would not work on cows or horses. The people who were doing the slaughtering got paid by the piece, so they worked as quickly as they could. But the organs had to stay with each carcass until the meat inspector had completed the inspection. The workers wanted to get as much work done as possible, while we students wanted to be slow and careful to be sure we were doing a good job. Sometimes we got a little behind. And when that happened those guys had a trick they used.

They were slaughtering pigs one day and I was doing my job carefully, as I had been taught, checking every lymph node. No one was going to get sick eating bad meat that I had approved. I was standing between two carcasses hanging from a rail, when *vroom!* Some of the slaughterhouse workers shoved the line forward, and before I could move I got caught between the carcasses, pushed inside a pig. I had to worm my way out. And from then on I knew to stand by the side of the carcasses—not between them—when I did my inspection. That's how you learn.

Many people wonder how it is possible to accept the slaughter of animals. People who work with animals—farmers, for example—understand that God made them on earth for us to use. Not abuse; use. In this case it meant finding a way to kill them quick and with no pain. The people who did this were skilled workers. It was just a different skill than you see from a carpenter or plumber. It's a gruesome job, but they did it in such a way to ensure that at least the animals didn't suffer. In a strange way I admired them, because I couldn't do their job. I think every vet will agree that the most difficult part of our job is putting down an animal, especially an animal that has been cared for and loved for many years. No matter how often I've done it, I still don't like it. And many times, tears come to my eyes too. I don't let people see me, but I do tear up. I also know when I do it that it is the best thing for the animal. I made a promise to myself while I was working in that slaughterhouse that I would never allow an animal to suffer. So when I do have to put down an animal, a dog or a cat or a horse, that animal is first getting an anesthetic. My animals get an anesthetic first. And only when they are quiet and at peace do I give them the final injection. There are others who do it differently. I don't care; this is my way.

I was very glad when I finished that phase of my training. You bet. I had gone to vet school because I wanted to learn how to help animals.

I was not the best student. I have always had a hard time learning from books. I learn best from watching. Show me how something is done and I'll remember it. Show me a surgery one time and I can do it the next time. What made it even more difficult for me was the fact that I'm color-blind. That made pathology especially hard. I couldn't make the diagnoses that were based on the color of the tissue. We sat in a dark classroom and the instructor projected color slides on a screen as he explained, "This is pneumonia. You can tell by the color."

Not me; I couldn't tell by the color. For our final exam they showed the slides and we had to identify the disease. I did just well enough to pass. But the next year they put organs on a table—all kinds of organs from all kinds of animals. We had to identify the animal, the organ, and the problem with it. That was easy for me. At the end the professor stopped me and asked, "You know everything that's here. Last year you had so much trouble. Why?"

"I'm color-blind," I told him, "and the teaching is backward. Last year it was, 'Here's a color picture of a diseased organ; tell me what you see.' It was backward for me. But this year it's exactly the opposite: 'Here is the diseased organ; what is the organ and what is the disease?' That I have no problem with."

I graduated from the school with my degree in veterinary medicine, a plan for my future, and an American wife. The wife had come first. I had come to the United States in 1961 as a high school exchange student, mostly because it was an opportunity to see my sister again. In 1955 my sister and her husband had moved to Ontario, Canada, because they had an opportunity to farm there. Canada needed farmers. There was just not enough land for farmers in the Netherlands. In those days transatlantic travel was not easy, so when people left Europe, there was always the fear that their family might not see them again. When the notice was posted offering an opportunity to live and study in Michigan for a school year, I paid special attention to it. I looked at a map of North America, and on that map Michigan and Ontario looked fairly close together. I told my parents, "Look at this. I can go to Michigan and you can come visit and we can go see Henny." I applied for the program and was accepted, and my life was changed forever.

Like most of my classmates, that was my first time on an airplane. While for many people the concept of going to live in America might be exciting or scary, the Dutch are pretty stoic; we tend to accept things as they happen without showing a great amount of emotion. I suppose I was nervous and excited, but I don't remember those feelings. Mostly I was curious. It took eighteen hours to fly from Amsterdam to Detroit. We arrived in the middle of August. I spoke a passable

British English. We were told that within three months we would be dreaming in English, but for me it was only two weeks.

I didn't know too much about America. My sister and her husband lived in a rural area in Canada—many of their neighbors didn't even have electric power—so I knew from her that life in North America was rough. The land was not as arable as it was at home, so instead of four crops a year they could have only two. Henny and her husband didn't complain; we had grown up on a dairy farm, so we had learned how to work hard. But they certainly didn't write to us that life was easier or better in North America than it was in Holland.

I stayed with the Dalrymple family in the small town of Mayville, Michigan. I was eighteen years old and in the same grade as their daughter, Diane. Some people wonder why a family with a teenage daughter would invite a teenage boy to live in their home, but this was a very different time socially. I don't remember anybody even questioning it then. Diane and I quickly became friends. I remember my first impression of her: *Man, she's tall.* We were very much the same in many ways, but especially in our love of animals. Her family had dogs and cats and chickens, although their neighbors didn't like the chickens waking them up early in the morning or scratching up their gardens. When Diane was in second grade, her school mascot was a wildcat, so her father went into the woods and caught a woodchuck. For a school parade he decorated a wagon, then put the woodchuck in a cage on the wagon and told everybody it was a wildcat. There is a wonderful picture of Diane's father sitting on the porch with his pet woodchuck right next to him.

I had my crippled chicken; when Diane was seven she got a pet duck. Well, it turned out to be two pet ducks. She had won the first little baby duck playing a game at the town carnival. She named her Patrick. Patrick must've thought that Diane was her mother, because she just followed her everywhere. There was a trapeze in Diane's backyard, but to reach it she had to climb up on a sawhorse that her father had built. One day she went to play on the trapeze and accidently tripped over the sawhorse, which fell on the duck, killing it.

Oh my God, you would have thought she had intentionally killed her . . . her pet duck. Diane was devastated. Her parents didn't know what to do, so they found another duck and brought it home. Its name also was Patrick. Diane and Patrick used to play tag. She would tap him and run away and he would chase after her and try to peck her. But by the time she got into high school, she didn't have too much time to play with her duck, so she gave it to friends who raised ducks. She would go over to their pond sometimes to make sure he was doing all right. The first few times he probably recognized her, but then he got too busy being a duck, and she lost track of him.

How could anybody not find a woman who played tag with her pet duck attractive? But we liked each other as friends so much, it didn't even occur to us that maybe we were also falling in love.

I didn't have any trouble adjusting to the American culture, if you want to call *The Three Stooges* television show culture. But one of my first memories was seeing one of Diane's girlfriends, a little tiny girl, driving into the yard in a big Buick. I looked, but I could hardly even see her behind the steering wheel. That impressed me; in the Netherlands every-body had a small car—Volkswagen bugs, for example—and I was more used to watching big people somehow managing to squeeze into these little cars. So watching this little girl drive in, my first impression was, *Wow, everything about this place is big.* There was so much space. That I liked a lot.

At the end of the school year I went back to the Nether-lands to start vet school and Diane went to college to study education at Michigan State. We wrote to each other every month, and both of us found that more and more the other people we were dating didn't measure up. During my first year of college, my father was diagnosed with bone cancer. Be-cause he couldn't get around so well anymore, we had to sell the cows; two of them sold for much more money than we ever knew they were worth. When my father was no longer able to take care of his cows I began to understand how seri-ous this was. My parents had visited America while I was there and met Diane and her parents, so when my father got sick, I wrote to Diane that if she wanted to see him alive again, she had better come pretty quick.

She came in the summer of 1964. While she was there, my cousin got married, my sister had a baby, and my father con-tinued to suffer and eventually died. Those last months of his life Diane and I sat by my father's bed late in the night making sure he had his pain pills if he woke up. My father didn't speak English and at that time Diane didn't speak Dutch, but they managed to communicate. He was a smoker and she filled his pipe for him when he couldn't do it any longer. Whatever he needed, she figured it out and got it for him. And when she wasn't helping him, she was doing chores in the house so my mother was more free to be with him. In hard times like that, you really learn whom you can depend on, who will be there when you need them. That was Diane, always quietly, always without a complaint, she would be there to help. We got close to each other.

My father died on the day Diane was scheduled to fly back to Michigan. She stayed a few more days for his funeral, then flew home. After that I spent a lot of time going back and forth between my house and the school, trying to help my mother. During that time I learned how to cook, how to sew—I almost learned how to knit—so I became basically a Jan of all trades. And for the next two years, while Diane and I were both still in school, we got to know each other better by mail. The mail was the only way to make a very long-distance romance work in those days. When I came back to America in 1966, we had already decided to get engaged.

For the next year we made all our wedding plans by mail. For example, Diane would write to ask me what color brides-maids dresses I wanted: pink or purple. I wrote, "No, I like yellow." She wrote, "Yellow?" I wrote, "Yes, it's a color I can see real good." The bridesmaids wore yellow. It was a very small wedding; Diane was an only child and she had several uncles and aunts. But it was a wedding with a lot of love in it. For our quick honeymoon, we spent three days at a little beach in the Thumb of Michigan; it's called that because the lower part of the state looks like a mitten—with a thumb. Then we sailed on a boat to Rotterdam so I could get back to school.

Looking back, that must have been devastating to her parents. At that time it wasn't so common to fly across the Atlantic. Their only child was going to live in Europe and they didn't know when they would see her again. But I already knew that we weren't going to be staying in the Netherlands. There was no need for more practicing veterinarians, and I wanted that feeling that I got when I put my hands on animals.

That was almost five decades ago. But I still have that feeling. It never went away.

There was no student housing at the school; the students lived in whatever apartment they could afford in the city. I could never afford too much, so I rented an apartment on the upper floor of the three-story home of Mr. and Mrs. Rietveld, very near the school. Just a few months after I'd moved in, Mr. Rietveld died of lung cancer, so I became the fix-it man for the next few years. If anything had to be fixed, it was my job. Mrs. Rietveld needed shelves put in: "Jan, would you put in the shelves, please." A switch had to be repaired: That was my job.

A lot of the vet students lived in the area, and here is something most people don't think is true: Vet students can be very wild. We were the rough-and-tumble school in the university. We were the young people who were going to work on farms, with big animals, so we had to be strong. Oh, we definitely were strong. Some of the other students thought maybe because we wanted to work on farms that we weren't that smart. We were smart enough to know better. Naturally when my friends found out that I had married an American lady, they all wanted to meet her. How do you meet in the Netherlands? With a beer party. I don't remember too much about it except we started the night with five hundred nice glasses and by the next morning only fifty were left. Even counting some of them twice.

We lived in my attic apartment, and Diane got accepted as a substitute teacher at the American Air Force base. As soon as we got to Utrecht, she started studying Dutch, which is not a simple language to learn, but within eight weeks she was able to read a Dutch newspaper and even have a conversation in the language. It took her six months to get a full-time teaching job. With the money she was earning, we were able to buy our first car; naturally, our little Volkswagen.

Our plan was to return to Michigan after I graduated. Animals are animals; they have a pretty good sense who to trust, even if you have a funny accent. I had written several letters to the state to find out what I needed to do to get my license. This was my first encounter with the American bureaucracy, and the bureaucracy won. All these years later, I still haven't stopped fighting it when necessary. Getting my license required passing several tests and getting letters of recommendation from practicing vets. Diane and I moved to Mayville and I started working with a local vet, Dr. Drysdale, who lived about a half block from Diane's parents; he didn't pay me, but he could write that letter I needed.

Dr. Drysdale was a very nice man. He was a Scotsman, and he looked like a large-animal vet; he was big and tall and very strong. When he made a farm call he never had a doubt he was going to be able to figure out the problem and fix it. When he couldn't, and that happened, he took it personally. Right from the beginning he treated me with professional respect, sometimes asking me to help him do something even before he knew if I could do it. One of the first farm calls we made was for a calving. At the college we had been taught that when doing a calving you had to get both arms inside the cow. Both arms! The professors warned us, you can't work with just one hand because then you might rupture the uterus. One time a student who couldn't get both arms inside had his ass kicked; literally, the professor kicked his butt. Believe me, ass kickings make memorable lessons. Dr. Drysdale had big, thick arms and this was not a big cow, so he was struggling to get both arms inside. After trying for about a half hour, he asked me, "Jan, can you spell me for a minute?"

I was already thinking, *What can I do?* I was a proud graduate of one of the best veterinary colleges in the world, so I had all my lessons in my head. I ripped my shirt off, got both of my long, thin arms in there, and felt around, trying to figure out what the problem was. In this case the calf's head was turned, so he couldn't be moved. I knew that problem; we had worked on it in the clinic. The calf's head had to be straightened out; the difficulty in doing that is when you grab the head with one hand you can't hang on to it. So what I had learned to do is take my middle fingers and put them in the eye sockets of the calf. Animals are a lot more resilient than people think: you can push those eyes way into the head without causing any pain or damage. So I got one hand in there; then I squiggled around until my other hand was in there, grabbed hold of the eye sockets with my middle fingers, and straightened up the head. Within five minutes we pulled it out, alive and pretty quickly kicking.

The farmer looked at Dr. Drysdale, then looked at me. Then he looked back at Dr. Drysdale. It was pretty obvious what he was thinking: This big guy spent a half hour working and he couldn't get it; this kid got it out in five minutes. I didn't say anything, but you bet I felt bad. It was embarrassing to Dr. Drysdale, but what else could I do? That calf had to come out or the cow was going to die; getting the calf out alive made me feel very good. All Dr. Drysdale ever said to me was, "Thank you, that was very good."

But after that there were a couple of times that he had a calving while he was in the middle of something else and he called me up and asked me to go do it. I wasn't legally allowed to do that, but the time is expired so I admit to it now. I passed the board exams in Michigan and Ohio; in Ohio I had to stand behind a podium while four people asked me questions. One of the questions, I remember, was what to do for a cow whose uterus is out. Well, I told them, first put something underneath to keep it clean because if it gets infected there isn't too much to be done. What I do is take it straight back, wash it up, and then carefully just knead it back in. I went through a very specific explanation. But then I noticed the people were laughing at me. I was wondering what the heck was going on. This was a very important examination and the people who had to pass me thought something I'd said was pretty funny. That wasn't such a good sign.

Then I found out the reason: My whole life I've talked with my hands. I need my hands to explain my words; that's probably why I never smoked. But as I was answering the question, I was doing it step-by-step with my hands. I was cleaning and kneading. Once I found that out, I started laughing too.

Once I passed the tests, I started looking for my first real job. At Utrecht they had taught us how to be good vets, but they hadn't taught us how to earn a living being a vet. That was not the purpose of the school. But from my father I had learned about the economics of farming, so I understood the needs of farmers and their sometimes-limited ability to pay for services. Farmers use vets for very specific purposes: pregnancy checks, health certifications, tests and inoculations, those things that have to be done regularly to keep the animals healthy. But it is the other problems, the unexpected problems, the difficult births, the infections, the accidents, and the mysterious illnesses that cause them to call the vet at other times. For a farm vet especially, most of the work is routine. When we go to a farm we don't expect to find a new disease that they can name after us: Dr. Pol's Big Infection. Those days are long gone, and anything that is new or different is going to be discovered in the laboratory, not the barn. But the job can bring with it great satisfaction. I couldn't wait to get started.

Diane and I looked around for a good place to start our career. Most veterinary practices consist of the owner and as many assistants as needed, depending on the size of the business. After a few years, the assistants move along for the same reasons people in any other profession move: a better opportunity. Unlike in the Netherlands, there were jobs available. We finally accepted a job as the second assistant to Dr. Arnold Hentschl in Harbor Beach, Michigan, for the salary of $10,400.

It was almost exclusively a farm practice; his clients were mostly small dairy farms, family farms—just what I liked: cattle, horses, and pigs. Dr. Hentschl taught me the importance of using brains rather than brawn to help make the farmers money. He liked to do the small animal work. Dr. Hentschl and his wife, Anna Marie, helped Diane and me learn how the business of being a vet worked. Harbor Beach was right at the tip of Michigan's Thumb; it was a very flat area with fertile soil—in some ways it was like Holland. I spent the first few weeks riding with Dr. Hentschl and his assistant Dr. Arbaugh, just getting to know the clients and letting them get to know me. Dr. Arbaugh was a big guy; in those days a lot of large-animal vets seemed to be big guys, but he was easygoing and very knowledgeable about the profession. He knew his animals. He was also the president of the local school when the teachers went on strike—and Diane was one of those teachers who walked out with them! We're vets, we agreed, and just didn't talk about that.

There were a lot of German and Polish immigrants farming in that area, and they were nice people, but pretty direct in their opinions. That worked well for me; the only way I knew how to do the job was to be direct and honest. There have been times when I've had to give my clients the worst possible news about their animal. That's never an easy thing to do, but it doesn't help anyone to be less than completely candid. My first concern has always been the animal; how do I keep the animal healthy, and if it is too sick, how do I make sure it doesn't suffer?

It was during those first few weeks riding with Dr. Hentschl that I learned a very important lesson that I have always taught to my own assistants: When you make a farm call, always turn your car or truck around before you get out. There are three reasons for that: First, all our tools are in the back, so this provides good access to them. Second, it seems there are always young children on a farm; this way you don't have to back up and risk an accident. And third and sometimes most important, if it should become necessary it helps you make a quick getaway.

TWO

A Practice of My Own

W hen you have a large-animal practice like Dr. Hentschl did in Harbor Beach, there is hardly a night when there isn't some kind of emergency. It seemed like our phone was always ringing and I would have to race out in the middle of the night to help with a calving or figure out why a cow was down. I don't claim that I am the best veterinarian, but having grown up on a dairy farm, I understood the importance of every animal and maybe tried a little harder. To some vets a cow is just another cow, and there is always another one to replace it. So if it's sick or gets hurt, they figure the farmer can just ship it out. But I understand that a cow has the potential to give a farmer up to $4,000 worth of milk in a year, and if the farmer loses that cow, he loses that money plus what it costs to replace her.

Once Dr. Hentschl sent me out to a farm in a very small town called Parisville. At that time there were still some

DPs—displaced persons, who had been chased out of Eastern Europe by the Russians—living in the area. This farm was run by an elderly couple from Poland and their children: one son and two daughters, who did the work. One of the daughters had called and explained that their cows were bloated. That isn't usually a serious problem. But it was to these people; to them it may have meant the difference between survival and losing their land.

It wasn't much of a farm, really. They had a few cows, which they milked by hand—there was no modern machinery on that farm—and a small garden. All they did was try to exist, try to stay alive. As soon as I drove onto the farm I recognized it in my soul. I understood their struggle; they hadn't been able to integrate into the community. Whatever money they were going to pay me was going to affect their lives. This is the kind of problem every vet has to deal with all the time. You can't forget you're running a business, and the bills have to be paid, but when you see the opportunity to help someone who could really use it, you try to find the right way to do so. My belief has always been that if you're passionate about something, the money will follow. For veterinarians, just like medical doctors, the first thing is always do no harm; but doing nothing because the owner cannot afford the treatment is doing harm to the animal. That was my belief, but it was Dr. Hentschl's practice. There were times we clashed about it. I understood that the money pressures on him were different from those I faced, and later when I opened my own practice and had to deal with those same problems, I tried to remember that feeling.

The parents didn't speak English. I looked at their cows,

and as their daughter had reported, several of them were bloated, blown way up. Just like a medical doctor, I usually began my examination by asking a few questions. The cause quickly became obvious. It had rained hard the night before; then the farmers had put the cows out to pasture, which was alfalfa. The combination of water and fresh alfalfa causes foam, and that foam was the cause of the bloating. It was easily solved with a big dose of mineral oil. To prevent it from happening again, I told them, "Don't let the cows out in the morning. You feed them hay in the barn first. When they have a bellyful you can turn them loose." That was it; they never had that problem again.

While I got my medical knowledge at Utrecht, I got my education during the ten years Diane and I spent working for Dr. Hentschl in Harbor Beach. I spent the first month I worked there going on calls with him, basically so he could introduce me to the farmers and show me how he did things. Then I began going out on calls by myself. Even though I had confidence, I have to admit I was pretty nervous. At first I continued doing things the way Dr. Hentschl had shown me because the farmers were used to it, but pretty soon I decided, *Oh, this takes too long; it doesn't have to be done this way.* For example, to take out the afterbirth, Dr. Hentschl put on a special rubber sleeve that fit all the way over his shoulder, and then he added an apron to it. You almost had to dress up to get the job done. After putting all that stuff on several times, I thought, *This is ridiculous. We have plastic gloves; they'll work just as well.* Sure, if a glove broke my hand would stink a little, so then I'd have to wash it, which I was doing already. A simple plastic glove got the job done just as well as the whole body sleeve and the apron, and nobody ever noticed the difference.

I started by doing the simple jobs, like pregnancy tests, and gradually began working more difficult cases. Then I began making my own diagnoses, and that helped build my confidence. When Dr. Hentschl began depending on me to help him when he was having a tough time getting a calf out, I knew I had the skills to be successful. At first I tried to do everything by myself to prove that I was capable, but one Sunday morning I got a call that a cow had a prolapse. When I got to the barn, the cow was standing still, but its uterus, which was about three feet long, was hanging only six inches off the ground. That's not an especially difficult problem—you can push it back in—but one person can't do the job. The people there were no help. They thought this was funny, which really ticked me off. I had them holding an apron under the uterus to keep it off the floor to prevent infection. I stood there and stuffed the uterus back into the cow, and just as I got it all in, the cow strained and it fell out. That caused those fellas to laugh even harder, which made me even more upset. I stuffed it in again; it popped out again; they laughed harder. Finally I was secure enough to ask for help. When you're starting out you don't like to ask for help; you want to prove you're capable of doing everything yourself. You actually have to be pretty secure to admit that you need some help.

Dr. Arbaugh had been at a party the night before, so his head wasn't completely clear. But he came by and together we managed to get the uterus back into that cow.

It was in Harbor Beach that I learned how to be a vet and run a practice. Be honest with your clients. That was always first. Work hard, and if you don't know what the problem is, don't be afraid to admit it. Tell the clients what you find and tell them what you think it is. They will respect you for that. If you don't know, treat the animal to the best of your ability and learn from that treatment. If you're not sure, go back the next day, and if that treatment didn't work, try the next thing that your mind tells you might be effective.

I learned what I thought was the right way to do things, but I also saw things that I disagreed with. Arnie Hentschl was a good vet, and he ran his practice in the way that was right for him, but it wasn't for me. For example, we were paid a base salary and a percentage of the business we brought in. I didn't like that because it encouraged us to charge our clients more, and even to sell medicines that might or might not have been completely necessary. There was absolutely nothing done dishonestly—nothing—but for me it made the financial aspect of the profession almost as important as the client. Even then I knew that when I had my own practice everybody would share in the profits.

Also, while everyone in the practice respected one another, there was not a lot of camaraderie. We were colleagues, not friends. Dr. Hentschl and I got along, but we got along better when one of us was out on the road. As much as I loved the work, it always felt like a job, and admittedly after all that time I didn't think I was being paid fairly for my work. I was doing the most work and getting paid the least. While Diane and I had been talking about starting our own practice, we realized it was finally time when Dr. Hentschl and I had serious argument. I remember the argument very well. What I don't remember is exactly what we were fighting about. I know it was about the way I had handled a case. He started yelling at me, "That's not the way to do it."

"Listen," I said back to him, "I have been here ten years. I know what I'm doing. If you don't agree with it, then you go ahead and tell me. But don't yell at me." Then I slammed my hand down on the table and walked out. I came in the next morning, and okay, everything was fine. Not an apology, not a mention. Okay, I thought, time to go.

Diane was also ready. A lot of people who have watched our show have asked me how we found Mount Pleasant. It wasn't that hard, I always told them; it was right there where it always has been, in the middle of Michigan. In fact, we found it by looking at a map of the entire state that pinpointed where vets had their practices and compared it with farm bulletins that estimated the number of animals in each area. We discovered several Michigan counties that seemed to be underserved. Isabella County, for example, was second in the state for beef cattle and third in the state for dairy cattle, but there were only three almost-retired vets in the area. There was a large-animal practice for sale in the small town of Coleman, which was in the next county, which we looked at. We went there in the springtime, and a lot of yards were flooded. It didn't really matter; the vet wanted more money for his practice than I thought it was worth. It turned out that he had been a classmate of Dr. Hentschl's, and when we decided not to buy his practice, he called Hentschl to tell him we had been there.

Dr. Hentschl tried to talk us out of leaving. That made sense for him; he had an assistant he could trust whom he was not paying that well. "You know," he said, "you're making

$40,000 a year. If you start your own practice, you have to make $80,000 just to live the same way." Well, I didn't know the numbers, but I knew it was time to leave.

We drove through several different areas. I remember the first time we visited one of those little towns. It had a population of a little more than three hundred people; the main street included a church, a hardware store—and two bars. As we went through it, I remember thinking, who in the world would ever want to live way out here in the country? But the area had a good feel to it. The people we met smiled easily, even with strangers. There was an older vet in the area, and we thought it would be right to speak with him before moving into the area. He turned out to be a strange bird, and he serviced only a very small area around his house. When you talked to him he wouldn't look at you; instead he looked directly at the button on my shirt. I was talking to him and he was talking to my shirt, so we didn't know how to figure him out.

But after we'd left he contacted the wife of one of his clients, a woman who was a local real estate agent and told her she'd better help us find a house there. It turned out this vet needed a quadruple bypass and two new knees, so he was more than happy to have somebody younger come in to take care of the area.

In Harbor Beach we'd bought an old house to fix up, which meant we never actually got done with the fixing part, so we wanted something a little newer. The real estate agent, Donna Murphy, found a nice house for us, which was more than we could afford, but her husband, Tom, a local farmer, helped us get a loan, and we settled in Isabella County. Just like Harbor Beach, this area was mostly family farms. What made it a little different was the fact that the Amish were coming into the area, which is a whole different culture I knew nothing about when we moved there. But we loaded everything we owned into an eighteen-wheeler and began our new life.

Starting a new business is scary, exciting, and challenging. When we started we turned the garage into our small-animal clinic, and people just waited outside. It wasn't much, but we didn't need much. No matter how much planning you've done, until the telephone starts ringing, there is always that doubt that you are going to be successful. We didn't get the double-wide clinic that people know from the show until five years later.

The first call came from Tom Murphy. For some reason his regular vet couldn't come and he needed help pulling a calf. That's an accurate description of the job, grabbing hold and pulling it out of the cow. I didn't even have my calf pullers unpacked, but I went on over there. I couldn't charge him for that—we'd used his tools and it didn't take long—but when I told him there was no charge, he admitted he'd never heard those words from a vet. Instead, he took me around the area and introduced me to some farmers. Fortunately he didn't say to anyone, "Use this guy; he doesn't charge you." Then I began unpacking and waited for the phone to ring. One of the first calls came from a farmer named Jim Graham, who asked, "Are you a veterinarian?"

"I am," I told him.

"Can you do pregnancy tests?"

"Sure," I told him.

He asked, "How many?"

"All of them," I said, as if that was ever a problem.

It wasn't that they had confidence in me or had heard anything good about me; I was filling a void. There were no large-animal vets in the area, and he needed a large-animal vet. The Grahams had artificially inseminated their herd and just wanted to do a health check. I had been doing pregnancy tests for ten years in Harbor Beach, so this was nothing new for me. After you've done enough pregnancy checks, you can pretty much figure out when the calf is due, which is important for a farmer to know. I reached inside the animal, closed my eyes, and told them, "This cow is pregnant this many days."

They knew when the cow had been inseminated, so they could determine how accurate I was. After the first few cows, they could see I knew what I was talking about, which built their confidence in me. When I had finished the job, Jim Graham asked me to go to his brother's farm. The fact that there was a new vet in town was big news in a small farming community. I never had to take out a single ad; the word of mouth was more effective than a notice in the newspaper. After more than three decades, the phone still hasn't stopped ringing. It turned out there was a tremendous need for a large-animal vet in this area. That first year I castrated forty horses.

It wasn't always easy. I have an accent. There are certain words I pronounce funny. In Harbor Beach there was no problem at all because a great number of our clients were originally German or Polish, so I sounded like their uncle. When we settled in this area, there were times when I could feel the mistrust because I was a foreigner. There were farmers I told, "If you don't trust that I'll do my best for your animals, I'm not interested in working for you," and there were people who, once they heard my accent, never called back.

But there were more people who didn't give a dang what I sounded like; they just wanted to be sure I was honest and that I knew what I was doing. One Monday morning, for example, we got a call from a beef farmer. People who raise beef cows don't call us as often because they have different needs. All their animals had to do was produce calves; the farmers raise those calves until they're ready to be sold, and then the process starts all over again. This farmer told me that his heifer had been trying to have a calf but couldn't give birth. When I got there I saw that the calf had been dead for a couple of days. It was big, still inside the heifer. "You have these options," I told him. "I can get the calf out and it'll cost you a couple of hundred dollars and she'll never have another calf again. She may not even live because of all the problems. If she lives you're going to have to sell her because she isn't going to get pregnant again. But right now she isn't sick. She has a normal temperature and there is no evidence of infection. Ship her out right now and take what you can get and call it quits."

He looked at me strangely. "What do you mean?"

I repeated what I'd said. This animal no longer would have any economic value to him. If he wanted to waste his money I'd do the procedure, but even if she survived it wasn't going to change anything.

"I think I'll ship her out," he said. The next day he sent her to the slaughterhouse. Later I learned he had told his daughter that this was the first time a vet hadn't tried to take him.

Word got around: This guy is honest. The next question people wondered was, How good is the new doc? One of my first clients was a farmer named Ray Wilson, who called and asked me to come over to do some pregnancy checks. Ray ran his place with his sons, John and Mike, and his son-in-law, Paul Hoover. As I learned, the Wilsons were known for being determined, straightforward people. You always knew how you stood with the family; and if they liked you there was nothing they wouldn't do for you. They had hearts of gold— but if something was wrong, they would let you know that, too. Mike Wilson once broke his wrist punching a cow. That cow did not want to get out of Mike's way, so he punched it. He sort of forgot that you can't hurt one of these big animals. The cow probably didn't even feel the punch, although it might've gotten a good laugh watching Mike jump around in pain.

Ray's herd had been artificially inseminated, but none of them had settled, which is the farmer's term for getting pregnant. I started asking questions, especially, "What are you feeding them?" A lot of problems start right there. "A lot of corn silage, some hay, grains," Ray told me.

"Okay, what kind of minerals?"

Turned out he didn't give his cows any minerals "because this guy who sold us a liquid silage additive said it already had everything in it so we didn't have to feed them anything else."

"Really?" I replied. "Who pulled your leg?" Because they were feeding their cows so much corn silage, I told them to get some dicalcium phosphate, which would supply all the minerals the cows needed. They added that to the feed on Wednesday, and on Friday the first cows were in heat. That fast.

I was feeling pretty good about my diagnosis, at least until the phone rang Sunday morning. "That mineral, that dical,"

Ray asked, "can you feed it free choice?" Meaning *Can you just put it out and let the cows eat as much of it as they like?*

"Sure, you can feed it that way." Cows will eat only what they need. I'd met Ray only once, when I'd been out to his place, but I could hear the confusion in his voice. "Why?"

"It says on the bag that it's for mixing purposes only."

"What's the matter, Ray?" I asked.

"Well, we have a dead cow this morning."

"I'll be there." That was the worst possible news a new vet could hear. If my prescription had been responsible for the death of Ray Wilson's cow, it would take me a long time to gain the trust of the local farmers—if I ever did. My professional reputation was definitely on the line.

I got there as fast as I could. There was a big, dead cow lying where it had fallen in the barn. It was possible that was my future in mid-Michigan lying there. I was upset, but I also was very curious. There was no obvious connection between the mineral feed and this cow's death. But something had killed it. When I see a dead animal, the first thing I do is lift up its eyelids. This cow's eyes were pure white. She had bled out. But why? I asked him, "When was she in heat?"

"Yesterday morning."

"Look at this, Ray," I said, showing him her eyes. "She bled out inside." There were a lot of possible reasons for that. I just took a guess. "Did she slip maybe? Did she fall?"

Ray didn't know, but he permitted me to do an autopsy. When I opened her up I immediately found a blood clot two feet long, six inches thick, and a foot wide in her belly. As I examined her I found she had been in heat, but it was clear she had slipped and done a split. A tiny blood vessel had busted in her groin area and didn't clot, so she'd bled out inside her abdomen.

"Well, look at that," Ray said. From that day on Ray was confident I knew what I was talking about. I have taken care of that family's cows ever since that day.

That first year I couldn't afford to hire any help or turn down any work, so I just kept going and going. It was just me and Diane; she answered the phones and made all the appointments, and I raced around. One day I made twenty-two farm stops, and one of those included fifty pregnancy checks. Today, because farms are larger and farther apart, that would be almost impossible, but at that time there were as many as four farms every mile, so I could get it done.

There were things that happened that first year that I've never seen again. There was no way to explain it; things just happened. It wasn't necessarily a bad thing; it helped spread the word that there was a new vet around. I did the pregnancy checks for Jim Graham's neighbor, Bob Neeland. When I was at his place in May, he asked me to look at a cow that was due to have a calf that month, but nothing was coming. I checked her; everything looked okay. "It's just a big calf," I told him. "She'll have it."

Next time I saw him was at the fair in August. He said to me, "You'd better come tomorrow, Jan. Remember that cow you pregnancy checked in May and said she was due any day?"

I didn't, I admitted.

"Well, she's finally trying to have that calf."

"What?! My gosh." Either this was the longest pregnancy in history or something was wrong. When I checked the cow the next morning, the first thing I saw was a calf's foot hanging out of her, and it was completely covered with long hair. I reached in and felt around, and, oh my gosh. What a big one. I figured out pretty quickly what had happened. The fetus's brain had not developed. Without a brain that fetus couldn't tell the mother, *Okay, it's time; I want to get out of here.* So instead of being born, the body just kept growing. The calf had been growing for almost three extra months. By that time the body was much too big to get out whole, so to save the cow's life I had to cut the remains into pieces. With Bob's help I got that calf out in sections. Unfortunately for me, the hair also had kept growing, and as I pulled out the pieces, strands of long black hair had stuck to me. By the time I got finished I was covered with black hair from head to boot. I looked a lot more like a werewolf than a vet. Bob didn't know whether to laugh or take my picture. It was the kind of situation that we were laughing about twenty years later: the day Dr. Pol became a werewolf.

I had to keep proving myself every day. The word had spread that I knew what I was doing with cows, but that had nothing to do with horses. One farmer, for example, used me to take care of his cows but wouldn't let me touch his expensive quarter horses. He had a special horse vet for that. But I was on the road one Saturday afternoon when Diane called me on the CB and told me to go right over to that farmer's place. He had a very sick colt and his regular vet was gone. I didn't like that too much; if that colt hadn't been in trouble, he would have waited for the vet he knew, and if I treated it and it died, I would get the blame.

This was a stud colt about six months old, a beautiful and

valuable animal. But it had colic so bad there was nothing I could do. It was much too late. I looked that man right in the eyes and said, "I can treat him, but it isn't going to make any difference. It's not going to live." "Do whatever you can," he said, and I did, but a few hours later that colt was dead.

I wanted to know why. I opened him up and he was just full of large roundworms. I could pick them up by the handful. I asked the farmer, "Why didn't you worm him?"

"We worm 'em all the time," he protested. I could see he was doubting I knew what I was talking about. He'd probably never had this problem with his regular horse vet. But he couldn't doubt the evidence.

"Well, it looks like this one got missed." Sometimes I wonder why God made certain animals so stupid. Stud colts have the dirty habit of eating their mothers' manure. Unfortunately, it's infested with worm eggs. So if the mama has a low level of worms and he eats her manure, he's going to be infested like crazy. That's what I suspected happened in this situation. By the time I had gotten to the farm, there was no way that colt could have been saved. Once the autopsy confirmed what I'd told the farmer, he began to think, *Maybe this young guy does know something.*

Those first few months I felt like I was always being tested. The only thing a farmer wants to know about a vet is, *Does he know what he's doing?* and *Is he honest?* I got called one day to go out and check a bunch of heifers getting ready to be shipped out. This was a pretty big farm. In those days they would get a good cow—a cow that was giving a lot of milk—and give her hormone shots. Instead of producing one egg, there would be multiple eggs on her ovaries. Then they would flush those embryos out of the uterus and implant them in recipients that would carry them to birth.

I didn't do the actual transplants; that was a time-consuming job done by experts. All I was asked to do was check the heifers and certify that they had been vaccinated. Those heifers that had been vaccinated had a tag and a three- or four-digit tattoo on an ear; without that tattoo they couldn't be shipped. Checking heifers is a pretty boring job, but I was happy to have the work. As I went through the herd I found a heifer with a tag—but no tattoo. When I showed it to the farmer, he told me, "Well then, we just got to put another tattoo in there."

I knew what I was being asked to do. He wanted me to help him out. Chances were pretty strong there was nothing wrong with that animal and we could have gotten away with it, but you either have principles or you don't. My integrity was on the line, and I didn't see any room for a compromise. "No," I told him, "no, we don't."

He nodded. "Okay." I've always felt that if I had done as he had suggested, he would've labeled me a cheat and put me off his farm. Instead, he never said another word about it and he and his family became very good clients.

The relationship between farmers and a vet has to be good; we may not be friends, but there needs to be a mutual level of respect. If a farmer doesn't trust his vet, it's better for both of them if he finds someone else. We need each other, so we have to work together. A large-animal vet isn't like a doctor who treats one patient at a time; I'll work with an entire herd. Most of the time, in fact, I won't even recognize my patients. Only if an animal had suffered some serious injury or disease that I treated will I even remember them.

When we first got to Mount Pleasant the phone rang all the time in the middle of the night. There was nobody but me to respond to it. At that time there were many more small farms in the area, so the phone rang often. When you're a small farmer with only thirty cows, losing one of them is a big deal; when you have three thousand cows and you lose one, it doesn't make a lot of difference. There were nights when I made a call at one A.M., then raced twenty miles to make another call at three A.M. In a one-man practice it wasn't unusual at all to be out two or more hours in the middle of the night, then be up early and on the road again the following morning.

I knew there were a lot of Amish farmers living in the middle of Michigan, but I didn't know what that meant. We hadn't had any Amish living in the Thumb. A person's beliefs never made any difference to me, I respected them all as long they were earnest about it, and professionally there is no such thing as an Amish cow. A cow is a cow; it has the same four legs. Even though to the Amish I was an "English," an outsider, there were never any restrictions put on me when I was working on an Amish farm. If they had a sick animal, I'd treat it no differently than I would any other animal. These people took good care of their animals: "That's my cow; you get it better. That's my horse; make sure it can work."

The first Amish farmer to call me was a man named Ike Swarey, an open-minded Amish who spent hours explaining his faith to me. I learned a tremendous amount from that gentleman, and it helped me a lot at an important time. The main thing about the Amish is that they intend to be self-sufficient. What was surprising to me is that there are as many different branches in the Amish community as there are in the Protestant Church, or in Judaism, and they follow somewhat different rules. Some groups are very conservative; they won't even use buttons on their clothing. They make all their own clothes and close them with hooks and eyelets. The more conservative Amish will not use anything self-propelled. They won't drive a car, for example. They can use a power mower, but only the type that has to be pushed. They don't use modern farm equipment; for example, they use horses to pull their plows and the hay baler. It has never been that unusual to have an Amish client arrive at the clinic in a horse-pulled buggy and tie his horse to a tree, although many of the traditional Amish now have friends and neighbors drive them in a car. (I'm always concerned about them when I see a buggy on the road, and there have been a number of accidents.) Among the Amish in our area, there actually are still working windmills that are used to pump water. When I visited Amish farms the Amish women would not talk to me because it wasn't their place, and before they got to know me the men weren't overly conversational either. Other Amish are a lot more modern; they use diesel engines to power generators and run their farms on electricity. Ike Swarey was one of the modern Amish.

The biggest misconception people have about the Amish is that they are stoic, quiet people. That's not accurate; most of our Amish clients smile and laugh pretty easily, and generally they have a real good sense of humor. In addition to being good farmers, a lot of them are very talented craftsmen. They hand-make beautiful furniture. In the work they do they are careful, cautious, and good. They work hard and long until the job is done.

They don't use modern technology. No TV or radio, though some of them do have cell phones. That was a problem for us once. Several years ago my assistant Dr. Kurt Kiessling went out to an Amish farm to examine a pregnant horse, and after he had done that the farmer asked him to look at two heifers that weren't doing well.

Dr. Kurt was a fine vet and he didn't have any trouble discovering the problem. One of the heifers had a twisted stomach on the left, so he wanted to roll the cow. That farmer had never helped roll a cow, so while he and his son wanted to help, they weren't quite sure how to do it. Making things even more difficult was the fact that this cow did not want to lie down, so Dr. Kurt had to give her two injections of a tranquilizer. By the time she finally lie down, she was basically pinned up against the wall, which meant there was no room to roll her to the right. "Here's what we're going to do," Dr. Kurt explained. "I'm going to stitch her stomach in place and then we'll move her away from the wall on her back. Then she'll roll the right way." But when they pulled the cow away from the wall, the farmers pulled her the wrong way. It made the situation just a little more difficult.

"You guys hold her head," Dr. Kurt said. "I'll get the back end and I'll roll her onto her side. You guys do the head and the feet." Dr. Kurt planted his back leg and reached down to pull the cow over. And when he did, his kneecap popped out of its socket right to the back of his knee. He went down to the ground in awful pain. He told me later it was the most painful thing he'd ever experienced. Meanwhile, that cow was starting to wake up and was flopping all over the place. Dr. Kurt was yelling, telling the farmer, "You got to get on the radio and call the clinic. Just push the button on the microphone and tell whoever answers that I got hurt and need some help."

Unfortunately, this was a traditional Amish. "Oh, we can't do that," the farmer explained. "We'll go get the neighbor."

The neighbors were a half mile down the road. The good news was that these cow pens are usually filled with mud and manure, but Dr. Kurt was lying on a clean bed of straw. While he was waiting for help he thought he might be able to put his own knee back in place. So he pushed down hard on his knee.

Well, that was a bad idea. Apparently the pain was terrible. He didn't try again. It took a little while before we finally got to him. But that was about the most serious problem we ever had dealing with an Amish client.

While we always keep the distance between our friends and our clients, as time passes and you continue to work with people, good relationships do grow. We had a special feeling for Ike Swarey and his family, who had been so kind to us when we arrived in Mount Pleasant, and Diane and I were honored when we were invited to his daughter's wedding. There was no invitation; as is tradition, we were just contacted a day before and told about the wedding. We had been invited to Amish weddings before, but the phone calls had always come too late for us to attend. This time we were invited three days in advance.

For us it was like walking into a completely different world. While the surroundings were familiar, everything inside was new to us. The wedding was held in a large barn-size structure. Backless benches had been arranged in sections: married women sat on one side; single women sat in another section; married and single men sat separately. Children sat in their own section. The back rows were for the outsiders, the "English." The bride wore a dark dress and a bonnet; the groom wore new work clothes. Three ministers spoke, and they spoke for a long time. Most of the ceremony was conducted in German, but we were able to follow some of it. Those sermons were very well done, but they were long. After the first few hours, believe me, those benches got plenty hard.

After the ceremony everyone walked up the road to another farm for the reception. This was a family-style meal; we all sat on those long benches and enjoyed homemade food—and plenty of it. That wedding could still be going on and they wouldn't have run out of food. There was no dancing and no entertainment, but it was a very warm and welcoming atmosphere.

When we started filming the TV show, we wondered how the Amish would react to the cameras. It turned out they didn't object the slightest bit to the crew filming on their farms, but for the most part they didn't want their faces to be shown. The crew had to come up with a special type of release that allowed the Amish farmers' backs and hands to be shown. As long as we've respected that, they've not only been willing to participate; they've been fascinated by it. In fact, a couple of them have actually seen the show. They went to a neighbor's house and watched it. One of them, I remember, was very pleased, pointing at me and scolding in a friendly manner, "You're going to make me a movie star, aren't you?"

Farmers tend to be loyal to a vet they can depend on to be there when they need him, day or night, and whom they trust. Diane and I had picked a good area, and the business was good right from the beginning. My own family background made me sensitive to our clients' needs. When it was possible I tried to teach my clients how to handle certain things to save money. When I was doing a calving, for instance, I'd show them: "This is how you do it." I'd teach them so I didn't have to come for every small problem. "If you need me, you call me," I'd tell them. "I'll be there. But there are things you can do by yourself." Ray Wilson's son Mike, for example, eventually got real good at calving, so the Wilsons rarely called me for that. It saved them a lot of money and it saved me a lot of time. Good for all of us. But one day in 1984, though, Mike called and his voice was shaking as he asked me to get over there as quick as I could: "I have a calf coming inside out."

I knew exactly what he was talking about. It's a condition called schistosoma reflexum, and it is exactly as he described it. For some reason a calf develops with its ribs bent the wrong way, and its heart, lungs, and intestines outside its body. But because the calf's heart is beating inside the uterus, it actually grows. When the calf is ready to come out, it dies instantly because it can't breathe. For a vet it isn't that rare—I've actually had many of them—but for a farmer it is a unique and very bizarre experience.

Mike and his brother, John, were waiting for me when I got to the barn. This took place just after the movie *Indiana Jones and the Temple of Doom* was released. In that film the bad guy reached into a man's chest and pulled out his beating heart. Anybody who saw that film never forgot that scene. When I got there I reached into the cow and I could feel the calf's heart still beating. I couldn't resist. "Look at this," I said, grabbing hold of that heart and tearing it loose. I ripped it out of the animal. Then I stood there holding a beating heart in my hand. And I smiled. "This could be the problem," I said.

Poor John went pale. "Darn you, Doc," he screamed. "What'd you do?" And then he bent over and almost threw up. Mike and I were laughing so hard we could barely catch our breath. It's that type of memorable, shared experience that long-term relationships are built on.

Actually, there was no way—no possible way—this animal could have survived, and this was the fastest way of euthanizing it. At that point the animal's brain and nervous system are not fully formed so it doesn't feel real pain. For the animal it's over almost instantly.

The practice was successful almost from the very beginning. Within the first few years we had outgrown the house and were looking for a bigger place. The man living next door raised racehorses on eighteen acres. He had a little house on the land as well as the horse barns. There was also a cement slab with a septic tank and electricity all hooked up. I took care of his horses for him. He knocked on my door one day and asked me if I wanted to buy his land—that afternoon.

"I'd like to think about it," I said.

There was no time for that, he said. If he didn't sell that afternoon, he explained to me, he'd have to pay big long-term capital gains taxes. We didn't negotiate much; we didn't have time for it. We went to see Donna Murphy again and explained the situation. She immediately drew up all the papers. That might have been the fastest sale in real estate history.

I pulled up the cement slab, dug out a basement, then put the double-wide clinic people know from the show on the land. I couldn't afford to build any other kind of structure. We moved the clinic out of the garage and into the double-wide. I planned it out so that the doors to every room were right across from another room, so we could move around comfortably. Six years later we had grown so much, even that space was no longer big enough. We had five vets working and the small-animal part of the practice was becoming more important. So we dug out another basement and put another double-wide on top of it. That's the clinic people see on TV. Maybe it's not so pretty, but there's enough room to get our work done.

Through the years I've watched as too many family farms have disappeared; in a few instances I've seen the whole house and barn literally pushed into a hole and covered up. Not only have we treated several generations of animals for the same family, but we've also treated the animals for several genera-tions of that family. One time when we were still getting the practice going, an elderly farmer who raised Belgian horses had a mare that was aggressive with her colts. There's no easy ex-planation for it; it happens. She had killed the first one and had tried to kill another one, but they'd stopped her before she could trample it to death. The farmer wanted me to put that colt down because there was no way he could protect it. That seemed like a waste to me, so I told him, "Okay, then, I'll take it."

The colt was only a few hours old. I didn't have a van, so I drove over to his place in my station wagon to pick it up. That colt weighed only about 150 pounds, and it was calm. I put its butt on the floor in front of the passenger seat, lifted up his forelegs onto the seat, and drove home. I drove with one hand and held its mane with my other hand. We started feeding it gallons of milk replacer and it grew like a weed. When it was three months old, big enough to protect itself, the farmer came and told me he'd take it back. I'd thought he'd given it to me, but evidently he thought differently, and it was his animal. He held its papers. He paid me a certain amount of money for taking care of his animal, and then he sold it. We never said another word about it, but I continued to treat all his animals, and all his family's animals. In 2013 a young woman came into the clinic with a small dog and introduced herself, explaining that she was the fifth generation of that family whose animals I had treated. Five generations of the same family and I couldn't begin to figure how many animals. Maybe five generations is a bit unusual, but I have taken care of three generations of many families. In some cases for those first generations I took care of farm animals, but after the family farm was sold, the family stayed in the area and I began taking care of their small animals.

When we first moved into the house, we had an Amish farmer build a small cubicle in the garage. That cubicle was about six by ten, and it's where I did all my routine small-animal examinations, vaccinations, and surgeries; somehow we even made room for a few cages. We kept that garage very clean and had regular appointments, but it was too small. Moving into the new clinic allowed me to expand that part of the practice. I finally had room in the basement to store supplies and the drugs we needed to enable the business to grow. That was very satisfying for me. I like working with small animals because the economics are so different; there is more we can do to help them.

There are times when the cost of saving a cow or a horse will be more than that animal is worth. If we can't bring the animal back into production at a sensible cost, the farmer will exchange it. Small animals are different; we will often work with them for their entire lives. In fact, some of the office staff know our clients by their pets rather than their own names; you know, Misty's owner, or that woman with that funny rabbit. And rather than an economic value, there's an emotional attachment. Some pet owners will spend much more than they can afford to treat their animal, and admittedly there are vets who will allow that to happen. There's a balancing act there, and the best thing I can do is be honest about the prognosis and give advice as if I was working with one of my own pets.

While the small-animal practice consists mostly of dogs and cats, just about the only types of small animals we haven't treated at least once in the clinic are porcupines and skunks— but as people who watch the show know, we often have to treat dogs that have had an unpleasant encounter with a porcupine. Here's the short verdict of how that confrontation is going to work out: The porcupine wins every time. Porcupines are nice animals; normally you can pet a porcupine with your hand and nothing will happen as long as you move with the direction of its hair growth. And they don't like to fight; they'll run. But when they're threatened they'll put their bristles up. They don't shoot them; instead, they flip their tails. Or a dumb animal tries to bite one and gets a bunch of those quills in his mouth. The porcupine just laughs and walks away; the dog's owner brings the dog to the clinic.

Those quills have barbs at the end. If you look at them

under a microscope, you can see those sharp barbs sticking out. People bring their dogs in with dozens of those sharp needles stuck in their muzzles, in their legs, their eyes, even their throats, and tell me, "You won't believe how dumb this old dog was. Can you take them out?"

Yes, I will, I'll tell them. It's painful for them, and it's probably a little embarrassing too. There's no easy or painless way of getting them out. We give the animal an anesthetic and pull them out one by one; usually, though, the dogs don't suffer any type of permanent injury.

Sometimes I do wonder how such a wonderful animal as a dog can be so darn dumb. I can understand a dog being interested in a porcupine—*Hey, what's that funny-looking thing?*—once. But after several dozen needles are pulled out painfully from their skin, you'd figure they'd be smart enough to know: *Maybe I'll just leave that little guy alone.*

Skunks, too, are nice animals. A lot of animals get bad reputations. Pigs, for example, like to live in a clean place and will keep their pen as clean as possible. Skunks also keep their homes clean. If they aren't threatened, they won't do anything to bother you. Skunks can be descented by removing the anal gland, though I did hear about a family who had a pet skunk that was not descented. It used to sleep in the bed with them and they never had a problem—at least not until the night their cat jumped up on their bed and landed accidently on that skunk. A week later they were still trying to clean that cat.

Only one time did I have an encounter with a skunk. My mother had come to visit and we were driving along a country road when I saw one of the biggest skunks I'd ever seen. They don't have skunks in the Netherlands, so my mother had never seen one. I thought I'd give her a little treat. "That isn't a cute kitty," I told her. "Watch this." So I stopped the car and we got out. "We'll stay over here," I said. I tossed a rock, which landed about six feet behind that skunk. The instant that rock hit the ground, two balls of smell shot out in that direction. Then the skunk turned around to see what was going on. I'd always been told skunks can spray only once; then they have to recharge. So I picked up another rock and threw it—and it shot two smaller balls. That guy shot twice, so that was a mythbuster right there.

The smallest small animal I've ever treated was a white mouse that probably weighed about fifty grams—not even two ounces. A little boy brought it in. He was concerned about it, so I was concerned about it. There isn't too much that we can do for a white mouse, but in this instance I was able to help. "That's a nice-looking mouse," I told that young man. When I looked at it I asked him, "What are those things that are crawling on him?"

"I don't know."

"Looks like fleas to me. Does your cat like to look at him?"

The boy nodded. "Oh yeah. Sometimes he even sits on top of his cage."

I put a little flea powder on that mouse and told the boy to try to keep the cat farther away from him, and another satisfied client walked out the door.

The fact is that we're never surprised by what comes in the front door. We've had several people bring in their pet rats for treatment. Believe me, they love their pet rats just as much as other people care about their dogs and cats. Normal people. Every animal and even every rodent has its own unique personality. People get to know and appreciate that personality, and when it's gone they will miss it. I haven't treated too many rats because they don't live very long, and they are susceptible to serious tumors. I had a very nice couple bring in their four-year-old rat, which wasn't doing so well. Four is already ancient for a rat. This one must've had some type of tumor in his brain because it couldn't walk anymore. It was no easier for me to tell these people that I had to put it down than it would have been for the owners of any other animal. And they cried just as hard at their loss as anyone else who has ever loved a pet.

We've treated only one alligator. I can be pretty sure about that because treating a pet alligator is not something I'd easily forget. A client came in carrying an alligator he kept in a fenced-in pond in his backyard. It was seven years old, he told me, but I looked at this animal and it was only two feet long. I asked, "What in the world is going on here? How come he's not growing?"

"Because he's not eating," the man told me.

I examined him and he looked to be pretty healthy. "The problem," I told him, "is that alligators are not supposed to live in Michigan; it's too cold for them." That alligator should have been sunning itself in the tropics. The best thing to do, I told him, was to heat the pond or get a rock heater so the alligator could sit on the warm rocks.

To confirm that, my son, Charles, and Jon Schroder found an animal behaviorist in California. Dr. Jill helps people to understand their animals. I think that's very important; if you understand your dog, it's easier to work with it. But the animal has to understand you, too. When Dr. Jill came to Mount

Pleasant, she took the opportunity to visit this small alligator. "How do you feed it?" she asked the owner. I hadn't even asked that question. He dangled dead mice from string in front of the gator, he told her. That apparently was part of the problem. Alligators do not eat off a string; they eat what's on the ground. She laid that mouse on the ground and yanked it a couple of inches, and *pow*! It was as if this gator had been introduced to fast food. I do have to admit, though, when I decided to be a vet I didn't think I'd have to be treating an alligator.

Many people have brought in their birds, too, mostly to have their nails trimmed or their beaks trimmed. I never thought I'd have to be a manicurist for a parrot either, but you learn how to do what's necessary. Birds require careful handling. It takes two people to manicure a parrot. If a parrot manages to clamp down on a finger, that finger is gone, so one person has to hold on to the parrot's head while a second person does the actual trimming. When people bring in their parrots, they always want them to speak to me; they want to show me how smart their birds are. They tell me their birds can understand the meaning of as many as three hundred words. But the truth is that a lot of parrots don't want to talk to me; they don't say a word. I understand that; I love animals, I want to help them, but too often they don't like me. They are in a strange environment, with people they don't know, and that is filled with scents they don't recognize. If they do have any memory of being in the clinic before, it is that *this is the guy who hurt me before*. It's like taking a child to a dentist—the second time. They may not remember what happened, but they do not associate that environment with anything too good. So I've never had a good conversation with a parrot.

I've also worked with many owls and hawks. One time the Michigan Department of Natural Resources brought in an owl with a broken toe, which prevented him from catching anything. They found him hopping around a farmyard, so I brought it to the clinic and started feeding it. Many creatures seem to understand when you intend to help them and they will let you get close. You just have to be deliberate about it. This particular owl was in a sorry state. Somehow his wings had gotten hooked together on his back so he couldn't fly. The worst thing that can happen to an animal is for it to know it is vulnerable. Every animal has some kind of skill that allows it to survive. When that skill is compromised—they can't run; they can't fly—they understand they have become exposed to danger. The fact that this owl couldn't fly meant he had terrible difficulty catching food or even getting water. He was starving. When I got him back to the clinic, I gave him some water, then put a dish upside down so he could sit on it. Birds don't like to sit on the ground, they want to be on a perch. Then I started feeding him venison.

Most of the time I start feeding an animal like this with an instrument that keeps a distance between the food and my fingers; whatever fears the animal has usually will be overcome by hunger. I remember one hawk in particular that I fed meat with a hook for several days, and then I took a chance and held a piece of meat in my hand. He picked it right out without touching me. So I began feeding him out of my hand. He never bit me. I continued feeding him by hand until he was finally strong enough to go to a rehabilitation center before being released into the wild. That animal wasn't going to bite the hand that was feeding him.

Most people bring their small animals into the clinic on a leash or in a cage, but probably the most unusual animal we had was a cat that came into the clinic in a car. I don't mean he was riding inside the car; that cat was in the car. This man came in one afternoon without an animal. "What can we do for you?" I said to him.

"It's this cat," he said. But he didn't have a cat with him. Then he explained, "He's caught in the frame of my car." We went outside. He was driving a big Suburban, which had a metal tubular frame with holes in it. As we stood there, I heard *meow, meow,* and it seemed like it was coming from the motor. This was a new one for me. I crawled underneath the car, and sure enough, there was a tail hanging down. The cat was right where the axle was attached. I reached through another hole and managed to grab hold of that tail and start pulling.

That was a very strong cat. And he did not want to come out. Whatever he was holding on to, he was holding it tight. I tried as hard as I could, but I couldn't pull him out. I said, "Okay, you asked for it." I got an anesthetic ready and crawled back under the car. I reached in there again and pulled his tail. He didn't like that and began moving. I saw his hind leg and jabbed. *Got ya!*

We waited probably ten minutes. Then I reached in again. That cat was nice and relaxed. I pulled it out by the tail and brought it into the clinic. It was a beautiful Siamese kitten, a tomcat. We castrated him and vaccinated him, and the people took him home. It wasn't their cat when they'd gotten in the car and heard that sound, but it was now.

Another afternoon a man came into the examination room carrying a pillowcase knotted at the top. "What've you got in there?" I asked.

"My snake," he said. "Watch out when I open this up. He'll jump right out."

We've actually treated a lot of snakes. Back in the Netherlands I had grown up afraid of snakes. We were always warned to stay away from them because their venom was poisonous. If I was going to be a vet, I had to get over that. In college I'd handled one. I remember it was cold and dry; it felt a little like sandpaper. But after that I wasn't afraid of snakes anymore.

At that time Dr. Rachael was working as an assistant. Before coming to Mount Pleasant, she had worked in a zoo in Saginaw and one of her jobs was cleaning the big snake house. So she was not afraid of big snakes. In fact, she used to wrap the zoo's twelve-foot boa around her body when she was cleaning the cage. It was harmless, she told me. A boa will constrict only if it's hungry or if it feels danger. She wrapped it around her body and cleaned the cage, then unwrapped it and let it go.

This man opened up the pillowcase, and *vroom*, just like he had warned me, that darn snake rose up high above the table. I knew it wasn't poisonous; I grabbed it by the neck with my left hand and pulled it out of the pillowcase, and it quickly wrapped itself around my arm. There was about six inches of it head poking out. Dr. Rachael looked at me and smiled. "I'll give you twenty bucks if you take it into the office."

Into the office? Into the office where Diane was working? Maybe I'd gotten over my fear of snakes, but my wife hadn't. She was wonderful with almost every animal—except snakes.

She was terribly scared of snakes. Why would I do that to her? (Besides the twenty bucks.) Of course, everybody knows the way to get me to do something is to make it a challenge: "I don't believe you'll do the sizzle reel for a TV show." "I don't believe you'll dress up as a woman for the local charity dinner." "I don't believe you'll take that snake inside and show it to Diane." I said, "You got a deal."

I walked into the office. Diane was working at her desk. I stood about a foot behind her and asked, "Diane, how do you like this one?" She turned around and that snake was about a foot from her face.

Here's one thing I guarantee: I won't do that again. Oh my gosh, that was the wrong thing to do. She was really scared and really angry. And she didn't hesitate to let me know what she thought. I definitely regretted that right away—except for the twenty bucks, of course.

It was a white-nosed snake and it had a snotty nose. For a snake, that can be a serious problem. Snakes don't cough, since they don't have diaphragms like humans do; the diaphragm allows us to cough and clear our throats. Same thing with frogs and turtles; if they get pneumonia, the dirty pus comes right out of their nostrils. And it's what can happen when a snake is in an environment that gets too cold. Snakes need to live in a very warm and moist environment. When a snake gets stuffed up, you just have to clean out its throat and make sure it's warm enough.

Out of necessity, I've learned how to handle snakes. The snakes in Michigan aren't poisonous, but you still need to be careful with them. One of the problems I've seen several times is sore lips. They don't have lips like ours; they don't need them because they can't talk anyway, but when it is too hot, they try to get out of their terrariums, and they bang their heads on the glass. So they get bruises and sores on the mouth. It hurts them when they eat, so they stop eating and they die. It's easily treated; disinfect the sores with alcohol or iodine and put a topical antibiotic on them. Then make sure the temperature in the terrarium is comfortable.

Some snakebites can be dangerous but not usually in our area. When the Christian Veterinary Mission sent me to New Mexico to teach basic veterinary medicine to ranchers, they told me a story, and I still don't know if it's true. At night, they said, snakes will crawl onto the blacktop roads because they retain the warmth from that day. That sounds right to me. Then, supposedly, when a snake senses the danger that a car is bearing down on it, it will curl up and open its mouth. As the car rolls over the snake, the tire pushes back the upper jaw and some of the hollow teeth become embedded in that tire. The driver doesn't notice that and keeps driving. But as the tire wears down, those teeth go a little deeper, eventually causing a slow leak in the tire.

I'm just repeating this story I was told. What happens then is when the person fixing the flat tire runs his hand over it to feel if there might be a nail stuck in it, he gets scratched by the hollow tooth; the snake venom gets into the skin and he suffers the damage.

I can believe it. It doesn't take much poison to cause a reaction. While I never saw that happen, I did once have a pretty unusual encounter with a snake—I treated a snake that was partially eaten by a rat. A woman who lived several hours away called and said she had a four-foot pet boa. She fed it live rats. She had put a live rat in the cage with the snake, but instead of watching it to make sure the snake ate it, she fell asleep. When she woke up, the rat had chewed the snake all along its backbone, but the snake was still alive. She had called her local vet, who told her, "No, I don't want to see it. I don't want anything to do with it." "Okay," we told her, "bring it in; we'll look at it."

She arrived carrying a large plastic container. When she lifted the lid, the stench that came out of it was terrible. I looked, and I had never seen anything quite like this. The rat had chewed the muscle right off the snake, exposing the spines of the vertebrae. The snake was still alive, but it was in obvious pain. In a case like this, you just have to do the logical things; we gave the snake antibiotics and applied a solution that would keep the wound moist while it healed. We showed this woman how to give the antibiotic shots to the snake and gave her the supplies she would need. She left, and we never heard from her again; she didn't provide us a phone number, so we couldn't follow up, and she never called. In fact, that is not all that unusual. There's always a little question in the back of my head—*I wonder how that snake did,* or *I wonder how that puppy did*—but sometimes we never find out.

When I first came to America to become a vet, it was kind of hard going. Diane and I worked hard to be able to have our practice, which was always our dream. When we moved to Mount Pleasant we took a chance and we spent almost everything we had saved. But it worked out; as viewers of the TV show see, it worked out really well. The practice continued to grow; at one time in addition to myself we had four vets working there, as well as the office staff. Diane got a call from the local bank one Friday afternoon several years after we'd opened the practice. Apparently a man had come in and made a large cash withdrawal. After giving him the money, the bank didn't have enough money for the ATM outside. The bank asked Diane if she would please make a deposit so they wouldn't run out of money over the weekend. Believe me, it's a nice feeling to be able to loan money to the bank.

THREE

Where Does It Hurt?

O ne morning we were in the clinic when a person came in with a dachshund. It was a nice dog, but it was struggling hard to breathe. Its breathing was raspy and strained. It was looking at me with the saddest eyes: *Think you can help me, please?* "We're gonna see what's wrong and get it fixed," I told her.

A common cause of this type of breathing difficulty is that the animal has eaten some rat poison and is bleeding in the lungs. In a farm area, there is always a lot of poison around to control infestation in the barn, and dogs especially seem to love it. There was one month when I treated six dogs that had ingested poison. Dogs, never cats; cats don't like the smell, either that or they're too smart. I began my examination by asking the owner, "Could she have eaten any d-CON?" No, he told me firmly. "There's none around?" Nope. "The neighbors didn't put some out maybe?" Absolutely not. *Okay,* I thought, *we'll see.*

There are different tests you can use to make this diagnosis. In this instance I took blood and then measured the clotting time. The blood wouldn't even clot. There was no question what that meant. I told the owner, "This dog has eaten d-CON. Did you have some behind a counter maybe?"

"Oh yeah, I forgot about that."

"Well, this is a dachshund; it's smarter than you."

That dog was in serious danger. She had probably eaten the poison as long as a week ago. Her rasping was almost definitely being caused by bleeding in her lungs. She needed a blood transfusion right away. Dogs have about fifty-six different blood types, compared to the six that humans have, but they are not unique, as each of our types is. There is a lot of crossover. There is universal blood on the market, but the problem with commercial blood is that you can't store it for any length of time. If you don't use it, it becomes useless. Instead I often use my own Great Danes as blood donors. They're big; they can give as much blood as we need. For many years, Charles had the sweetest dog, a Dane named Maeson, who knew exactly what she was supposed to do. I'd bring her into the examination room and tell her to sit down. She'd look at me, and I knew exactly what she was thinking: *Oh no, not again.* But then she'd actually stick out her front leg and turn her head away, as if she didn't want to watch, like little kids do. I could have 60 cc of blood in thirty seconds when I needed it.

I always start a transfusion by giving the recipient just a tiny bit of the blood to see how the animal reacts. If it starts breathing heavily or shows any sign of distress, it means it is having an allergic reaction, so then I quit right away. No damage done; that little bit won't hurt it. It's a little bit old-fashioned, but it has always been effective, and I like it because it has enabled me to save a lot of dogs. In this case the dachshund did not reject the blood, and as soon as she had her transfusion I could see the difference: her ears perked up a little bit; she began showing some curiosity about her surroundings; her tail even swished a couple of times. It was like a person waking up from a daze and asking, "Hey, where am I? How'd I get here?" That little dachshund survived. She was very lucky; some of them don't survive. We were able to save this dog because we'd seen other animals with similar symptoms and recognized them.

It would make a vet's job a lot easier if a sick animal could just sit down in a chair and describe its symptoms. That would be nice: *I've got just a little bit of pain in my rumen, Doc.* Or, *I think I bruised my fetlock. I got this throbbing ache in my loin that won't go away.* It would help if I could just ask, Where does it hurt? Or, do you feel anything when I touch you here? The most an animal can do to let you know how it feels is try to kick you when you touch the wrong place.

How can you make a diagnosis when your patients won't tell you what's bothering them? I never try to convince anyone that animals talk to me. I'm no Dr. Dolittle; even parrots don't talk to me. But animals do have a way of conveying a message that, to me, is plain to see. So if you're very careful, if you look and listen and even taste and smell, they will let you know what's bothering them. It would be impossible to estimate how many animals I've examined, but I know what a healthy animal looks like and acts like, and when an animal is behaving a little different or has a problem, I can often pick it right up. I can use my own senses. For example, when I see a cow with its hair slicked down just like Elvis, I know right away that's a sign of lice. Cows with lice turn in circles, maybe hold their tails funny, and keep licking themselves, which slicks down their hair. I'll take out a tuft of hair and the lice will be there. We'll treat the problem, but there's no way of getting rid of it entirely. It's just a perpetual fight.

Lice can do very serious harm too. When I was just getting started, we got a call one day from a farmer who told Diane that his heifer had been killed by lightning; he wanted me to examine it and write the letter so he could collect the insurance. Sometimes people call and tell me what the problem is, but I don't usually pay that much attention to them. I listen, but I need to make my own examination. Cows do get killed by lightning; they're standing out there in an open field and get struck. For insurance purposes it's considered an act of God so the farmer gets paid in full. But the insurance company won't pay a penny unless a vet confirms it.

Before I went out to his farm, I asked Diane if she remembered the last time we'd had a thunderstorm. "Last spring, I think," she said. If that was true, that cow had been dead for a long time. When I got out to the farm I didn't even have to do an autopsy. That cow was lying out in the pasture and there were no obvious signs of a lightning strike. In fact, there wasn't any obvious reason she should be dead. There were no wounds of any kind. So what could have killed her? I lifted up one eyelid—you can tell a lot just by looking at the color of the eyes—and that was all I needed to see. I took my knife and scraped it along the hide, then held up the blade. "Look at this."

It was absolutely covered with lice. This animal had been sucked completely dry. The lice had taken all the blood out of it.

I told the man, "I'm sorry, but I'm not writing a letter for the insurance. Can't do it."

It's possible he was being honest with me. The cow was out in the pasture, she was healthy, the night before she was eating without any hesitation, and the next morning she was dead. A lightning strike makes sense. But what he couldn't see was that the cow was very low on blood; the lice on her had been there for a long time. Suddenly for some reason the number of them just exploded and they killed her. It's very believable that the farmer might not have had any idea she had lice. If he had, he would have called me before he lost her.

It isn't that unusual to get a call from a farmer telling me he has an animal that is down and not getting up. I hear this all the time. "I don't understand it, Jan. She was fine last night, but when I went out to the barn this morning, she was just lying there and wouldn't get up." A down animal obviously means there is something wrong and the vet needs to get out there and figure it out while there's still a chance to save the animal. There's an old saying on the farms: "A down horse is a dead horse, but a downed cow doesn't mean as much." That's usually accurate.

A horse's primary means of defense is running away; horses don't fight unless they have to. So when a horse doesn't run, or can't run, it's in trouble. There are a lot of things that I can look at that might tell me the problem. For example, we've had several cases of West Nile virus: A horse is normal at night, but flat out on the ground the next morning—and still eating. If you put hay in front of it, the horse will lie on its side and start chomping on it. Well, we know what that means: encephalitis. The horse is paralyzed. It can't stand; if you got it up, it would just flop over. By the time a horse with encephalitis goes down, it's too late. If the farmer happens to notice the horse is acting a little abnormal before it goes down, we treat it with massive doses of cortisone. That fights the swelling, and some horses can be saved. But after the infection sets in and the brain swells, there's nothing that can be done. It's sad, but the only thing we can do is put the horse out of its misery.

But horses do go down for other reasons. A nice local lady had an old Belgian that had helped her get over a serious problem. She called Diane one day and told her I needed to come quick, that her horse was down. The two of them were close, so I dreaded what I was afraid I was going to have to do and the impact it might have on the woman. I went out there and began examining the horse. There was no paralysis, no sign of anything serious at all. That suggested one thing to me: "He doesn't want to get up," I told her. "I think he has some arthritis, but he can get up fine." That horse needed a good talking-to; I put him back on his brisket and made a lot of noise to get his attention. Then I slapped him on the butt and pulled his tail. *Okay, okay, I'll get up.* That horse just scrambled to his feet so the crazy vet would go away and leave him alone.

A down cow doesn't mean the same thing at all. Some people see a cow lying there and not getting up and assume there is something terribly wrong. When examining a down cow, if there is not something that I spot right away, the first

thing I'll do is grab hold of her ears. That's my natural thermometer. If those ears are warm, her blood circulation is
okay. But if they're cold, the next thing I'll do is shine a flash-
light in her eyes. If her pupils don't shrink, that means she is
low on calcium and probably has milk fever. Milk fever is a
pretty common condition; it happens after a cow has had a
calf and starts making milk. The milk gland takes calcium out
of the blood to maintain the consistency of the milk. But calcium is used to conduct the electrical impulses between nerves
and muscles that result in movement. When there is not
enough calcium, cows can't move those muscles, so they go
down and stay down. Untreated, the condition can be fatal. It
can be treated successfully by giving the cow large doses of
calcium, though. Within a short period of time the cow will
go from near death to perfectly okay. When I opened the practice, we were always treating cows for this—and it isn't something that can wait even an hour. Regardless of what other
problems might be going on, I'll correct that imbalance first
and then start looking for other possible causes. As long as a
cow is crawling, it has a chance to get up. Cows have thick
skin; they're not going to do any damage by moving along the
ground. But smart farmers realized that they could save valuable time and money by treating milk fever themselves.

I hate seeing an animal down; not only is being vulnerable
like that scary for them, but I think it also embarrasses them
a little. The advantage for me is that it's easy to get close
enough to them to try to diagnose the problem and help them.
You don't have to catch a down animal. But I always put a
halter on them and tie it to a back leg. I don't want the animal
suddenly trying to get up and hurting me, or hurting itself.

Many times the first thing I have to do when I make a farm call is catch the animal and restrain it enough to allow me to conduct my examination. That can be very time-consuming, frustrating, and dangerous. When an animal feels vulnerable, it becomes much more defensive and it'll strike out at anything it doesn't know. Like me.

Catching and restraining animals was not something we were taught in school. They told us at school that when we got to the farm, the cow better be tied up. The horse better be tied up. The pig better be in its pen. Maybe that was true in the Netherlands, but I learned pretty quick when I started working for Dr. Hentschl it didn't work that way in the Thumb. Most farmers have small pens that prevent an animal from moving too much. They're too narrow for them to turn around in and not long enough for them to get up any speed. What we try to do is funnel the animals from larger pens into those smaller pens. But if they're not in a pen or tied up when I get there, we've got to figure out how to get them under control.

I'll never run after an animal; I'm not going to do any fifty-yard dash. Besides, it wouldn't do any good; the slowest animal is still faster than me. And if I did catch up with one of them, what was I going to do to make it stop? Can't run away from them either. They'll catch you every time. Before I go into any fenced-in area with an animal, I've already figured the quickest way out. You can't go to the middle of a pen and be sure you're going to get out of there alive. They'll get you. I always stay close to the fence, and if they come at me I hop over it. But if for some reason I can't, with large animals you can usually just do a quick sidestep; cows and bulls aren't especially agile. If you do a sidestep, most animals will just keep going straight and miss you. Most animals aren't vindictive: they don't want to hurt anybody; they just want to get away from you.

So one of the first things I had to learn when I got to America was how to rope an animal. Back in the Netherlands I had seen all the American Westerns, but that didn't make me any kind of cowboy. I can throw a lariat, but as anyone who has seen me try on the show will agree, I'm not exactly Wild Jan Pol. I just make the loop as big as I can and get as close as possible before tossing it. Then I get ready to toss it again. I'm pretty good with cows because they don't move too quick; horses are a lot more difficult because their reaction time is a lot faster than a cow's. When a horse sees that rope coming, it'll move; cows will just stand there wondering, *Now, what the heck are they doing to me?*

One of my favorite moments in filming the show took place when I had to rope a Texas longhorn that needed to have a calf pulled. It was a beautiful animal; the points of its horns were at least six feet apart. I made myself a big loop and threw it. It landed over one horn, then settled over the second horn. That wasn't the toughest part, though. The toughest was acting like I wasn't surprised. And I will never forget what I was thinking: *I really hope they got that one on film, because it isn't going to happen so easily a second time.*

There are times when I trick the animal; I'm still smarter than most of the animals I deal with. One Saturday morning I had a farmer ask me to come out right away because his beef cow needed a calf pulled. This was an angry cow with big horns, and she was dangerous. She was roaming around in a very large fenced-in area. Every time I got into it, she came toward me. I couldn't help her if I couldn't catch her and tie her up. And I couldn't get close enough to get a rope over her head. So what I did was stand on the wooden fence and pester that cow: *Come on, you dumb cow, get over here.* I picked up a couple of small pebbles and tossed them in her direction. Finally she got real irritated and came running at me. As she came running past, I dropped the loop over her head and pulled it tight. *Gotcha!* Oh, she was mad. She started bucking, but we were able to lead her into a much smaller pen, where she couldn't turn around. I put another rope on her and tied both ropes around posts. She still had fight in her and pulled so hard she almost strangled herself, so we had to loosen the ropes. And when she finally got calm, I pulled the calf, which was dead. I told the farmer, "Listen to me. This cow does not leave this pen until Monday morning, and then she goes right to slaughter." Then he told me that this cow had actually killed another heifer that had just given birth, trying to get her new calf. She just wanted a calf. That animal was no longer controllable, and when that happens there aren't any options.

About a year later that same farmer called again. Another one of his cows was having trouble giving birth and he needed me to come right away. "Where's the cow now?" I asked.

"Oh, she's running along the river with the rest of the herd."

"Okay," I said. "You call me when it's caught and I'll be right there." I never heard from him again. I can only do so much; if a farmer doesn't want to help me, I don't mind just walking away.

The most important thing to remember when trying to

catch an animal is that the potential for danger is always present. That's true for every type of animal. Most people believe cows are docile creatures, for example; people think they are all like sweet Elsie the Cow. That is definitely not accurate. Cows are big and incredibly strong; pound for pound they are much stronger than horses. In fact, one of the most fortunate things for people who have to work with cows is that cows have no concept of how strong they actually are. Also, there also are some wild cows. I have actually seen cows jump over a gate without touching it. Just about the first thing I teach young vets coming to work with us is that they should never turn their backs on any animal at any time for any reason.

I've never had to rope a pig. It hasn't been necessary. Everybody has seen funny movies of people falling down trying to grab on to a pig; one thing I know is that pigs don't want to wrestle. But if a pig is loose, there's no use chasing it. In Harbor Beach we used to let a pig run until it stopped on its own. Then we would slowly approach it, talking to it softly, and when we got close we would put a plastic pail over the pig's head; that got it confused and it just stood there. Then we used four-by-three-foot boards to direct it wherever we wanted it to go. I learned from Dr. Arbaugh's experience that maybe that wasn't the best way to do it either. Dr. Arbaugh was trying to restrain a pig one day and put the pail over its head. Pigs don't look like they have necks, but they do have enormously powerful neck muscles. When the pail went over its head, that pig tried to throw it off, and he rammed his head up. The edge of the pail caught Dr. Arbaugh right underneath his nose; it knocked all his front teeth loose. He had to have several teeth basically reimplanted, and he was in bad pain for several days.

I've had some run-ins with big pigs. There was a gentleman in the next county who wanted six pigs castrated. "How big are they?" I asked.

"About a hundred pounds or so," he told me.

I told him I needed a fifty-five-gallon drum. When I got to his place, I saw that this farmer's "or so" was about a hundred more pounds. These were big, strong animals. They should have been castrated months earlier. As soon as they saw me, they started running. Who knows, maybe they figured out why I was there. It wasn't hard to catch them. We put the barrel at the end of an alley and ran the pig into it headfirst; as soon as he was completely in the barrel, we picked the barrel up so he was basically standing on its head. Then we just grabbed the hind legs and spread them and I cut off the testicles. It's not especially painful for the animal. When I was done, we threw the barrel down and the pig backed out and took off—fast. We got all six done real quick.

It was a little strange, though. As I was working, the farmer asked me to keep the testicles clean. Okay, that's not so unusual, except when I asked him what he was going to do with them, he told me that he was going to cook them. "They're delicious," he said. And then when I was done he invited me to stay for dinner. I didn't get out of there as fast as the pigs did, but I was still pretty quick.

Goats are easy; most of the time it's not difficult to catch goats. We probably dehorn an average of a thousand goats a year. Goats usually don't run away; they are very curious. When you walk through a herd of goats or sheep, they're all nice to you because they want to know what you've got in your pockets, or if you have something in a pail for them. If you want to make friends with a goat, give it something to eat. And goats will eat anything. There's an old joke, "Do you know goats helped settle the Sahara Forest?"

"It's not the Sahara Forest. It's the Sahara Desert."

"Oh sure, *now*." Goats are generally easy to handle, and once you have them, they stand still. Their attitude is, *Okay, you got me—go ahead and do whatever you're going to do.* But years ago, before farmers began dehorning their goats, they could be dangerous. I remember having to deal with a goat whose horns were at least a foot and a half long, and that goat scraped them against a rock wall to sharpen them. Those points were like daggers. Unfortunately, there was a horse on the other side of that rock wall, and one day that horse just looked over the wall to see what was going on and that goat poked its eye right out.

Sheep will run. Sheep are herd animals. Their only defense is being in a group and running as a group. One sheep may just stand there; a flock of sheep will run around you or, if necessary, over you.

I certainly remember the most unusual animal I've ever had to capture. Somebody called one day and told Diane in a nervous voice, "Could Jan come over pretty quick? There's a very big bird looking in my kitchen window."

A bird looking in the kitchen window? Well, that wasn't so unusual; we have birds on trees or even sitting on the sill that seem to be looking inside. But when Diane asked the caller to describe the bird, she said, "It's standing on the ground and looking in the window. It's about seven feet tall."

"Uh, okay. What kind of bird is it?"

"I don't know. That's why I'm calling you."

My son, Charles, was just a little kid at the time. We got into our Jeep and drove right out there to see this seven-foot bird. It turned out to be an emu. Some farmers had just started raising them. Emus are tall birds; they don't fly, but they run and jump. I've actually had several emus as pets. I like them a lot—they're silly; they make me laugh. I had never handled an emu before, but this poor guy—or gal, because you can't tell the difference—was pretty sad looking. It was pretty obvious it was hungry; that's probably why it was looking into the kitchen. It was a little skittish; I walked up to it very quietly and put a sock over its head. I pushed it a little and it squatted down. Just like ostriches, they think when they put their head in the sand, nothing can happen to them. It's an odd kind of behavior. Maybe they think if they can't see you, you can't see them. But they're seven feet tall—you can't miss them! It just means they can't see the danger. I picked the bird up and carried it back to the car. "Hold him down, Charles," I said. As we drove, every time that bird tried to raise its head, Charles pushed it down.

We put it in with the horses. The horses looked at it nervously. *What the heck is that thing?* At first it just ran away from the horses, but then it got comfortable, and later it came and ate out of our hands. Another time I got a call from the animal control officer. Another emu had gotten loose in Clare and was running along the highway. Somebody had called the dog pound—I guess because they didn't know whom else to contact. The dogcatcher went out and spotted the bird but didn't know how to catch it. "So," he said to me, "what are we going to do?"

"I'll get it," I told him. By that time I had learned a little bit about emus. When they feel like they're in danger, these birds stand up straight, but when everything is safe, their bodies are horizontal to the ground. Straight up, danger; bent over, safe. So I started to approach the bird. It looked at me, wondering if I was a danger. It wasn't sure, so it started moving away from me. Right then, instead of standing straight up, I bent over at my waist as far as I could. The bird tilted its head—*What the heck is that guy doing?* Then it decided, *Okay, I guess everything is fine,* and it bent over. We stood there for a minute, bent over and looking at each other. Then I slowly walked toward this bird, staying horizontal until I got close enough to put a dog lead over its neck. "Come on," I told it. "Let's get out of here." I led it to the car like that.

When she was safe, the dogcatcher asked me, "What was that all about? Where'd you learn to do that?"

I told him, "They taught me."

Some vets use a tranquilizer gun to get control of animals. Not me; I don't even have one. Tranquilizer guns are gas-propelled guns that can shoot a vial with a needle point as far as fifty feet. I know they can be effective, but they're not for me. If I carried one every time a farmer has a cow that's running loose, he would expect me to use it. I'm just not going to tranquilize animals other people have not been able to catch. That's not my job.

There are times, though, when tranquilizing an animal is the only way to contain it. One time, eight beef cows got loose in Claire County and ran into the woods. People think cows are slow, lumbering animals that might not even be able to survive in the wild. That isn't true; cows will fool you, and those cows adjusted to being in the wild pretty quickly. They were able to elude people trying to catch them. Those cows lived in the woods for months. People were trying to shoot them with tranquilizers but never got close enough. Finally some people drove them out of the woods, where a hunter was waiting for them. That time he shot them. He put all eight of them down.

If I do have to tranquilize an animal, I'll find a way of jabbing it myself. There was a woman nearby who owned a farm around here with her two sons, and they had a real mean bull. She was one of the few women around running her own farm. A few years before, her husband and his friends had been caught tearing up a golf course with a four-wheel drive. He was afraid that he was going to be sued for damages and lose the farm, so he signed it over to his wife. He must not have been so nice to her, because three months later she kicked him out.

Usually what we do with a mean bull is put a ring in his nose and attach a chain to it. But this was one tough bull. If you wonder where the word "bully" came from, this could have been the guy. My problem was I couldn't get close enough to him. "So how can we catch him, Doc?" the woman asked.

"Just watch me," I said, but then I added, "Pick me up if he gets me first."

He was watching me too. I walked slowly into the pen. There were several cows there and I was careful to keep them between the bull and me. Cows don't bother me: I push them a little bit; they push me. I kept moving, using one cow, then another as a shield. Finally I got close enough to his butt so that I could suddenly reach over and hit him with the tranquilizer. He turned fast, but I was gone already. I got myself out of there. Then we watched and waited. Five minutes later he was getting woozy. Another five minutes and he was sleeping peacefully. I walked right up to him and put the nose ring in, put the chain on it, and walked away. Then I saw something I have never seen before. Didn't know it was possible, in fact.

That bull must have been awfully mean to those cows, because when they saw he was down and not moving, they went after him. Oh, were they angry. They butted him with their heads; some of them climbed right over him. Man, they beat him. I said to the lady, "I guess you'd better go and help that guy before they kill him."

"I think so too," she said, but I also thought that maybe she was glad those cows had the chance to get a little even. Who knows, maybe she was thinking about her own life. Anyway, she and her sons chased the cows to the other side of the barn and locked them out.

When I was in the pen with that bull, we never took our eyes off each other. The way he was looking at me, it was pretty clear he was curious but didn't trust me at all. His body language was warning me to stay away from him if I knew what was good for me. If you pay attention, animals will tell you how to handle them. You can look an animal in the eyes and pretty much tell what it's thinking about you. The look in its eyes will tell you whether that animal is angry, afraid, or friendly. You just have to be experienced enough to under-stand their body language. A few months after I started to practice, I was doing a health test on the Murphy Beef farm. At that time they had a herd of heifers. We got a few of them in the pen, and I remember jumping into that pen and trying to run them into the head gate, where they would be easier to handle. I was flapping my arms and yelling at them. This one heifer turned and looked at me once, then twice, and the next thing I remember is being smashed up against the gate. A couple of men reached in and yanked me out of there. "Doc, didn't you see that?" one of those hands asked.

"See what?" Mostly I was seeing stars.

"When they give you one look sideways and then another one the other way, get the hell out of Dodge, because they are going to charge you."

That's exactly what she did, and I wasn't ready for it. That was the first time I was hit by an animal. After that I got a lot better at reading animals: When a cow gets angry, she will swish her tail really fast; that's her way of telling you, *Just go away and leave me alone.* Horses will talk to you with their ears and their body posture, but the ones you have to watch are horses that snort and open their nostrils. That means they are not interested in being examined or treated by you.

Just like large animals, small animals will make their intentions known if you look for the signals. Except for cats; cats keep their own secrets. But I've found that as long as you can maintain eye contact with most animals, they will rarely try to bite you or charge you—except Chihuahuas. I don't know why, but I've just never been successful in understanding a Chihuahua.

The way I work is to get the story from the animals and the people, do my examination and make a diagnosis, explain what the prognosis is going to be, and then install treatment. There are a lot of different things I look for when I start my examination. While I pay attention when people tell me what they think the problem might be, sometimes it goes in one ear and doesn't stop till it's going out the other ear. "Well, yeah," I often tell them, "you could be right. But I think it could be something different." Then I make my own diagnosis. People want to help, but they miss a lot. Or sometimes they play down the symptoms because they don't want to admit that their pet is seriously ill.

A lot of people know about me and Pol Veterinary Services in Weidman, Michigan, because they've watched the show, so they call the clinic to ask questions. I can't legally do very much on the telephone, but I try to be helpful. I had a call from an Amish farmer who lived at the end of our practice area. "Doc," he told me, "I have a cow that's off her feed. What can I do?"

Well, that doesn't tell me too much. "Do you think it could be hardware?" I asked him. Had she swallowed something?

"It could be," he said, " 'cause they were pasturing. But it could also be pneumonia. She's been acting strange and her production is way down."

From this description it could have been anything; the symptoms of a variety of problems, including hardware, pneumonia, and a twisted stomach are very similar. Sometimes the animals run a temperature, sometimes they don't. But this is typical of the way people describe their animals' condition. After asking him a few more questions, to which he gave me the same types of general answers, I told him, "If it was me, I'd put a magnet down. Then I'd put her on antibiotics and see how she does for a couple of days." Hardware is very common. Putting a magnet down doesn't cause any damage in case the cow's problem is something else entirely. It won't make the cow any worse. The magnet is just dropped down into the second stomach, the reticulum, which is a small stomach that holds mostly water. Usually it's about six inches across, but it can contract real fast to as little as two inches. If there's hardware in there—a little piece of wire, for example—when that stomach contracts the wire could go through the wall, and that hurts, and the cow stops eating. But if it is hardware the magnet will pull it right out.

Two days later he called again. "Still not good. Can you come out? I'd hate to lose her."

When I got there it was easy for me to diagnose the problem, but there was no way he would have been able to. The cow had a twisted stomach on her right side; that's a serious problem. Normally I would have told him to send the cow to market, but because he had given her antibiotics, she couldn't go. Surgery wouldn't have helped her even if he could have afforded it. When you do this surgery, only one in four animals survives, and this animal wasn't going to be a survivor. If the farmer had been just a little more accurate in describing the symptoms, I never would have suggested he give that cow antibiotics. That's why I never depend too much on what people tell me. The cow's problem was completely different from what I thought, but I never just walk away without trying to do something. "We're going to roll this cow," I told him, which in some situations can resolve that problem. I'd done it before and it had worked some of the time. So we pulled the cow down with ropes and let it lie on its back for about five minutes. I could hear the gas in the twisted stomach being released, which is a very good sign.

The most important question I always ask is, What is this

animal doing differently? Animals like doing the same things the same way every day; when they change their behavior, there is definitely a reason for it. One of the things they told us at Utrecht was to use all of our senses when we're trying to figure out what's going on. Look at it, touch it, listen to its heartbeat and its breathing, smell its breath, even use your sense of taste. By this time I've examined enough animals to know what a healthy animal looks like, feels like, sounds like, and smells like.

Obviously the first thing I do is just look at the animal. I know what a healthy animal looks like and what it feels like, so if something is changed, hopefully I'll see it or feel it. Usually by the time someone calls me, the animal is pretty sick. When people get that sick, right away they go to a doctor, but until an animal begins showing symptoms, there is no way of knowing it isn't well. So we don't get the chance to treat a problem early. When you look at a sick dog, for example, you can see that it doesn't feel good. Its eyes are not clear; its heartbeat isn't good; its color is bad. Then I'll run my hands over its body, feeling the lymph glands, the resiliency of its skin, seeing if I find any lumps. In big dogs I've found lumps as large as six inches across. All these things taken together usually will allow me to make some kind of preliminary diagnosis.

Usually. Sometimes the symptoms are so general I can't make a good diagnosis. This lady once brought her rat in, and I ran my hands over it, and every milk gland, both sides, was swollen. Rats are notorious for tumors, but these weren't tumors; there actually was fluid in the nipples. The only thing that was logical was a false pregnancy, which we see quite a bit in dogs. But I'd never seen a rat with all the milk glands swollen. That was the symptom, but the cause of it was almost impossible to diagnose. I could have run a lot of tests, but there was no guarantee I'd be able to identify the problem, and even if I could, it probably wasn't curable. So there wasn't much I could do for it. I suggested she use cold compresses and wait. Later on the same lady came back with another rat and told me that the sick rat hadn't gotten better so she'd taken it to another vet, who told her they were tumors and killed it on the spot. Whatever the cause, those weren't tumors, but he didn't know what to do either; it was a rat, so he killed it.

I'll always smell an animal's breath. Cats and dogs often have stinky breath, but it's a normal stinky. But with small animals, when their kidneys aren't working right you can smell the urea, which can tell you a lot. You can also smell if its teeth are bad, if there is an abscess or sores in the mouth. All of those things have different smells, which you can pick up.

One problem that can usually be determined from smell is ketosis, a metabolic disorder that can cause a variety of problems in a herd. Some people can smell the presence of acetone in milk; it's like a dirty sweet smell. Not everybody can smell it; for some reason women are more sensitive to it than men. In fact, on family farms when both the husband and wife did the milking together, it would most times be the woman who picked it up. I had good clients like that: The wife would detect and tell her husband, "Call Jan; tell him we got ketosis." If only one of six cows in the milking parlor had it, she could pick it out. But for a long time I couldn't. Believe me, I tried; it's a valuable skill to have. Then suddenly I was doing a check and smelled a cow's breath and said, "Wait a minute. That's ketosis." There was no reason I know of that I suddenly became sensitive to it, but that's exactly the way it happened. Now I can smell it.

Mastitis is a very common infection of a cow's milk glands that causes a high white cell count and spoils the commercial value of its milk. The fewer white blood cells in the milk, the longer its shelf life will be; the longer it can stay on the shelf, the more valuable it is. So farmers are always looking for ways to lower the white blood cell count. If mastitis spreads on a dairy farm, it can be financially disastrous because the farmer can't ship any milk. When I was working in the Thumb, a lot of dairy farmers used an old type of milking machine; these machines weren't much more than a bucket and a very thin galvanized line that supplied the vacuum, but for the amount of milk cows were giving, it was sufficient. But over a period of years farmers had learned how to increase production so much that those small lines just were no longer good enough. There wasn't sufficient airflow. The farmers just didn't know it, and as a result mastitis became pretty common. Several of those farms actually were in danger of going out of business.

There are different ways to diagnose it; sometimes when you feel the animal's milk glands, they are a little harder than usual, or when you look at the milk you see some flakes or the milk is watery rather than pure white. But a lot of times there are no obvious symptoms; the cow just seems lethargic. An old farmer back in the Netherlands told me once, "If you think the cow has mastitis but you can't see it, go ahead and taste the milk." So that's how I diagnosed it in the Thumb. I would squirt just a little bit of milk on my hand and taste it with the tip of my tongue. I didn't drink enough of it to make me sick. But I could taste the difference from normal milk;

the milk tasted a little bit salty. I could tell right away what it was.

We convinced the farmers that they had to upgrade their milking machines; then we treated their entire herd. The farmers were able to begin shipping milk again, and they were able to stay in business.

I learn a lot by listening too. An animal can tell you a lot just by the way it's breathing or the way its heart is beating. There are times it's obvious. A farmer named Dave Livermore called the clinic and asked me to get right over to his place because one of his young alpacas was choking. I raced right over there. It was a little guy and it was struggling to breathe; the breaths were shallow and strained. It was obvious that something was stuck in its esophagus. I asked him, "What kind of grain you feeding it?"

"Oh, I give them pellets," he said.

I figured. Pellets basically consist of different dehydrated grains, which can include corn, oats, barley, and soybeans. The problem is that those pellets are hydroscopic, meaning they attract and hold water. Sometimes an animal eats some pellets too fast; the animal can't produce enough saliva when it swallows and the pellets expand and get stuck in the esophagus. I felt around the neck until I could figure out exactly where these pellets had gotten stuck. When I found a hard spot, I pinched it as hard as I could, crushing it; the alpaca swallowed and I could feel the grain just disappearing into the alpaca's stomach. I didn't even have to put a tube down its throat. Within a minute that alpaca was breathing evenly and easily again.

I told Dave that he shouldn't be feeding just pellets; he also needed whole oats. All he had to do was mix the oats with the pellets and he'd never have this problem again.

An animal's body is supposed to sound a certain way. Sound will bounce around the body in a very recognizable way, and when that sound changes, it tells you something has moved. Something is different. This is sort of a human sonar system. For example, sometimes cows go off their feed and there is a drop in their milk production for no obvious reason. I can't tell you how many times I've been told, "I don't know what's wrong, Jan. She just isn't herself. And she's not producing like normal." In those instances, while listening with a stethoscope on the left side, I'll put my fingers near the stethoscope and flick the spot, then listen for a certain sound, sort of a ping. If I hear that sound, it tells me that this cow has a twisted stomach on the left. That's not unusual; giving milk is a hard job. It requires getting a lot of nutrition. Sometimes when cows are eating a lot of high-energy foods, their abomasum, or fourth stomach, tends to flip over; instead of being on the bottom of the cow, it gets displaced and floats out of position and gets stuck there.

Basically, this fourth stomach is the closest of a cow's stomachs to the human stomach. It's filled with different acids and gas, which normally might cause it to rise. But it stays in place below the much larger rumen, just like a balloon doesn't move if there's something heavier on top of it. If for any number of reasons the rumen gets small, that balloon will roll out from underneath it and the gas will make it float upward. Usually it displaces to the left, which is easier to fix than if it displaces to the right. There are different methods to fix this displacement. I learned the roll-and-stitch method: You put the cow on its back, which will cause the abomasum to float up, but this time it's actually floating up to the bottom. You suture the stomach in place against the body wall so it stays there, and then you roll that cow over until she is sitting back on her chest. It can take several strong people to roll a cow. Don't try this at home. Cows can't figure out what the heck you're trying to do, but whatever it is, they don't particularly like it. The stitches hold the abomasum in place until the rumen can get filled up and blocks it from floating again, and about a week later you can take the stitches out.

There are a lot of good tests and tools that we can use to help diagnose an animal's problem. I love new tools, and when a good one comes along we'll get it right away. When I got started there were only a few reliable ways of diagnosing an animal, but now there are so many do-it-yourself tests that let us check for all kinds of different conditions. For example, when a cat was lethargic and not so responsive, we could only guess, *Maybe it's feline leukemia*. To confirm the diagnosis, we had to send a blood sample to a lab, and it took as long as a week to get the results. Then the SNAP test was invented. All we do is put a sample of the patient's blood in a little plastic container with porous paper in it, add a reagent, and *snap!* The reaction of the blood and the reagent on the paper will tell me whether the blood is positive or negative for feline leukemia. Instead of a week, the test takes about eight minutes, and it costs a lot less. There are similar tests to confirm a lot of different diseases.

In the clinic we have an X-ray machine, ultrasound machine, a blood chemistry machine, a surgery laser, and a therapy laser; we even have a gas anesthesia machine. And we now have a very good microscope with a camera on it. For certain problems, each of those machines is very good. But for me, even though there are things I can't do under a microscope because I'm color-blind—I have to get the slide ready and ask someone else to look at it for me—there still is nothing better than the microscope. My main use of the microscope is for intestinal parasites. I had a call in the middle of the winter from a young man living about sixty miles away telling me, "My goose is sick and my local vet won't even look at him."

"How come?" I asked

"I don't know. He just told me not to bring him in."

"Okay, go ahead and come on over."

He was raising this goose for his 4-H project. I have always been a big supporter of the 4-H. He walked into the clinic carrying his goose under his arm and put it down on my examining table.

"Hello, goose," I said to him, rubbing my hand over his body. "What's bothering you?"

That goose stood there letting me check him over. It was surprisingly tame. Its temperature was normal, but when I felt his breastbone I noticed there wasn't too much muscle. "What are you feeding him?" I asked.

As the young man started to answer that question, that goose did what geese do best, and he did it on my examining table. "Okay," I said, "Thank you very much. That's exactly what I want." For a vet this is a very good thing. I took a sample—believe me, there was no shortage of sample material on my table—and examined it under my microscope. Aha! It was loaded with worms. That was the problem. I asked the young man, "Where do you have him housed?"

"In the barn right now because it's so cold out."

Meanwhile, that goose was honk-honk-honking away happily. He was having a fine time. I showed the young man the sample under the microscope and he saw the worm eggs. "This is the wormer," I said, handing the product to him. "Treat him with it and make sure his pen is as clean as possible." I never heard from him again, so it must have worked.

Sometimes, though, even my microscope isn't sensitive enough. A heartworm is a parasite that grows in the hearts of mostly dogs and cats. It is spread by mosquitoes; when an animal is infected, the worms travel through the bloodstream, and they can cause severe damage to the heart, lungs, and other organs. It's a serious disease that can be effectively treated—but if it isn't treated, it can be fatal. Years ago, heartworm was almost unknown in Michigan, but we see it more often now. Heartworms can be a foot long, and they don't lay eggs because they are living in the circulatory system, which is enclosed; instead, just like some snakes, they give birth to live worms—what are called microfilaria. We used to test for heartworms by examining a drop of blood under a microscope; if we saw those little wiggly things, then we knew, *Oh yeah, this guy's got it*. But even if we didn't see them, depending on the symptoms, we still took preventive measures. Now, instead of looking for microfilaria, we test chemically for the presence of the antibodies that the animal produces to fight the heartworms. This test allows us to positively confirm the presence of heartworms much earlier than we were previously able to do and to start treatment to safely eliminate them. These are the type of do-it-yourself tests that we do all the time now, making it possible for us to check for a lot more things than ever before. They provide more information and they do it faster and, in many cases, less expensively than in the past.

The temptation is to rely completely on these tools and just go ahead and ignore decades of experience. I don't do that; I can't. Young vets today depend way too much on diagnostics. An animal comes into the clinic and they run $500 worth of tests, hoping something will show up. In the human medical business doctors run every possible test because they're worried about being liable if something unexpected should happen. That's a problem that vets don't have; cows don't sue. I try to use my experience to make a preliminary diagnosis, and based on my examination and my experience, then I'll use a specific test to try to confirm it. If the test results don't back up my diagnosis, then I'll reconsider that diagnosis.

I pay attention to test results, but I never depend on them solely. I've seen that machines don't always give you the right answer. There have been many times when I did the blood work on an animal, and all those modern tools told me the animal's liver was not bad at all. After the animal died I opened it up, and the liver was completely shot. There was just enough liver function that the enzymes tested normal. As I had learned when I was just starting, even an X-ray, which in many situations can be very valuable, can't provide all the answers.

Back in Harbor Beach, we didn't even have an X-ray machine. One day, a woman brought in her dog, which had stopped eating. That's not a clue that leads in any specific direction diagnostically. We checked the dog over and didn't feel any problems during the physical examination. We did all the regular tests, and everything showed up pretty normal, but that dog wouldn't eat. Dr. Hentschl was on the board of the local hospital, and sometimes they let us use their X-ray machine. Most of the time we anesthetized the animal so it would stay still during the procedure. These days we hardly do that just for X-rays. For me there's too much risk involved, so we'll just hold the animal still. It takes a little bit longer to do it that way, but that's just the way I want to do it.

The X-ray technician was very good. He took the X-ray and looked at it. Nothing there. Okay, let's try again. The next day he took another X-ray. Again, didn't see a thing. We didn't do barium studies in those days because that would force us to take repeated X-rays every few hours. Finally, the dog died. When an animal dies for reasons we don't understand, I always want to do an autopsy. I want to learn from that animal. As soon as we opened up the dog, the answer was right in front of us. He had swallowed a chestnut, and that chestnut had completely closed his intestinal tract. But it hadn't showed up on the X-rays. It was just like the broom bristle in Utrecht. I was the third man in the practice so I didn't speak up, but what we should have done was open up that dog and find out the problem. Dr. Hentschl was very conservative in his treatment, though, so this wasn't something he usually did. I understood that—operating would have been expensive without having any idea whether it would make any difference.

One problem with X-rays is that not much shows up on them except bones and stones; soft materials don't show up very clearly. Sometimes, though, even when you can't see anything specific, the X-ray tells you what you need to know. When we look at the X-ray, for example, we might see a pocket of gas in front and nothing behind, so obviously there is something there that is plugging the intestinal tract up. In that situation we'll put the dog on the table and open it up. Often, there it is.

"So are you missing a glove?" I said to the owner.

"Oh my gosh. How did he eat that?"

I had opened up the dog, took out a whole glove in one piece, and sewed him up. For two days we gave him no food, kept him on an IV, and then sent him home happy.

I tell owners that dogs will eat anything, especially if it has blood on it. That glove had been worn when the dog's owner was skinning an animal, so the smell of meat was on it. Believe me, sometimes even I don't believe what we find inside an animal: socks, nylons, and we even sometimes treat dogs that have eaten rocks. This guy brought his hunting dog in with the usual complaint: He's just not eating. When I ran my hands over his gut I felt something hard in there. We didn't know what it was until we opened up the dog and found three rocks in his stomach. The dog's owner figured out what had happened. He had to butcher a deer on some rocks and blood had dripped on them. *Hey, that's pretty good,* this dog must've thought, and then swallowed those rocks. Then when they got caught in his stomach and intestine, he didn't feel so good.

If an object smells like food, a dog will eat it. There are plastic plugs that parents put under the nipple on a milk bottle so the milk doesn't drip out until you're ready to feed a baby. I took five of those rings out of a dog once. He had smelled the milk on them and decided that tasted pretty good. "Where'd he get all these rings?" I asked the owner.

"I don't have any idea," he told me. "We just knew they were missing."

I've never treated a cat that had eaten a rock; instead, cats eat stringy things. A professor at a small private religious college brought his kitten into the clinic just after Christmas. That kitten had quit eating. *Uh-oh*. I know what's around the house during Christmas. I felt the animal's body, and its intestines were very thick. That meant there was something inside, because if something gets plugged in there, it pulls everything together. "She was playing in the Christmas ribbons," he said.

"Oh, did you miss any?" I was pretty sure I knew the answer to that question.

"Well, we couldn't tell." We opened her up and I took out a piece of tinsel maybe a foot long. It was shiny and looked interesting; why wouldn't a curious cat eat it? Fortunately it hadn't done any damage. We sewed her up and she bounced right back to normal in a day.

After all the years I've been doing this, I know when to take an X-ray, but there are still people who think it's always necessary. On one segment in the show I treated a calf with a front leg that got broken when a cow stepped on it. I couldn't even guess how many broken limbs I've treated, so when I feel a broken bone, I know exactly what's going on. In most situations an X-ray isn't going to show me something that I don't already know, and it's going to cost the farmer as much as $200 to fix a calf worth $100. It's cheaper for him to shoot it. That's harsh, I know, but that's the economics of farming. They brought the calf into the clinic, and I could feel where the fracture was; when I straightened it out, you could actually hear the snap. The camera crew winced. After the bone was back in place, I wrapped the leg in cotton, encased it between two pieces of thin, pliable bushel-basket wood, and taped it up. Boy, did I get criticized for that by some lady watching the show. She complained to the state that I didn't take an X-ray. *How could you fix a broken bone if you can't see it?* she wanted to know. But I did see it—with my hands. Oh, I was angry when I was notified about that complaint.

I never hesitate to use a good tool if I feel I need it, but if it isn't going to give me more information than I already have or can get in an easier way, I won't use it. A lot of large-animal vets use ultrasounds to do pregnancy tests on cows, for example. It's the hot way of doing this test. But I'm not one of them. For me, at least, using an ultrasound would take longer and would cost a lot more to get basically the same information that I learn by hand. Also, the ultrasound is a good tool, but it does not work if the cow is more than three months pregnant. If a cow is one or two months pregnant, it's very nice. If a cow is three months pregnant, you can still do it, but there are many times we do pregnancy tests for cows that are four or five months pregnant or more. I had a couple of heifers that were six months pregnant or more and I examined them with an ultrasound and showed the results to the farmer. "What do you see?" I asked him.

"I have no idea," he admitted.

"Well," I told him, pointing to a hazy image, "that's the leg of the fetus."

He squinted his eyes and said, "Oh yeah. Now I see it."

I get the same results when I do the test by hand. I reach inside there—admittedly, sometimes I have to dig out some manure, which is not my favorite thing to do—and I go right to the uterus, and within ten seconds I know if that cow is pregnant or not. Then I palpate the uterus to confirm that and see how far along she is. I still have to confirm it because I've made some mistakes; there are times when the uterus is enlarged and has good fluidity, and I come to find out that the uterus is full of pus. One time, I examined a cow that had more than a gallon of pus in her uterus. We got it out and she's fine; she survived.

Most of the time when I finish my examination I have a pretty good idea what's causing the problem. Then I make my prognosis; I tell the owners what to expect. I'm always completely honest with them about that. If the problem can be treated, I tell them the cost. If there are options, I tell them all the options. There are many times when people ask me, "Are you sure, Doc?" I tell them, "I'm as sure as I can be." There have been a few times when people tell me they disagree; okay, in a short time we'll find out who's right. If the cow gets better, thank you very much.

Sometimes people say I'm too blunt, but I can't lie. I can't tell them, "Here's a bunch of pills. Just give them to him, and in a week he'll be better," when I know that isn't what's going to happen. I want people to be prepared for what to expect. We'll always do everything possible to keep the animal alive, but we are not God; we only can do so much.

When I'm treating small animals especially, there are always people who don't want to hear the truth. Sometimes they have no idea how sick their animal really is. Many, many times, people have told me, "Oh, it's just a cold," or "It's just a kidney infection," and I end up discovering the animal has cancer and will live only a few more weeks or months. I make it as easy as possible for them, of course, and I'll do whatever is possible to make the animal feel better and to take away the pain.

With our animal patients, just like with humans, there are times when all the symptoms add up to nothing that makes sense, and I can't make a diagnosis. That is really frustrating: We know there is something wrong, but we just can't figure out what it is. Then I'll tell the owner, I don't know exactly what's going on with this animal. When that happens I'll treat the animal symptomatically and see what happens. If an animal is dehydrated, for example, maybe I'll give it Gatorade. I know there are vets who say Gatorade is no good for animals, but I've been using it for a long time without it ever causing a problem. It works just as well in animals as it does in people; it rehydrates and replenishes lost minerals. Dogs don't drink it usually, but when they're throwing up and have some diarrhea, that's what I give them. For that purpose, Gatorade is fantastic. For certain viruses, just keeping animals hydrated over a period of time is enough to make them better. Maybe I should do a commercial for Gatorade.

Sometimes the best treatment is aspirin. Aspirin is an anti-inflammatory painkiller that works in most animals just like in people. There are aspirins for cows that are about three inches long and about eighty times stronger than the aspirin we buy in the drugstore. One time, I remember, I was on the road, and I had such a splitting headache that, oh my gosh, I had trouble driving. I got mad at myself because I didn't have any regular aspirin with me. Then I thought, *Wait a minute.* I stopped the car, opened a jar of aspirin, and licked a cow aspirin. A few minutes later, I was good to go. The headache went away. Anyway, a lot of times when I'm not sure what the problem is exactly, I'll recommend aspirin and see what happens.

I also give animals Pepto-Bismol and Kaopectate. Kaopectate actually comes in gallon jugs, and I use it with calves all the time. I mix it with milk or any other electrolytes they're being fed, and it coats the intestinal tract. Both medications remove acidity and coat the intestinal tract, so once the calves quit throwing up and start keeping fluids down, we got it made.

I'll try anything that makes sense and won't hurt the animal. When a treatment doesn't work, we'll just try the next one. There's a disease that only horses get called uveitis, or moon blindness. As a result, horses go blind, usually in one eye. The history goes all the way back to Alexander the Great, when it was thought the blindness was caused by changes in the moon cycles. It starts as an infection that progressively gets worse if it isn't stopped. I've seen several cases in the Amish horses in Michigan. My sister had it on her farm up in Canada too. Usually we try to treat it with antibiotics, but most of the time that treatment doesn't help very much. When we found uveitis in an Amish farmer's herd, I just decided to improvise. We have a vaccine for a bacterial disease that dogs get called leptospirosis, or seven-day fever. We don't have a lepto vaccine for horses, but I could get the dog vaccine. I bought a 25 cc dose and sent it to the Amish farmer, and it seemed to work: He had no more horses come down with moon blindness. Sometimes you just have to think outside the box and cross your fingers.

I don't give up easy. If I try something and it doesn't work,

I'll try something else. I never run out of trying. When nature tells me there is nothing more I can do, I'll reluctantly accept it and do what I can to make the patient comfortable. But if there's hope, I always tell my clients, if they're willing to try, I'll do it. I've got nothing to lose.

There are times when my clients don't want to accept my diagnosis. There was a fantastic gentleman, a Korean War vet named Rupert, who came in one day with his small dog. Rupert had been a client for a long time. He'd had another dog that he loved for a long time, and that dog had gotten diabetes. We'd kept it alive as long as possible, but finally we had no choice; we had to put it down. Honestly, when I did that, I thought, *This is the end of Rupert too.* But I was wrong. Instead he spent several months going from dog pound to dog pound and to all the animal control centers until he found a dog that looked just like the one he had lost. It was wonderful, as if he had gotten his best friend back. The two of them came in to see me one day while the crew from Nat Geo Wild was filming. As the cameras were rolling, Rupert told me he was there because his dog was not eating.

It wasn't all that hard to see the problem. That dog had gained too much weight. I examined him and I didn't find any physical reason that would cause a substantial weight gain. I asked Rupert, "What have you been feeding him?"

The dog basically ate all the same things he did, he told me. "He's eaten chicken breast with me; he's eaten steak with me . . ."

That was the problem; he was killing that dog with love. I remembered what I had learned in school so many years earlier. "He isn't sick. He isn't eating because he's just not that hungry. You can't feed him off the table like that," I told him. "It isn't good for him."

"But he likes it," Rupert replied.

"If you want to keep him healthy, you have to stop," I said.

It was obvious that wasn't what he wanted to hear. In fact, as he and his dog walked outside, the camera crew followed him all the way to his car as he explained the problem to his dog, muttering, "Dr. Pol's trying to tell me you're too fat and that I shouldn't feed you. D'you hear that? You're too fat . . ."

As usual, the dog did not say anything.

FOUR

A World of Wondering

Early one evening a man came rushing into the clinic carrying a very sick dog. It was a beautiful animal; it must have weighed as much as 120 pounds. But this dog was totally lethargic, he had a very high fever, his breathing was strained, and he had a lot of fluid in his belly. "What in the world happened?" I asked.

"Don't know, Doc," he said. "He just got that way. I rushed him right over here, soon as I noticed it. Whattya think?"

"I don't like it," I told him. "I don't know exactly what's wrong with him, but it's not good." There wasn't too much I could do at that time. "Let me keep him overnight. I'll work with him, see what I can do." I did the few things I could to make him more comfortable, then went home for some dinner. I went back to check on him a couple of hours later and he seemed to be resting a little better. But when I got to the clinic the next morning at seven thirty, the dog had died.

There was no obvious reason why this animal had died. I called the owner and told him what had happened. Then I asked his permission to do an autopsy. I wanted to know, I wanted to learn from this if I could. He gave me permission, and as soon as I opened him up I saw the cause right in front of me. The owner wasn't going to like it, but I had to be honest with him. "Did you have a party recently?" I asked.

I already knew that answer. Of course he had. "And did you serve hors d'oeuvres?" Of course he had. I knew it because I'd found a six-inch-long wooden skewer in the dog's stomach.

They had used skewers with sharp points for the cheese and whatever else, and when they were finished, these long sticks had been thrown in the garbage. These sticks had a strong food smell on them, so the dog did what dogs do: He dug into the garbage and swallowed the stick. The sharp point had gone through the intestinal wall and resulted in peritonitis. It was like a person having a ruptured appendix. If they had brought the dog in sooner, there are treatments that could have helped him, but by the time the symptoms became noticeable it was too late to save him.

Accidents happen all the time, and when they do, instead of calling 911, people call their vets. In a small town, the vet never really keeps office hours. If there's a sick or an injured animal, I'm there. You have to be available anytime an animal needs care, and you can't be squeamish. Sometimes you see things that you never even thought possible, things that can break your heart. One night a farmer called and asked me to come right out to his place: "I've got this cow with its foot cut off."

When I got there he brought in the cow, and I could hear

it coming; it sounded like someone walking on an old-fashioned wooden leg: *Tonk, step,* step, *tonk, step,* step. This poor animal came hobbling in walking right on her bone. But she was trying to make it. "What happened?" I asked.

The cow had been in a free stall, he told me. There are basically two types of stall: a tie stall, where the cow is tied up and can't get out, or a free stall, in which cows can choose whichever stall they like in the barn to lie in while chewing their cuds. This cow had been in a free stall and got up and walked out to get something to eat while they were scraping the alley. The manure alley runs the length of the barn, and it's where cows do their business. This farmer used to clean the alley by scraping up the manure in a metal bucket in front of a tractor. The problem was that eventually that bucket's edges would get razor sharp from being pushed along the cement floor. It was like a big, sharp razor blade. What happened was that cow backed out of its free stall, slipped on the manure-covered floor, and kicked the bucket. If the tractor had been two feet farther away, nothing would have happened. Funny as that might sound, it wasn't funny at all. The farmer barely even noticed it and kept scraping. When he finished, he went back to his other chores.

In the evening the cow came limping into the milking parlor to be milked. He heard her coming. That's when he looked at her leg and discovered that the whole bottom of her foot had been sliced off. She was just walking on bone. It wasn't anybody's fault.

There was nothing I could do for that animal. There was no way it could survive with that foot missing; she looked fine and the bleeding had stopped, but eventually that open wound would have got infected. I told the farmer to take her to slaughter while she was still healthy so he could get something for her.

An animal that can't support its weight and move around can't survive. Putting down that cow was the most humane thing we could do for her. But I treated a horse for a similar injury and he did fine. This could have been a much more terrible accident. An Amish farmer was giving his granddaughter a ride in the wagon for her birthday. Somehow the tongue got loose from the harness. The tongue is like the brake on a wagon, and without it, it's difficult to stop. When this tongue broke loose, the wagon started running into the butts of the horses. In that situation I probably would have pulled hard on the reins to stop the horses, but the wagon might have run right into them; instead, trying to protect his horses, the farmer was trying to stop by making a wide circle going up a hill. Unfortunately, they went through this old metal fence and ran right into a pile of metal garbage. At least a third of the horse's hoof had been ripped off. It was gone and I didn't know how it could be repaired. After examining it I told the farmer I wasn't too sure what we could do for him. "This is a sweet horse," he told me. "He's well broke, and if there's something we can do . . ."

"We can try," I told him. There was enough there for the horse to balance himself on. "If it doesn't work, we'll have to put him down, but let's give it a try."

As with every injury, you have to be concerned about stabilizing the animal, preventing further damage to the injured area, then stopping infection. Many animals survive the original accident but end up getting an infection and fighting for their lives. This damage wasn't quite as severe as the injury to the cow, who had lost her whole foot, but it was a serious injury. There was nothing I could do to repair the damage; there wasn't anything to work with. I cleaned out the wound and made it as sterile as possible, then wrapped it and gave the farmer a lot of medicine and good instructions for what to do with it. When I left I told the farmer, "Don't give up; he's got a lot going for him." Within a few weeks the horse was walking. His hoof was flopping a bit; he probably had broken some tendons, but that would scar over. The most important thing was that the animal was able to put weight on his hoof.

When an injured animal comes into the clinic, you never know whether or not you'll be able to save it. You know you have to make quick decisions and just hope that they end up being right. In a rural area it isn't uncommon for us to see dogs that have been hit by cars. One of the most controversial episodes on the show started when a nice couple brought in their Boston terrier, which had been hit pretty hard. Mr. Pigglesworth was in bad shape. He had taken a big wallop in his head, he was all cut up and bleeding, one of his eyes was hanging out of its socket, and I suspected he had some internal injuries. The woman was crying—that's something we have to deal with a lot—and asked me several times if he was going to be okay; that's a question I usually don't like to answer. I didn't want to lie, so I gave her the best answer I could: "That's what we're here for." Then I gave her a hug, which she needed badly, and went to work.

My son, Charles, was working with me. Each of our three kids, Kathy, Diane Jr., and Charles, had been helping out since we opened the practice in our garage. Kathy wanted to be a nurse and loved helping with the surgeries, even though she had to stand on a bucket to reach high enough. Charles had been riding with me since he was four years old, so he knows how to be helpful. After giving the dog anesthesia, I took a series of X-rays to determine the extent of his internal injuries. Because of the visible head injuries, the owner was afraid he might have fractured his skull. I didn't think so; the dog was walking fine. You walk, you're not brain injured. That's just common sense. The X-rays showed that he had a broken pelvis, which I could see would heal nicely by itself, and no head injury. That's when I knew I could save this guy.

But there was no way I could save his eye. So I gently cut the tissue around it and removed it. That sounds a lot more gruesome than it really is; a lot of animals adjust very well to their physical limitations. When Charles asked me about it, I told him, "With one eye he still can see better than you with two." Then I remembered Charles wears glasses, so I added, "Or four."

After cleaning up his cuts and sewing up his eyelid we put him in a cage to recover. Within two hours he was sitting up and, except for that eye, looking pretty good. He looked at me out of his one eye as if to ask, *So, Doc, what the heck am I doing in this cage?*

After the segment was broadcast, another vet complained pretty loudly that I had done everything wrong: Supposedly I didn't give the dog sufficient anesthesia or pain medication, the treatment area wasn't sterile enough, and I didn't intubate the dog, meaning I didn't put a tube down his throat so he could breathe more easily.

When I heard about those complaints I just had to shake my head. I know that there are always people who are going to complain, but that dog had been seriously injured and could have died; instead he walked out of the clinic wagging his tail. Believe me, after all these years I know how much anesthetic is necessary, I know how the dog is going to react. I don't get angry that often, but when a person accuses me of not caring about animals, that gets me angry. I've spent my whole life caring about animals. I can't bear to see an animal mistreated in any way. One time, for example, when we were still living in the Thumb, Dr. Hentschl sent me out to a farm to do about a dozen pregnancy checks. I had never seen a farmer so mean to his cows. He was yelling, screaming at them at the top of his lungs, and hitting them. Finally I had enough. He was a lot bigger than me, but I didn't care. I got in his face and I told him, "You don't stop hitting these cows, I'm going to beat the tar out of you." I darn well would have done it, too, if he hadn't stopped. That was the last time I was there, because he had to sell his cows: He was mistreating them so they were not milking for him.

I would never hurt an animal, and no animal is more vulnerable than when it has been seriously injured. That Boston terrier was in shock, which complicated things, but the way he reacted to what I was doing told me that he wasn't feeling pain. One thing I've learned is that animals react differently to pain than humans do. Another dog I treated had been hit by a car; his front leg was broken and dangling, but he had managed to run home. He was wagging his tail when the owners opened the door and saw he was hurt. I'd like to see a person come running home with her arm dangling and still have a smile on her face. Believe me, when Diane broke her wrist, she wasn't smiling at all.

Anyone who complains about nonsterile conditions has never worked with animals in an emergency situation. How do you make a barn sterile when a cow's insides are hanging out? That little dog had been ground into the dirt; his eye was hanging out. The treatment area wasn't sterile, and it was impossible to make it completely sterile. I've treated a lot of dogs that have been hit by cars. One dog—I remember this guy very well—was brought in with his intestines hanging out. Can I make him perfectly clean with his intestines hanging out of him? Of course not. In that emergency situation I gave him the anesthetic, washed up everything as best as I could, found out where the hole was, and pushed the intestines back in. Then I gave him some antibiotics and some painkillers, and that was it. That dog did just fine.

People like that woman veterinarian who complained try to humanize animals. They want to give an animal the same level of treatment they would give to a human being. But they're not human beings; they're animals. You do what you can do to save their lives.

An associate, Dr. Kurt, was on call at about midnight one night when we got an emergency call. A hunter was bringing in his dog, which had been badly hurt. Dr. Kurt could hardly believe the dog was alive when he got there, telling me, "It look liked this dog had been in a battle with a can opener. From inside the back leg, all the way up the leg to the abdomen, this dog was just spread wide open."

We have several clients who hunt for profit; they especially do a lot of varmint hunting. Most of them maintain a whole kennel of valuable hunting dogs. These are rough, tough men and you wouldn't think they would show too much emotion, but they get closely attached to these dogs. This hunter told Dr. Kurt, "I don't care what it costs. Whatever we need to do to put this dog back together, that's what I want to do."

"What happened?" Dr. Kurt asked him.

"This dog has a tendency to hunt really hard," the owner told him. "She was chasing a raccoon and thought she could climb a tree. She actually managed somehow to get up in that tree about fifteen feet. The raccoon jumped from one tree to the next one. This dog thought she could do the same thing. When she did, a branch got her just behind her tendon." The dog was impaled on a tree branch. It had taken a long time to get to her because they couldn't find her. They heard her screeching but didn't look up in the trees. By the time they got to her, she was badly hurt.

Dr. Kurt started cleaning and sewing, cleaning and sewing. There wasn't too much else he could do. The treatment was expensive, but fortunately it was successful. That dog was in and out of the clinic several times in the next few weeks. She ended up with a nasty scar, but within another month she was out hunting again.

I know my own limitations. After all this time, I'd better. I know what I can do and when an animal needs more help than I can provide. The McConnells were among my very first clients when we moved to Michigan. I've been treating their animals all these years. John McConnell's main business was the slaughterhouse, but he also had some cows, and his wife, Diane, had just a few very valuable quarter horses. One of them was an expensive stallion she'd brought to Michigan from out west. During a big storm, this horse was hiding in a little lean-to type of shack, and the wind blew the shack over. Exactly how it hit him we never knew—accidents happen—but the timbers caught him square on the right shoulder. The McConnells called me early in the morning and asked me to come over quick. I ran over there and took one look and thought, *Oh my gosh.* The falling shed had almost cut the neck band, the strong tendons that hold up the horse's head, right above his shoulders. There was a hole there at least six inches deep, there were some bones broken, and it looked like several spines of his vertebrae had broken off. I had never seen that kind of wound. I did what I could right there; I flushed out the wound as well as possible and took out some pieces of broken bone and hair. Then I said, "Unh-uh. This is too much for us to handle here. You need to take this guy to Michigan State, where they have much better facilities." We put the horse on antibiotics and painkillers and they took him there.

They treated him there for more than two weeks, and he survived. He had a divot in his neck and he walked a little funny, but he could still breed. The McConnells are the kind of solid people who support the whole neighborhood, and the most help I could give them was to admit that I could do only so much.

Horses have a tendency to heal really well. Unlike dogs, for example, horses don't chew on their sutures; they let their bodies heal. I've worked on some really ugly wounds. I remember one horse that went through a high-tensile wire fence and got a spiral cut on one side from the shoulder almost all the way down to the hoof. In that situation all you can do is suture, suture, suture. I gave that horse a tranquilizer—actually, a combination of three tranquilizers—and just kept sewing. One way of preventing infection is to continually hose off the wound with cold water for three or four days; that'll wash out a lot of bacteria and reduce the swelling. It works.

It's amazing how tough horses are. I've seen horses injured by running into something, and the owner doesn't even know it because the horse doesn't show any distress. It comes when it's called, it eats, and everything is normal—until the owner notices a wide-open gash. The horse doesn't care: *Food's here, I'm eating.* I work at the fairgrounds in Mount Pleasant when we have some kind of competition. I was there one time and I got a call that one of the horses had tried to crawl underneath the trailer door and ended up with a big hole in his butt. It was right on top. It was an angled cut with each side about six inches long, and underneath some of the meat was gone. I gave him a tranquilizer, pulled everything together, and started suturing. Then the owner tells me that the competition was starting in two hours and he still wanted to participate. Two hours. "Well," I told him, "I think you're going to be all right." And two hours later the tranquilizer had worn off and he went into the ring with that horse and won first prize. It was so exciting they could have made a movie out of it.

Most of the time people don't care how an animal's injury or a wound looks after it heals, as long as it heals. But once I had a show horse that hooked his nostril on something and ripped it open. A flap of skin from his nose was just hanging there. Normally that wasn't a big deal and would have been an easy fix, but this was a real expensive show horse. And this competition was like Miss America for horses, which meant that the entries couldn't have even small blemishes. The owner wanted me to suture the skin back into place. I told him, "No, that won't work; there's no blood supply left in there. But I can fix it."

I never thought I'd end up being a plastic surgeon for horses. I cut the ripped piece off and sutured the skin from the inside. Good as new. After it healed, no one could tell it had lost skin on that nostril.

Every accident creates a different kind of challenge, and you have to be able to adapt to the situation. Sometimes that means being creative, finding different methods to help the animal. In another episode of the show, a farmer brought a two-day-old calf with a broken leg to the clinic. I could feel where the fracture was, and I set the leg, wrapped it in cotton padding, and then rather than using a solid cast, I taped bushel-basket staves around it to keep it in place. I've been using bushel basket wood for a long time with great success. I've got as much of it as I need; it's wide and thin; and it doesn't bend much, but it curves around the leg easily.

The splint can be left in place for several weeks, it stretches with the animal a little, water doesn't hurt it, and after the leg is healed the farmer can just take it off and the animal is fine.

Broken legs are very common with cattle, and unlike in horses, in cows they often can be fixed well enough for the animal to live a long life. A local farmer was trying to load an adult cow in a low trailer, and the cow hit her front leg on the edge of the trailer and broke it. "She's a good cow, Doc," the farmer said to me. "I'd like to save her if we can."

I'm always going to try. We gave the cow an anesthetic, laid her down, and set her leg with basket staves. I had to use a lot more cotton and tape this time, because this was a big animal. She did fine, though. Her leg healed up a little crooked, but that cow had a solid leg to support her and lived a full life.

There was one calf that we healed that turned out to be special. There was a good client of mine who pulled a Jersey calf one day. When it was about a week old he had put it in his truck to take it to the county fair for the calf parade. He thought that calf would lie down in his truck, but it didn't; instead, it jumped out of the truck and broke a front leg. Some people would have killed that calf—it cost more to fix it than it's worth—but these are nice people. He brought it to the clinic and asked if I could do something with that leg. We set the leg just like usual, and when it healed he told me if I wanted that calf I was welcome to it. Yes, I wanted it. So I took it.

Elsie, as we named her, was about the tamest animal you have ever seen. She grew up to be a big, pretty girl. When she was a year old, my daughter Kathy took her to the county fair, and little kids rode all around on her. The second year, as she was walking around the ring to be judged, Elsie just decided to sit down and relax. So she did, right in the ring. Nobody was going to get her to move until she wanted to move. So she just sat there looking around at everybody and maybe wondering why people were laughing. We milked her for four years, but by then the kids were in high school and couldn't give her the attention she needed. I was busier, too, but most important, Diane said we had to sell her because her milk was 5 or 6 percent butterfat so we were all gaining weight. We sold her to a Jersey dairy farmer who we knew took good care of his animals.

One of the more interesting segments in the show started when a woman brought in a little Schnauzer named Zeke, who was limping so badly I thought for sure he had a broken leg or a displaced hip. "He's mean," she warned us. "Be careful. He's really mean." Well, I know how to handle animals, but she was right—this was a mean little dog. That dog tried to bite anybody and everybody who pointed a finger at him. Maybe he was mistreated as a pup—who knows what happened to him?—but he didn't like anybody getting too near him. It's okay to have sympathy for animals, but being sorry for an animal goes away pretty quick when it keeps snapping at you. Even after I gave him an anesthetic he was fighting it; he did not want to lose control. Finally he was out, but even then he was causing trouble; when animals are under anesthetic they can't control their bladders, so as Charles was carrying him upstairs from our X-ray room, Zeke let loose on him.

That little dog didn't know how lucky he was; there are a whole lot of people who wouldn't have put up with that attitude, much less spent their money taking him to the vet. I didn't care about his attitude; I've been nipped by bigger dogs than him, and I didn't have to live with him. The first thing I did was take X-rays. But when I looked at his leg and his hip, I was surprised; everything looked okay. He was much too young for arthritis, so that wasn't causing the limp. I needed to take a good look at him.

"Next time you see him," I told the woman, "he's gonna be bald." Zeke was covered with long and thick hair, which had matted and knotted all over the place. I thought for a while it might even be wrapped over his butt, preventing him from defecating. I had actually seen that before. That wasn't it, though. I had to cut through his hair; the woman told me Zeke had bitten his groomer more than a year earlier and no one had been able to get close enough to him to cut his hair since. I definitely could believe that.

Charles and I started trying to clip his hair. At first we were using regular small animal clippers, but they didn't do any good; the hair was too badly matted, so I put them down and used cow clippers. And when I got most of the hair cleared away from his leg, I discovered the problem: His hair had been wrapped so tightly around his back leg that it had literally cut through the skin. He had a big, open hole in his leg. I had never seen anything like that before. I cleaned up the wound and stitched it up.

A lot of vets will improvise; most times there isn't only one way to solve a problem. I like to say that if you never try to do something, you'll never be able to say to yourself, *Hey! It worked!* So as long as it isn't going to hurt the animal, sure, I'll try anything that seems to make sense. Some people brought a Great Dane in with a broken leg. It was a bad break and I had to put a pin in it to hold it together. The pins we had were too small, so I called the local hospital and told them, "Hey, I need some human pins for a dog."

"For a dog?

"Sure, why not?"

"Okay, Doc," they said, "we'll fix you up."

They gave me a whole tray of huge pins. I put one of them in the dog's leg and told the owners to keep him quiet.

The dog came back a week later. The pin was bent; that dog actually had bent the steel rod in his leg. "You let him run too much, didn't you?" I said.

They told me that he'd gotten away. It was frustrating. I couldn't take that bent pin out, so the leg healed with it in there. As I told them when I checked him for the last time, "As long as he doesn't try to go through airport security, he'll be fine."

The danger to an animal doesn't end when the damage is repaired. There are a lot of problems that can take place during that healing process. We used to have a Jeep Wrangler, and Charles's dog Maeson, my blood donor, loved to ride in that car. Maeson had come to us from a couple in Lansing who just couldn't keep the dog in town. She just wanted to be outside. One day I put her in the car and slammed the door just as her tail came whipping around, so it got caught in the door. I opened the door right away and the back end was flattened just a bit. That's not the most unusual injury, and while it can be painful for the animal, it isn't life threatening. And the loss of part of a tail doesn't affect a dog at all. A dog's tail doesn't have an important function; we cut the tails off hunting dogs to make it easier for them to move in the brush without getting their tails bloody. I treated Maeson's tail and bandaged it, but she wouldn't leave it alone. She kept licking it, preventing it from healing. She did serious damage. I had to cut pieces off it three or four different times. She just wouldn't leave it alone. From then on to the end of her life, when she was mad at us or if she was left alone too long, she'd start chewing on that tail. She definitely showed us!

Through the years I've seen some memorable and unbelievable things. Several years ago I got a call from a young farmer who was trying to work a small dairy farm with very little help. "Doc, can you come right away, please?" he said. I happened to be close by and I raced right over there. I got there within five minutes and I couldn't believe what I was seeing. The free stalls in his barn were divided by metal pipes. One of those metal dividers had come loose; either it rusted off or hadn't been properly connected, but as a result there was a pipe close to a foot long sticking out of the cement. This cow had slipped or fallen onto that pipe and ripped her belly wide open. But what was amazing is that she was pregnant and actually performed her own C-section. Her uterus had opened and her calf had come out. The calf was lying right beside her, completely healthy and awake, and shaking its head, while the cow was lying beside it. She wasn't bleeding, but she was hurt bad. I asked him, "What do you want me to do?"

He shook his head; he didn't know.

There was nothing I could do. Her insides were torn apart, her intestines were lying on the ground, and her uterus was split. There was no way of stitching up that cow. And even if I tried, there was no way of preventing infection. I had to be blunt with him: "Go get me the gun. You want meat; you got meat." People ask me if I feel bad when something like that happens. The answer is of course I do. I feel bad for the animal and especially for the farmer. Farming is a hard business, and it has gotten a lot harder since I've been in practice. For the small farmer especially there isn't a lot of profit to be made, and every dollar makes a difference. This was a hard-working young guy who was doing his best to work a living out of small operation. There wasn't a lot of extra money to buy another animal or pay vet bills. But you know what? All I can do is try to help them keep their animals healthy and fix them when they get sick or hurt.

But the reality is that accidents happen and sometimes there is no way of saving the animal. At one farm we were doing regular pregnancy tests. This farmer's barn had no stalls; the heifers just lay down in the hay wherever they wanted. To do the checks, we ran the heifers behind a gate. We'd done four or five without any problems at all, but this one cow just wasn't interested in cooperating with us. She just would not be caught. We started running her to one side, which meant she had to turn the corner in order to get behind the gate. This younger guy was running beside her, but instead of turning the corner she ran straight into the cement wall. She broke her neck. Her body twitched a few times, but there was nothing that could be done for her.

That time there was no question about what killed that animal. But sometimes we do everything we can do and the animal dies and we don't know why. Many times I'll ask permission from the owner to conduct an autopsy. I don't charge; I want to know what happened. Many times, an autopsy gives closure to people. After the death of an animal, people often wonder if there was something they missed or something else they could have done that might have saved their pet. In the summer of 2013 I had a man bring in a dog that had been fine in the morning, playing happily, and late in the afternoon it suddenly collapsed. It was alive when he got to the clinic, but it died before we could do anything. The owner needed to know what happened, for his own peace. The first thing I did was flip up the lip to look at its gums. The membranes in his mouth were pure white. That meant the dog had died by bleeding out; his tissues weren't getting any oxygen. But why did that happen? I started feeling around its belly. The belly wasn't swollen, but I wasn't surprised when I felt a lump. "Feel this," I told Dr. Sandra. Dr. Sandra was real smart coming out of vet school, but like a lot of young vets starting their career, she wasn't too sure of herself yet. Cases like this one helped her get the experience she needed. When I pushed a little on that lump, it almost disappeared. That was strange. "Let's do an autopsy," I said. Even after practicing all these years, the way the body works, and why it stops working, still fascinates me.

I did the autopsy. The lump I'd felt was in the spleen, and when we'd manipulated it we'd busted it. So the whole spleen was just mush. It had been what is known as a splenic hemangiosarcoma, a blood tumor, in the dog's spleen. It had broken and the dog had died in less than an hour. There was absolutely nothing the owner could have done. In some cases, it's possible to do surgery for this, but the outcome rarely changes. We would have had to remove the whole spleen, and even if that was successful, most of the time the sarcoma has spread to other organs, so after surviving a couple of not-so-great months the animal will die anyway.

It isn't at all uncommon for people to feel guilty when their animal dies. It makes them feel a lot better to know that there was nothing else they could have done, that what happened wasn't their fault. For farmers, it's very important for them to know the cause of an animal's death, because they need to make sure that whatever it was doesn't affect the rest of their herd. When Dr. Ashley was working with me, we got a call one day from a farmer in Clare who wasn't a regular client. He normally used a vet farther away for some reason. That's okay; people form relationships with a vet, and when they trust that vet there is no reason to change. But suddenly he called us. Four of his forty cows had died in one week, and some of the others were showing signs of distress. Could we get right over there? Dr. Ashley and I got there as quick as we could. I liked working with her; she was a fast worker and a hard worker; some people said she was one of the few people who could keep up with me. She had very small, strong hands so she could work inside an animal. She stayed with us at the practice for ten years before moving to North Carolina and opening her own practice. We walked through the herd, and a lot of those cows were just breathing heavy. It was obvious they were struggling. The farmer took us to the body of the last cow to die, and I cut it open. That cow's lungs were almost solid; there was barely any lung tissue left. "You got pneumonia," I told the farmer. Pneumonia is pretty easy to recognize. The lungs lose all their elasticity and the animal can't breathe. Sometimes a small strip is still functioning; if the cow's lungs are a foot deep, there's not more than four inches, sometimes as few as two inches, working, and it's impossible for the cow to get enough oxygen from that little piece of lung, so it dies.

Once we had learned what was killing the cattle, we had to figure out what to do to stop it. We had just heard that there was a new vaccine for this pneumonia. We hadn't used it yet and didn't have any. We called the manufacturer on a Saturday and told them we needed it overnight if possible. We got the vaccine pretty quickly and vaccinated the rest of the herd. We also had the farmer open the barn a little more, change the climate inside, and put the surviving cows on an oral antibiotic. He didn't lose any more animals.

Back in Harbor Beach we did a lot of autopsies, especially when we hadn't been able to diagnose the problem. Dr. Hentschl encouraged it because we all learned from them. We were Quincy, Animal Coroners. With farm animals we'd usually seen them before, so we knew what their symptoms were, and we'd remember the causes. The next time we saw that set of symptoms, we had a pretty good idea of what the cause might be. And if it was possible to treat it, we had a good head start.

Sometimes the symptoms are obvious. When a cow has diarrhea, for example, we know we have to test for bovine viral diarrhea, a virus that can be deadly. A lot of farmers will send a calf's ear notch to be tested to make sure it is negative for the virus; if the test is positive, the calf probably is going to die at a young age.

But a lot of other things are much harder to diagnose. Sometimes during the autopsy we found an abscess just hanging on the liver. An abscess can be caused by different bacteria, and when it's on the liver or lungs, it can be very difficult to diagnose. The body tries to keep it under control by fighting it with white blood cells, which make pus, and in turn that pus produces toxins that go through the body, causing the symptoms. Suddenly the animal doesn't feel good, even though there are no obvious reasons for it. The first few times I saw an abscess I had no experience in recognizing it. But as time passed I would see a sick animal, I would treat it, it would die, and during the autopsy I would find the abscess. And after I had seen enough of them I suddenly got smart. *Okay*, I thought, *now when I see these symptoms I know what I'm looking at.* And sure enough, another farmer had a big fat steer that just was not in good shape. After examining it I told him, "This steer has a liver abscess."

"How do you know?" he asked me.

Well, I certainly couldn't see through the animal's skin. "The symptoms," I told him. "There's no temperature, but the animal is dull; yes, it eats a little and drinks a little, but the manure is pasty instead of normal. That's not good. My suggestion is to butcher her and see if the meat is good." They took the steer to the slaughterhouse and butchered it. They had to throw away the meat, though; they told me there was an almost football-size abscess hanging on the liver.

A lot of time when diagnosing an animal there isn't that much you can tell just by looking at it. Sometimes after you open up an animal you discover things like cancer of the spleen that make you wonder how in the world this animal lived so long. Early one spring an Amish farmer asked me to look at one of his horses, which had no obvious symptoms, but according to the farmer, it just "wasn't right." It wasn't eating; it had a little temperature; it was a little lethargic. The symptoms were so general and vague that there could have been a long list of possible causes. We put it on antibiotics to see how it responded. The next day it was dead. "Doc," the farmer said, "I just want to know what's going on."

This was a big animal. It was lying out in a field, and I started hacking away at its hindquarters. As soon as I opened the horse up I saw what had happened; this horse had died of peritonitis. I'd considered that diagnosis but couldn't find any reason for it. And even as I looked at the horse's body, there still didn't seem any reason for it—until I cut open the large intestines. It was just full of tapeworms. Coincidently, as I was doing the autopsy, it started snowing. Tapeworms in horses are white, short, and wide, just about the same size and color as the snowflakes. There were white spots all over the horse, a weird mix of tapeworms and snowflakes. What had happened was that one of those tapeworms had made a hole in the intestine, and bacteria had leaked through and killed the horse. It was very unusual, but obviously it was something I've never forgotten.

Sometimes an autopsy is the only way of solving a mystery. Another horse I was called to look at was carrying a colt and was constipated. That's not terribly unusual, but it's something worth paying attention to. I treated the horse over the weekend: I gave her a whole gallon of mineral oil and about five gallons of water to chase it. I told the farmer, "Okay, let's see if anything comes out."

By Monday morning, nothing had come out. That was a very serious problem then. The farmer asked me what I wanted to do next, and I told him, "This is all I can do. Why don't you take her over to Michigan State and see what they say."

The people at Michigan State did surgery and found what is called a fecal stone, or fecalith, a ball of stool that is rock hard and blocks off the whole gut. "Okay," I said when they told me, "now it makes sense." That was the problem. The farmer brought the horse home and it did fine for about a month. Then it developed diarrhea. So I went back there again. The horse's temperature was normal. I treated it as an infection and it got a little better. But it wasn't completely right. It would eat a little bit and then be uncomfortable. Dr. Brenda, who began working at the practice after graduating from

Michigan State in 1992, went over there and ran a bunch of fluid IVs. The horse didn't get any better.

The farmer didn't want to take the horse back to Michigan State. It hadn't done any good, he told me. I went back because I've got the longest arms in the clinic, and I reached inside and found another one of those big hard balls of manure. I could barely reach it; I used the tips of my fingers to scrape it apart and then pulled out the pieces. Behind the stool the manure was regular. It was just blocked from coming out. After I finished clearing out the hardened manure, I said again, "Let's see what happens." It was a real mystery.

A week later they called to tell us that the horse had stopped eating again. It had drunk a little water, but it was getting very weak. They had decided it was time to put the horse down. Sometimes that's the best course. This animal was suffering, and there was nothing more we could do to treat it. I agreed that Dr. Brenda would do it, but I asked if I could do an autopsy the next morning.

When I opened up that horse, I saw that the intestinal tract had become completely atonic; in other words, the colon, which is normally about eight inches across, was at least twice that size, and it was just full of manure. It was unbelievably big; I'd never seen anything like that, so there was no possible way of diagnosing it. There was no way that the gut could contract enough to move food through it. While I'll never know for sure, what I suspect happened was that the first fecal stone had extended the intestine so much it damaged the muscle; the muscle could no longer do its job, which is to contract and push the food through, so the food just stayed there. The more the horse ate, the bigger the colon grew. The intestinal tract stopped working and slowly filled up with food.

I also could see that the surgery they did at Michigan State was perfect: There was no infection, no adhesions, no nothing. It wasn't anybody's fault. It just happened, and there is no way anybody could have diagnosed that problem.

An autopsy will do some good only if you understand what you find. If the cause of death is obvious, like hardware, for example, then that's easy to understand. But usually in an autopsy you have to determine what's not normal in the animal and then try to figure out what caused it. One of the sad cases I had was a young farmer who lost eight out of his nine cows, and there didn't seem to be any specific reason for it. These looked to be big, fat, healthy cows; then, *boom*, they were dead. When I began doing the autopsies, the one thing I discovered that they had in common was that their livers were yellow. There were a few things that could cause that, so I started asking questions. What I discovered was that the reason these cows were so fat was because they were being fed corn silage and ground corn almost exclusively. The soil in Harbor Beach was so good, it was easy to grow corn, and farmers used it for feed. In steers that's okay; the bigger they are, the more they're worth. But in dairy cows that was a bad thing, as he was raising his pregnant heifers with his steers. The heifers tried to mobilize the body fat and use it as energy, but their livers couldn't digest it too well. They do much better digesting hay. That body fat could be only partially digested, but was also partially stored in the liver, and eventually it just got to be too much. He was feeding them to death. When I told him the reason his cattle had died, he kind of shook his shoulders and said, "This is what we got, Doc."

I told him, "Well then, get some more hay next year or you're gonna be burying more of these heifers." I guarantee you he didn't make that mistake again the next year.

On one of the episodes of the show I did an autopsy on a pet chicken that belonged to a nice woman who actually had several pet chickens. Some people wonder how anyone could have a pet chicken, but every animal has its own personality, and people become attached to them. To most people it's just another chicken, but to this woman it was a pet and she loved it as much as anybody else loves a pet dog or cat. She cared enough about this chicken that when it was unable to walk she brought it to the vet. When I examined the chicken, I felt a huge lump in her belly. The way it felt, where it was, made me pretty certain it was a tumor. "There's no way to cure it," I told the woman. "She should go." The kindest thing to do was euthanize the animal. She agreed, reluctantly, but wanted me to return the remains so she could bury it in the chicken's special place. I asked permission to do an autopsy first.

When I cut the chicken open, I was actually very surprised at what I found. First thing, I didn't find any tumors. An egg yolk had broken inside, causing peritonitis, a deadly infection. What I was feeling were pieces of egg yolks. Her belly was just filled with dried egg yolks. "There was nothing you could have done," I told the owner. "Nothing we could have done. No way to cure it."

"At least she didn't suffer," the woman told me, sad but satisfied she had done her best.

Actually, I've done many autopsies on chickens. Most

farmers in the area keep a flock of chickens. When one dies, it's okay; the farmer isn't too upset. It happens; chickens don't live that long anyway. But when the next chicken dies, the farmer thinks, *Wait a minute, this is too many. I don't want all my chickens to die.* They usually call me after the second chicken has died, and they do it to learn how to treat the rest of the flock. In the winter of 2013, a farmer brought in three dead chickens. They had died overnight, and they hadn't shown any signs that something was wrong. I opened them up and didn't see any obvious problems. The comb, the fleshy crest on the top of a chicken's head, was dark red, which can be a sign of oxygen deprivation. As I examined the organs I found small rocks in the crop, where the food collects first, then in the stomach, or the gizzard. It didn't make too much sense, so I started asking questions.

It was a typical central Michigan winter, cold and snowy. One icy afternoon the farmer threw out some special salt, which he'd bought to melt the ice that supposedly was safe for animals to walk on. Regular salt can irritate an animal's paws. But no salt is safe for animals to eat. Now, chickens will swallow pebbles and sand and store them in the gizzard to help them grind up food. The chickens thought the salt was pebbles or food and pecked it up, causing salt poisoning. They ate so much salt that their blood became hypertonic, which means it just goes to the periphery of the body, so it seems like it just disappears. That's why the comb was so dark red; a lot of blood had settled there. As a result there was not enough blood circulating to provide the oxygen they needed to breathe, and that's why they died.

One of the strangest situations I ever had to figure out

started with a call early one morning when a farmer told me he woke up that morning and had three dead cows. "I'll be right there," I told him. I actually had been out to his farm the previous afternoon to look at a cow. He hadn't been there, but when I examined the cow I saw she had a twisted stomach, an LDA, or left displaced abomasum, which is usually treatable by rolling the cow. But I couldn't do it without his help, so I left word I'd be back the next day. Now that cow was dead and this farmer was upset like the dickens with me. Whatever the problem was, he felt I should have figured it out.

As I rode over there, I wondered what had happened. The cow had a problem, but there was no reason in the world an LDA would have killed her. And there were two other dead cows, too. It had been a bad night: All night it was over eighty degrees and very foggy, with 100 percent humidity. The air just felt so heavy. Some breeds of cows don't do so well in extreme temperatures. Holsteins, for example, are the most comfortable between fifteen and fifty-five degrees Fahrenheit. When it goes above that, they get stressed, and when the humidity goes way up, they get really distressed. When it gets up to eighty degrees, they quit eating and milking. When we get several days in a row of very high temperatures, milk production will drop as much as 25 percent. So right away I was worried the heat and humidity might have had something to do with these deaths.

When I got there, I told him, "Let's open them up and figure this out." Sure enough, the first one—the cow I had looked at the day before—had a twisted stomach. She wouldn't eat, and under the stress of the warm and foggy night, she died. When I examined the second cow I found an infection around her heart, what's called pericarditis. She had scar tissue two inches thick around her heart. Normally the heart is in a sac with a little bit of fluid around it, like a lubricant, so that it can beat easily. Because of the scar tissue, the heart didn't beat well enough, and in the heavy air the cow couldn't get enough oxygen and died. The third cow also had a twisted stomach, but this was an RDA—the twist was the wrong way, which is very difficult to fix and causes other problems. The extra stress had killed that cow too. So this farmer lost three cows out of sixty, which was too many, and all three deaths were caused by the combination of high humidity and high temperature.

That farmer got even with me in his own way. He went bankrupt and never paid his bill.

There are times, unfortunately, when an autopsy reveals that we missed something. I had a pretty ordinary case in which a cow had a calf and did not get rid of the afterbirth. That happens; a retained placenta usually isn't an especially serious problem. I went over there and found a very sick cow. She had a 104-degree temperature and a very badly infected uterus. I put the cow on antibiotics to treat the uterus. I told the farmer to keep her on the antibiotics for the next three or four days, and hopefully that would clear up the problem.

She died two days later. That didn't make sense to me; that uterus should not have been so bad that the cow died. I did an autopsy and I saw the real cause of her death right away. "Oh my gosh," I said. "Look at this." I held up a piece of wire that I'd found in her stomach. "Who would have thought?"

This farmer fenced in his pasture with woven wire, squares of wire that come in a roll and can be as much as six feet high.

A lot of times people use it to keep deer out. It's not like barbed wire, which cuts anything that touches it. Woven wire doesn't have sharp edges; it just makes a barrier. When it's in good condition it's not dangerous, but when it gets old and rusted, it breaks off in six-inch pieces. These small pieces are cow killers. They are the worst; they are just long enough to get into the stomach and just sharp enough to go through the stomach wall into the heart. If a farmer mows hay in that field and doesn't know those pieces are there, they can get picked up in the bales of hay. This is exactly what happened. The cow had swallowed a piece of wire that was hidden in her hay. She had a bad uterus, but when she was straining to deliver her calf, the pressure pushed that piece of metal through the wall of her stomach into her heart, killing her.

I had missed it; it was completely masked by the infection in her uterus, which could have caused those symptoms. There really was nothing anybody could have done, although it does make me a lot more wary when I see anything similar. Fortunately, there is a way to avoid most of that hardware problem. While farmers try to be careful, it's surprising how many small pieces of metal are just lying on the ground. So when the farmers start chopping hay or corn, the machine should have a big magnet in it, and everything that's chopped up goes right over that magnet and any metal in the feed sticks to it.

There are times when you don't have to do a full autopsy to get the answer you need. In addition to everything else that we do in the practice, sometimes we get brought into a legal situation and are asked to do a forensic investigation. *CSI: Weidman!* That's us. In the afternoon of a very hot summer day in about 2003 a man went to the casino on the other side of Mount Pleasant. He left a long-haired German shepherd under the canvas cover in the back of his pickup. He didn't think he was going to be inside very long; he was just going to make a few bets and then go home. It turned out to be his lucky day, he thought. He couldn't lose. But while he was inside, a guard walked by his truck and saw the dog having seizures, so he opened up the truck and pulled the dog out. After a couple of more seizures, the dog died. The casino called animal control, which blamed the death on the owner for leaving it in the boiling-hot truck bed, and wanted to bring charges against him. They brought the animal to the clinic so we could determine if hyperthermia was the actual cause of death.

The dog's body was lying in the garage. Dr. Eric began making preparations to open him up. Dr. Eric loves working with small animals, especially dogs and cats, so this is what he does at the practice. I asked Eric, "Did you take its temperature?"

"No," he said. "The dog's been dead more than four hours."

"Let's do it anyway," I said. Four hours after its death, that dog's temperature was 114 degrees. One hundred and fourteen degrees. Oh my goodness. Granted, the animal's long hair acted as kind of insulation to hold in the heat, but geez, that's twelve degrees higher than normal. Of course the dog died from that heat.

The prosecutor from Isabella County told me, "I'm gonna get that guy. He's going to be in jail for three months."

I asked, "Why? That guy was stupid. He forgot about his dog 'cause he was winning. Just take all his winnings away plus extra. Give him that big fine and make it that for five years he can't have a dog."

The prosecutor went along with my suggestion and they told me that the owner was really upset about not being allowed to have a dog. If you're used to having a dog in the house and suddenly you're not permitted to have one, it can be very tough. I wouldn't know what to do if I couldn't have a dog in my house for five years. So I thought that was a much worse penalty than three months in jail.

There have been times when even an autopsy hasn't helped figure out why an animal died. Those are the most frustrating cases of all. When I was working in Harbor Beach, all of a sudden milk production went way down. It wasn't just one farm; it was happening all over the state. And then cows started dying. This went on for almost three years. We didn't see too much of it, but even a few cases were too many. Every vet in Michigan was getting called for these cases, but there was nothing anybody could do about it. Nobody could figure out what it was. The autopsies didn't show anything unusual. No matter what people tried, it kept spreading. Finally a farmer in Battle Creek who had a PhD in chemistry noticed that the mice and rats in his barn were dying. Like rodents do, they were eating spilled grain. He sent them to the lab at Michigan State; they autopsied these mice and rats and didn't find anything. But then they used a sophisticated process called color chromatography, which breaks down a sample into all of its chemical components. They found a mystery chemical in the fat that they couldn't identify. Finally they had an expert from New York look at it; fortunately he had seen it before.

It was a chemical named polybrominated biphenyl, PBB, a fire retardant that was used in children's clothing at that time, and in the same family as polychlorinated biphenyl, which is a toxic substance. But the question was, How in the world was a chemical used primarily for making kids' clothing fireproof spreading among cows in Michigan? It took some detective work, but the state finally found the cause. A chemical plant near Saint Louis that was manufacturing the chemical was also making a mineral called calcium phosphorus, which went into cow feed. They put them in the same color paper bags, but the fire retardant was called FireMaster, while the feed was NutriMaster. So they ran out of bags for FireMaster in that factory and some smart aleck told them, "Oh, let's just put them in the other bags. It won't hurt." They started shipping this PBB out to Michigan in NutriMaster bags.

It wasn't the fault of the people selling the feed, but it was a serious problem. It was the kind of chemical that could affect humans who drank the milk or ate the meat of cows that had been feeding on it. The officials were especially worried about it causing cancer and birth defects. The rats that ate it did develop cancer. The officials knew the chemical was showing up in people when it was identified in the breast milk of a woman who had just given birth. As soon as we were told what to look for, we began testing animals. We had to take fat samples from cows before they went to market, and if the samples contained more than three parts per billion of this chemical, the cows had to be destroyed. Unfortunately, we found quite a bit of it.

Thousands of cows had to be euthanized. The problem was that because this chemical was a fire retardant, incinerating the bodies would only have released it into the air. So the bodies had to be buried. The state dug a large clay-lined pit up on a military base in Kalkaska County. Being curious, I wanted to see it. I decided to take my whole family up there with me.

Some families go to Disneyland; we drove up to Kalkaska to see where these cows were being buried. I went to a local police station to find out exactly where this pit was located. I told them that I was a vet and many of my clients' cows were being buried here and I wanted to see it. "Well, sorry, Doc," they said, "this is a state matter. We can't tell you." Okay, they were honest. I stopped at a local gas station and asked, "Where are they putting all these cows in the ground?"

"Over by Gera," a man told me.

"Okay, thank you very much. We're going to Gera."

The town of Gera was dead. We couldn't find anybody to tell us how to find this pit. *It's got to be in the military preserve,* I figured, and we went over there. Then I noticed a dirt road that recently had been widened. *Look at this,* I thought. I backed up and started driving down this road into the woods.

I kept going for about two miles and suddenly I saw several generators and trailers; before I could do anything, a huge National Guardsman holding a gun approached our car. This guy had to be seven feet tall and weighed three hundred pounds. "Oh my gosh," I said. It was like we had discovered some secret government operation. I kept my hands right in front of me and walked up to him. I said the same thing to him that I'd said to the police officer: "I'm a vet. My clients' cows are buried here. I'd like to see it."

"Can't let you in," he told me. Well, okay, at least he wasn't going to shoot me. I turned the car around and drove back about a hundred yards, then stopped and took some pictures. But a car followed me all the way back to the highway. *All right,* I thought, *maybe the next time we will go to Disney-land.*

FIVE

On the Road Again, and Again, and Again

I 've spent my life on farms. There's no good reason to be a farmer; no matter how hard you work, you have to do it again tomorrow; nature is always fighting you and there's never been much profit in it. My brother, also named Jan Pol, always said that farmers live poor and die rich. But if it's in your blood, there's no other place in the world that makes you feel content. My dad had forty acres; we had thirty cows and several Friesian horses, we were raising pigs, we had chickens for eggs, and we grew our own potatoes. Sometimes we had sugar beets. Those were the cash crops. There was always wheat and oats. When we moved into our area, my dad was considered a progressive farmer, and there were people who resented him. They weren't looking for change. But he had a milking machine rather than doing the milking by hand, as it had always been done. And then he bought a machine that fluffed up the grass; in the Netherlands it's hard to make dry hay, and this machine fluffed it up so it would dry faster. That was something people had never used, and there was some controversy about it, but when the other farmers saw how well it worked, they all went out and bought those machines too.

My main chore was milking the cows in the afternoon. After school I was always playing out in the field, so when it was time for me to do my job, we'd unhitch the horses and instead of walking them back to the pasture, I'd jump on the first one, hang on to the other one, and ride bareback as fast as I could to the first gate. Then I'd jump off. I was a kid; I never saw any danger. I started riding when I was six; when no one was looking, I climbed up on a wagon and got on a horse's back and didn't fall off. Even today I can't ride in a saddle; give me a bareback and I'll be fine.

All of our cows had family names. If they were descendants of Dina, for example, they were Dina 3 or Dina 4. I got to know animals very well, especially cows. I learned that there were some milking cows that wouldn't mind anything—they didn't mind being bothered—while other cows were just waiting for me to be in the wrong place so they could lift a leg. I had to be very fast to avoid them. If you have a really good look at my nose, you can see that I wasn't always fast enough.

While every small farm may look different, the feeling of being in a place like this is always the same. If you've been lucky enough to grow up on a farm, there is a feeling of comfort and belonging that you get the instant you step into the barnyard. There's a language that farmers speak; it's the total of farming history and experience, it's based in respect for the land and the animals, and if you speak it you're welcome on pretty much any farm. Because of my upbringing I've always been comfortable working on a farm. And when the practice first got settled, I spent almost all my time making farm calls. If you're interested in wearing clean clothes or smelling good, then you can't make farm calls. We've worked in every possible condition, from the heat of a Michigan summer, when you work up a sweat just getting out of the car, through the blistering cold of a Michigan winter, when the only way to stay on the road during a blizzard is to follow the telephone poles.

A large-animal vet needs four things: the tools to do whatever the job entails, the skills to do it, the ability to ignore foul odors, and a really good washing machine. It's never a question of whether or not you're going to get dirty; it's a question of how dirty you're going to get. If you work with animals, you are going to end up smelling like animals. I've spent my days and many, many nights walking through mud and muck; lying on cold, dirty floors; and feeling my way around the inside of an animal. You can't ever pick your working conditions; you have to work wherever you find the animal. It seems sometimes that it's always too hot or too cold, too cramped or too dark, too muddy or too dusty; it's always too something. One time I had to check a bunch of sick pigs on a farm, and the farmer was keeping them in a lean-to beside the barn. There is one thing I have never understood about pigs: Why did God make an animal stink so bad but taste so good? As I walked around looking at the animals, I suddenly stepped into a hole about two feet deep. It was filled with pig manure

Kampeerboerderij „Pol" Wateren Zorgvlied

This was my family's house in the Netherlands. It was here where my father taught me the simple values of honesty, hard work, and respect for all living things that have made all the difference in my life.

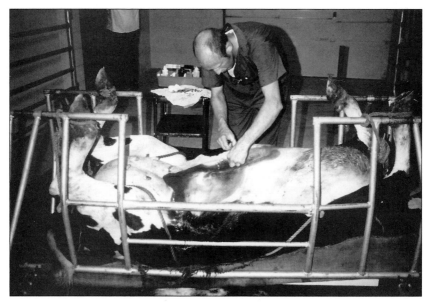

I learned how to be a large-animal vet working for Dr. Arnold Hentschl in Harbor Beach, Michigan. It was here I learned to treat the two patients in every case: the animal and its owner.

The staff of Pol Veterinary Services in 1995. From back left to right: Diane Pol, Andrea Warner-Matta, Jan Pol, Diane Pol Jr., Dr. Kurt Kiesling, Dr. Ray Viele, Malissa Miller, Barb Van Raalte, and Dr. Brenda Grettenberger. I'm happy to say that Dr. Brenda and Malissa still work with us, and I still didn't have hair back then!

This is the staff of Pol Veterinary Services, taken in 2010, along with the crew from National Geographic responsible for making our TV show. A lot of people didn't think a TV program about a farm vet would be popular—and I was the first one to think that. But the love for animals shared by the staff, the crew, and all of our viewers has made the show more popular than anyone could have imagined.

This 1997 photo of my associate, Dr. Ashley LaRoche, and me was taken after we'd struggled to deliver a Percheron foal. The animal unfortunately was dead and needed to be cut out of its mother.

Working with large animals often requires the assistance of several people. In this picture, Dr. Ashley LaRoche and I are fixing a hernia in a Belgian colt. While sometimes this work requires a lot of muscle, other times we need to be able to work in very small areas that require dexterity.

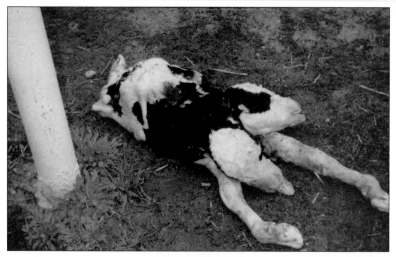

Yes, that is what you think it is: a two-headed calf that I delivered at a local dairy farm. This was the second two-headed calf I have delivered, and unfortunately, neither one could live. Just when I think I have seen everything during my long career, I get surprised by something different.

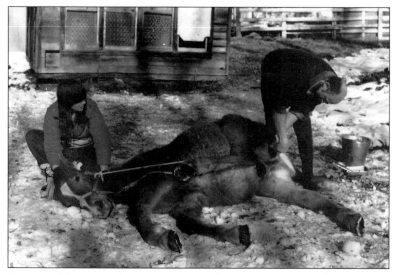

There are different methods of castrating a horse, as I'm doing with this Belgian yearling. Some vets do it while the horse is standing, and that's fine, but this is the way I learned to do it. While people think it must be painful for the animal, it's only minor. If it hurt, the animal would let you know it. Usually the animal is up and walking within a few minutes, and afterward it is a lot calmer and easier for the owner to handle.

I do have a special love for my horses. When one of my clients had a Belgian mare that was being overly aggressive with her colts, I put the colt in the front seat of my station wagon and drove it home. We raised it for three months, until it could protect itself, and then the farmer took it back.

Among the many pets we've had are dogs, peacocks, and sheep—and always horses. Always. I imported these two Friesian mares from the Netherlands. Friesians are big and strong and smart animals that tolerate people very well!

This is me at a goat seminar teaching how to dehorn a goat. While goats are generally pretty friendly, they can use their sharpened horns as a dangerous weapon, so we cut them off when the animals are young. They don't miss them.

I've spent a good portion of my life with my arm inside an animal's butt. It sounds a lot worse than it actually is, and it is absolutely necessary to make a variety of diagnoses. In this picture, I'm checking a sick cow for hardware, although Charles standing in the background looks like he might be the uncomfortable one. When I offered the members of the film crew the chance to do it, some of them jumped at the opportunity—while others jumped in the other direction.

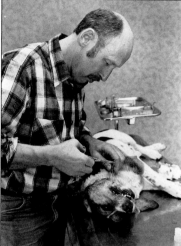

If cats are so curious, why is it that dogs keep getting facefuls of porcupine quills? We have to pull the sharp quills out one by one, and it's painful for the dog. But they don't learn, and sometimes we see the same dogs back again with more quills.

When we opened the practice, we treated mostly large animals. But the farming industry has changed, and now we treat more small animals in the clinic than farm animals. This little cat broke its leg and I had to set it. Almost without exception we've treated every type of pet imaginable.

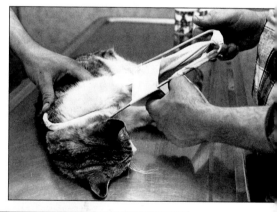

Many of my clients are too big to come to see me, so I have to make a farm call. Every large-animal vet carries his office with him in the back of his vehicle. Through the years we've driven through every type of weather, always communicating with Diane in the office on the intercom radio so we know where to go next.

Photographs this page courtesy of Werner R. Slocum

Many of the calls we get are routine and easy to handle, but even a simple problem can be deadly for an animal if we don't correctly diagnose it and treat it. In the picture at left, I'm running an IV of dextrose to a cow with ketosis, a common and easily treated condition that can lead to more deadly conditions when not treated quickly enough. On the right, I'm fixing the hoof of a cow that went lame.

and the manure went all the way over the top of my boot. Smells don't ever bother me—I can stay places nobody else can bear to be—but this was strong even for me.

"I'm sorry," the farmer said. "I forgot to warn you about that. We were going to put some more beams in here and never got to it."

What do you do when you're standing up to your knee in pig manure and the farmer apologizes to you? I just accepted it, took off my boot and washed it inside and out, washed off my leg, and drove home with bare feet because everything else stunk so much. Then I took a long, hot shower and went back to work.

Working in manure, getting it all over your arm when you reach inside an animal—that's part of this profession. Cows are never housebroken; they go to the bathroom as they're eating, so every barn has an alleyway behind the row of stalls, which is where cows mostly do their business. Farmers used to clean these alleyways by pushing a metal bucket in front of a tractor. That process grinds the side of the bucket until it has a knife-sharp edge, and as a result accidents—like a hoof being sliced off—happen. This alleyway was a problem because if you didn't clean it regularly, a couple of inches of manure and urine collected in the alleyway, and it was slippery. Cows would be slipping and sliding all over the place. Several times I almost slipped too. I got called one day to treat a cow for milk fever; when I got there, that cow was just sitting there in the alleyway. She'd fallen and she couldn't get up. I had no choice; I had to stand in the manure to treat her.

After I was done, that cow tried to stand up but couldn't get her footing; she kept slipping and sprawling. It was really sad watching this animal struggling to stand. In fact, the US government did a $2 million study of the problem, and after all their work they reported that manure is slippery. Thank you; any farmer could have told them that. "That's enough," I told the farmer. "Go get the tractor." Cows have very strong necks; I mean, you can't hurt them around the neck. We tied a long chain around her neck and attached it to the back of the tractor. "Just run with it," I told him. We positioned the chain so her nose would be held up. The farmer started pulling that cow, and it was just sliding along the alleyway with its nose in the air like it was water-skiing, pushing a wave of manure in front of it. When it got to the end of the alleyway, we unhooked it, and the cow stood up and walked away.

There was a man from this area named Don Mensch who came up with the idea of cutting those giant tires from construction and mining equipment crosswise and then in half again so you got sort of a giant curved rubber scraper, which could be pulled behind a tractor. He got a patent on the invention and it took off like crazy; now every farmer in this area uses one to clean the alleyway.

In this job you get used to bad smells—there aren't a lot of sweet smells—and like a pig farmer, after a while you just don't even smell things anymore. But there are terrible smells you never forget. Steve Fox's family dairy farm had a cow trying to have a dead calf. A couple of legs were hanging out of her, and there was some funky smell. The cow was fine; she was running around. We managed to get a rope around the calf and started pulling it out. Steve Fox was helping me and he said, "That really stinks, Doc, doesn't it?"

I said, "Man, this is terrible. Dead calves never stink that bad. I don't know what kind of bacteria is in there to make it rot like that, but it's awful." I pulled the calf out in pieces and I had to wash out that rope several times before I could put it in my car.

Maybe the worst one was when a farmer called me to come look at a cow that had a sore foot. I tied up the cow, fixed the foot and bandaged it, and I was done. But as I was going to the car, the farmer said, "Long as you're here, I want you to check a cow. She was supposed to have a calf more than a week ago."

Sure. No different than anything I'd done countless times. I got the cow calmed down and reached inside. I felt two feet. Well, when you feel two feet, you pull to see what comes out. I pulled.

That was a mistake. That was the plug that was keeping everything inside her. The cow mooed, and suddenly an entire liquefied calf came out of her. There were pieces of bone, pieces of hide; there were things—I had no idea what they might be, and the smell was worse. It formed a puddle two feet across and six inches deep right behind the cow. We all sort of looked at one another; I think we were all too embarrassed to throw up in front of everyone else, so we sort of swallowed hard; sometimes not throwing up is a matter of pride. *I can take it!* But I guarantee you if one person had thrown up at that moment, we all would have. But I wasn't done; I had to go back inside that animal and make sure everything was out. So I reached in and found several small skull bones and pulled them out. Then I gave her a strong antibiotic and she did fine.

Believe me, every large-animal vet—and his or her wife or

husband—can tell you stories about the weird things that have gotten all over him or her. For a few years we were giving cows injections of bovine somatotropin, a hormone that makes cows eat more, because when a cow eats more it gives more milk. After a few years the government made us quit, so we don't do it anymore. The injection had to be given in a little hollow right beside the tail that's filled with fat. The tail is always covering the anus, so it's always full of manure. Cows don't wipe their butts, so many times they get infected and develop a little abscess. One afternoon I was having a conversation with the farmer while I was doing pregnancy tests. As I started checking one cow I noticed a large abscess on her butt, and just as I put my hand in there, that abscess popped and that pus just went all over my face and in my mouth. That farmer started laughing and he couldn't stop. I said, "Man, that does not taste good." But I'll tell you, in all the years I've been doing this, not only have I never thrown up once; I've never even *almost* thrown up.

But sometimes my assistants have. And Charles? Well, Charles is certainly Charles. Just like I can remember the day when I decided I wanted to be a vet, Charles can remember the day he knew for sure he didn't want to be a vet. We each happened to be about twelve years old when we made those decisions. After dinner one night in the winter we got a call from an Amish farmer that his horse was having trouble with the foaling; that's an automatic emergency, and whatever you're doing, you go. It was miserable outside; it was freezing cold and we were having an old-time blizzard: the wind was blowing so strong that the snow seemed like it was coming down horizontal. There were drifts almost as big as the car. I told Charles I wanted him to come with me. If I went off the road or got stuck, I needed him to help me. We plowed through drifts; I just put my foot down on the gas and slammed through them. The foal had already been dead for probably a whole day when we got there, but I still had to get it out. I put chains on it and yanked it out, and that's when the smell that had been trapped inside burst out in one big, foul wave. Oh my goodness, was it terrible.

I looked at Charles and his face turned white and he tried hard to hold it in; then his whole body shook just a little, and then that was it. Out it came. He didn't say a word; he just turned around and went back to wait in the station wagon. I think at that time any other place in the world was better than being in that barn. That's the day Charles decided that he wasn't going to be a vet.

Probably the most important thing about getting to a farm is being able to get there in every type of weather. A large-animal vet's car becomes an extension of him- or herself. There is only one thing every one of them has in common: They ain't pretty. They are always dirty and beat-up, sometimes they don't smell so good, and any vehicle with less than a hundred thousand miles on it is just getting broken in. In Harbor Beach we drove mostly small trucks, but they didn't last. When I opened my practice I started buying used Buick or Oldsmobile station wagons because they were made so well and would just last forever. They stopped making station wagons in 1996—when SUVs filled that need—but we kept our wagons for ten more years. People still ask me, "Dr. Pol, what happened to your station wagons?" and I tell them, "They finally bit the dust."

Then we started buying used Jeeps. We have seven of them in the clinic; we use five and have two for backup. They last. The one I've been driving on the show has 240,000 miles on it. The springs go pretty quick, but nobody cares about that, but when the back axle goes, that's a problem. We usually just put another one on.

One time in February a farmer called and asked me to come right out because he had a pregnant cow that was getting ready to freshen; that means that she was getting ready to give birth. Well, she wasn't due till April, so I knew she was aborting. "Can you get her in the barn?" I asked him.

"I'll try," he said. But when I got there she was tied to his tractor in the middle of the snow-covered field. The snow was probably a foot deep. There were tractor tracks, but they were wider than my Jeep's axle. I just put it in four-wheel drive low and drove right out a quarter mile through the snow into the pasture, delivered a set of dead twins, got back in the car, and drove home. No problem. These old Jeeps get me where I need to go.

My office is the whole back of the truck. Medical doctors carry little black bags; large-animal vets drive large vehicles. All large-animal vets have to carry the whole office with them. Everybody arranges it differently, but the important thing is to put the same tool back in the same place every time, so you can find it when you need it, even in the dark. There's nothing more frustrating than needing a tool right away and having to search through a pile of stuff to find it. Charles tries to help me. He takes things out and cleans them, but he doesn't always put them back in the same place. One time he cleaned everything up so well and put everything in so neatly and orderly that I couldn't find anything. I told Charles, you got to clean out that Jeep because I don't know where anything is anymore. So we had to take out all these clean instruments and tools and put them all back my way. My way is my way, and it's different from Dr. Brenda's way or Dr. Kurt's way.

Same thing for the tools you carry with you. All vets carry the tools they are most comfortable using. When we were starting here, there was an ad in the *Michigan Veterinary Journal* from a small local vet who was selling his equipment. He turned out to be an older man with a bad artery in his heart. When he walked fifteen feet he had to sit down. I asked him, "How much you want for everything?"

"I don't know," he said.

So it was a contest to see who was the worst negotiator. That was one I could win. "Give me a number and we'll see," I said. He gave me a number and I agreed. He had all the equipment from his years of practice spread all over a damp basement. Diane and I told him we would clean it out for him: "If it's good, I'll use it; if it's not, I'll junk it." I love tools, and it was a memorable experience just walking through his storage rooms finding all this wonderful equipment. We mostly built the practice with those tools. Some of them I'm still using; I couldn't even guess how old they are. One well-made piece of equipment, for example, was a double-action nipper used to cut down a horse's back teeth. Now, many horse dentists say you cannot do that, that you shouldn't take more than one-sixteenth of an inch off the teeth; then you have to come back again in three weeks. I'm sorry, I don't have the time and many farmers don't have the money.

Normally a horse has smooth teeth, which rub against

each other so they don't grow too long, but as they get older, if a tooth breaks or gets damaged, the opposing tooth just keeps growing and growing and eventually pushes into the gums of the opposing jaw. And then the horse can't close its mouth, it can't chew, and it doesn't eat right. That's when I use my big nippers. I cut the tooth off right by the gums. For an older horse that means, "I'll see you in five years; you'll be fine till then."

That old vet also had an old-fashioned mouth speculum, a big, heavy, metal contraption that keeps a horse's mouth open so you can reach in safely without worrying about getting your arm bitten off. If the horse swings his head and hits you with this speculum, it'll knock you silly, but it does prevent you from seriously injuring your hand. Once the mouth is open, I come in with my nippers, put them around that tooth, and then try to close them. Those teeth are hard; I usually can't do it just by pushing my hands together. Many times I put one bar hard against my body and then pull with the other one, almost as if I were pulling an oar. That usually snaps the tooth right off.

This old doc had the knives they used long ago to cut a calf apart inside a cow, and he had a tool for spaying mares, meaning taking the ovaries out, which we don't even do anymore. That procedure was necessary because carriage horses won't stand still when they are in heat. The tool was essentially a chain that would crush the blood vessels to the ovaries, and they would just fall out into your hand. Never done one of those in my life.

He also had a lot of old drugs, but most of the pills were

outdated or too damp to be used. Diane and I picked up everything, and as we were picking through the boxes and piles, I saw some jars way in the back. Diane picked them up, blew off the dust, and examined them. The vet's wife had been very industrious, and during World War II she had done a lot of canning. There were cans of maple syrup on the shelves. One was dated 1942, the year I was born, and another one was dated 1944, the year Diane was born. "We've got to have those," I told Diane, and the vet was nice enough to give them to us. We still have them, too.

A few of my tools have been in the back of many different trucks. There's a feeling of comfort I get from using those old tools. I know what I expect from each of them and how to use them. In the back of the truck, and on and under the seats, I carry needles and syringes, my thermometer and stethoscope, and the suture material that I use for cows with twisted stomachs; I've got bottles of calcium, antibiotics, tranquilizers, and the other drugs I might need; I've got topical solutions and some mineral oil to use as a laxative in case a horse or cow is plugged up. I've got a cooler with my vaccines and a big plastic cabinet with three drawers where I keep all my different pills and various-size needles. I have a toolbox filled with those things I use for foot problems: knives and hoof cutters and scissors and my surgery kit. I have my calf puller, my chains, and a plastic garbage pail and a stainless steel pail. Sometimes I have my wood bushel basket, a balling gun to give pills orally to cows, two regular nylon lariats, and my halters. I keep the calf cutter under the seat with the plastic fiberglass cane I can use to push cows. When I want to move a cow, I can tap it on the head with this cane, and if it doesn't want to move, it kicks—but because of the cane it can't reach me. Too bad, Elsie; *boom*—she kicks; then I tap her again.

Most of the time I'll have whatever I need in the truck or I'll be able to adapt another tool to the job. Years ago we sold a lot of medicines, and that was very profitable, but now farmers and even small-animal owners can fill prescriptions through a direct mail-order service or one of the large pet supply chains for a lot less than I would have to charge them. I don't carry a lot of medicine anymore, so naturally that's what someone will usually ask for.

Keeping my tools available this way has worked very well for me for forty years. Wasting even a few minutes when an animal is in pain is a terrible thing to do to that animal. Instead, as I have been doing for my entire career, I go out to the truck and grab what medicines I need, then get a dose of it into that animal as fast as I can. And then I do my job. An animal in pain is very dangerous, and until I get rid of that pain, I can't do an examination.

Many large-animal vets drive pickups with what is called a Bowie box on the back. This is a fiberglass box made especially for vets. It looks very professional, very nice. It has a whole bunch of drawers, doors, a back door where you store the big items we use; it's even got a heater in the back. Everything is so neat. They're expensive, but they last longer than the truck, so you have to take it off the old one and bolt it on the new one. In the ten years I was in Harbor Beach, I went through three trucks and kept transferring the Bowie box. I didn't particularly like it because it wasn't good on dry dirt roads. It was always full of dust. Every month I had to vacuum it out because the medicine bottles were so dusty I couldn't sell them. I didn't even use the space in the back because when I opened it up there was always a layer of road dust on the bottom. So when I came to Weidman, I decided I didn't want the Bowie box; I wanted a station wagon.

At different times I've carried more than tools in the Jeep. Usually when a new assistant starts, he or she rides with me for a while so we get to know each other. Spending time together going on farm calls gives us the opportunity to get comfortable with each other. Overall I have been incredibly fortunate in the people who have worked with me. I don't even have written contracts with them. I tell them at the beginning, "All I expect is that you work hard and you're here for at least a year," and we shake hands on it. They have all been very good vets—except one. It was a lady who was here for a little while, and she did not know what to do. I realized pretty quick it wasn't safe to let her make emergency calls at night, so I always went with her.

One night she had a calving, for example, and I went with her. I was trying to help her build confidence. This was a big calf that needed a pull. "Okay," I told her, "there's nobody here to help you and you have to get this calf out of this cow." Then I went outside the pen. My hands were just itching to help her, but nope, she had to learn. So I just held on to the top rail to keep myself there. Normally, you begin by tying up the cow so she cannot walk away. Then you get the chains and pull the calf. Most people, when they're shown how to do it once or twice, pick it up pretty quickly.

This assistant struggled with it. She managed to get the cow behind the gate but did not tie her up. She was struggling to get the chains on the calf. The problem is that you need one hand to hold the gate and two hands to put the chains on. And she had only two hands. She kept going back and forth, back and forth, but finally managed to get the chains on. Then she got the calf puller and tried to pull the calf. Well, that needs two hands too, so when she grabbed it with two hands, she couldn't hold on to the gate. *Follow me*, that cow said, then started walking through the pen with this vet stumbling behind and holding on to the calf puller trying to get that calf out. It took a while for the cow to get bored, but finally she stopped and strained, and that calf popped out. Just then the farmer walked into the barn and saw the live calf lying there. He turned to me—I was still leaning on the rail—and said, "Oh great, we got a live calf. Nice going."

I think if I had responded, that vet might've hit me! Her problem was that she really knew the material in the books, but she couldn't translate it to the job. One Saturday night a couple brought in their dog, which had been hit by a car. It had a big cut right underneath the armpit. This young vet was in the clinic while I was on the road. On the radio I told her, "Give the dog an anesthetic and clean it up. I'll be right there and we'll sew it up." But by the time I got there it was already done. "Good," I told her, "you got a drain in there?"

She had a drain in there.

"What stitch is holding that drain in place?"

"Uh, this one, I think. This one. Maybe all of them."

"When do you take the drain out?"

"Two days." She knew her stuff.

"When do you take the stitches out?"

"Ten days." Uh, whoops. That was a problem. She couldn't take the drain out without taking the stitches out.

As we took the stitches out, I just happened to ask her, "Did you put sutures underneath there to close up the hole?"

She shook her head. "I just sutured the skin."

So when I removed the stitches, I found a big hole under the dog's armpit. I opened it up and started scrubbing everything down because she hadn't even cleaned it. I closed the big space underneath the skin. Suddenly this young lady started talking: "Yes, you have to close up subcutaneous spaces; otherwise, you get infection . . ."

My mouth just dropped open. I said, "If you know all this, why didn't you do it?"

She never answered. If it was in the book, she knew it, but she couldn't do it on a live animal. Eventually she left and joined a regulatory agency, where she has done a very good job. If not for having to work on animals, she would have been a wonderful vet.

Charles used to ride with me sometimes too; that was a time when I was working so hard that I didn't get enough time to spend with my family, so I wanted him to come with me so we could spend time together. Charles felt a little different about it; he wanted to know why he couldn't stay home and watch television. So we compromised—he came with me, but I let him stay in the car when we were at a farm. Diane also sometimes goes out with me on a farm call. She takes care of the business, keeping track of the cattle we test or treat and handling the billing.

And in addition to that colt I drove home in the front seat, occasionally I do have to transport an animal. I've had big dogs and cats in the car with me, and I've definitely learned one thing: Never transport a cat that isn't in a cage. I probably learned that from the people who came in with a cat under their dashboard; it wasn't happy there but didn't want to come out either. But there was one animal I didn't even know was riding along with me. A farmer named John McConnell allowed raccoons to stay in his barn in the winter, and by spring the family made pets out of the young ones. I made a farm call to his place one hot summer day and left the windows open while I did the job. When I finished, I packed up and drove away. I was about a mile down the road when suddenly a raccoon leaped out of the backseat onto my neck.

"Geez!" That surprised me. That tame raccoon had been hiding in the backseat, just being nosey. The shock lasted a split second, but almost instantly I knew what it was. I looked in the mirror, and sure enough, his nose was right next to my ear. To me it looked like he was telling me, *Turn this thing around. I want to go home.*

John McConnell was standing in his yard when I got back. "Hey, John," I told him, "train your raccoons not to climb in people's cars, will you?" I opened the door and this thing hopped out and ran into the barn.

No matter what type of weather we're driving through in central Michigan, the one thing we've always got to watch out for is deer. Deer are pests, but the good news is that they are edible. There are just so many of them running onto the roads and getting hit that in our area they're known as "Michigan mile markers." Everybody who has driven Michigan's roads for any length of time has hit a deer—or much more likely, a lot of deer. When I first got here I was driving pretty carefully—I wasn't going to hit a deer. In those days I could make as many as twenty or more farm calls in one day, but I had to keep moving. There was one afternoon when I finished doing pregnancy checks and my old station wagon wouldn't start. It needed a tune-up and I'd flooded the engine. The farmer had a brand-new Blazer, and he told me to drive it back to the clinic and bring it back later. "Okay," I said, but I was thinking that with my luck I'd hit a deer. So I drove back to the clinic real careful. I examined some small animals, I did a few surgeries, and at nine o'clock that night Diane got in the spare wagon and followed me back to the farm.

By that time the gas had evaporated and the old wagon fired right up. We started hightailing it back to the clinic because I still had work to get done. In those days on the roads the speed limit was generally whatever you could crank it up to. I was about a quarter mile ahead of Diane when I saw a pack of six deer running full speed across the road. There was no way I could miss them. That's the only time I've hit two deer at the same time. All I could do was yell into the radio microphone, "Diane! Deer!" She didn't think I was just being affectionate, so she slowed right down.

Both of them were dead. The only damage to the wagon was a few broken headlights. There wasn't any sense just leaving the carcasses there, so we put them on the roof and took them back to the clinic. The next day I took them over to the slaughterhouse, and the butcher prepared them for us.

I do feel sorry for the deer because some of the time they're not instantly killed. The last time Diane hit one, it was lying in a ditch when I got there, still alive but dying. A police officer came along and shot it, and we loaded it on the car and took that one home too. The saddest thing is when a car hits the doe and the fawn is left standing alone. A lot of times when that happens, the local responders bring the fawn to me. I'll treat it and an official from the Department of Natural Resources brings it to a deer ranch.

I've been called to just about every type of farm you can imagine, from the Amish farms, where just about everything is done by manpower, to the modern operations, where they use the newest technology. I remember one of the first farms I visited when I started in the Thumb belonged to Harvey and Evelyn Deer, the nicest people, who had very good registered animals. That's not why I remember it, though. Harvey was a small guy, and when he built his farm he put a stainless steel pipeline inside his barn that was high enough off the ground for him to walk under easily. But I was a lot taller than him, so every time we'd go into his barn, he'd walk underneath the pipe and turn around and warn me, "Watch the pipe." That first time, every time, I'd remember to duck right under it, but then I'd get busy and I'd be carrying my tools and a pail and we'd be talking as we walked along and . . . *bam!* Got me again.

"You okay, Doc?"

"I will be eventually." I can't count how many times I banged my head on that pipe. That is the only time that the cows could have been laughing at me.

I've seen some pretty unusual things in barns, but only one time did I see a cow flying. This was inside a very modern-type barn with free stalls. This cow was way forward in the stall; normally for a cow to get up, it has to rock forward and the hind legs get up first; the problem was this cow had no room to rock forward. She was much too big for us to move her. Normally if a cow is down in a free stall we can take the stall apart and turn the cow around, and she'll get up. But in this barn the free stall sides had been bolted in place, with steel on the outside. We couldn't get to the bolts at the wall end. That cow was trapped in that stall. "I got an idea," I said. "Get the tractor and the chains." The farmer had a big John Deere, a beautiful machine. I crawled into the stall and put a very short chain around the cow's neck. Then I got out of there. I told the farmer, "Okay, lift her up." He looked at me as if he was asking, *You sure?* "Go ahead," I said again. He shrugged and put that lift into gear. That cow weighed, I would guess, fifteen hundred pounds, and that tractor just picked her straight up in the air. It didn't hurt her at all; that neck is so strong, nothing will hurt it. Her butt was barely touching the ground. He lifted her up between the rafters; stretched out like that, she probably was ten feet long or more. He pulled her away from the stall, turned her around, and put her down gently on her butt in the alleyway. When we took the chain off, she got up and walked away. No damage.

I can still see that cow moving through the air, her head almost between the rafters, and not a complaint out of her. Far as I could figure, that was the only way of getting her out of the free stall. It was made so well, we couldn't possibly get it apart or give her more room.

While those modern-type barns include all the elements that make it easier for the farmer, they also can cause unusual problems. The Grahams were one of my very first clients, and I watched their operation grow. They took good care of their animals, so those animals rewarded them. Eventually they had 120 cows producing an average of eighty pounds of milk per cow every day. They were doing so well that they decided to build a brand-new milking parlor. It was fantastic: They put in state-of-the-art everything; I used to call it the stainless steel palace. But after they got it going, they discovered a strange problem: When they milked the cows at five A.M., they got full production, but when they milked them in the afternoon, production was way down. Production fell from about eighty pounds to fifty pounds, which doesn't pay the bills. They couldn't figure out what could be causing this, so they called me and asked me to come out there.

I checked the animals: Their minerals were good, their energy was good, there was nothing wrong with their feet, and they were eating; they just weren't milking right. At that time there was a problem in several places with stray electricity running through a barn and upsetting the herd. The Grahams' farm was only about a mile away from the little town of Rosebush. When we couldn't find any other possible cause, we suspected that could be the problem. I had a little cut on my finger and I put it up against a metal part of the stall then stuck a finger on my other hand in a wet drain. When I did, I felt the mild electric surge running through my body. Okay, I knew that wasn't supposed to be there.

If I felt it, the Grahams' cows definitely could feel it. Cows' hooves are very sensitive. If every time they put a hoof down they feel a little tingle, it makes them uneasy, antsy, and they start dancing back and forth from one foot to another. They don't stand still and give milk. The Grahams hired an expert in stray electricity, and he came over from Wisconsin and tested the parlor for them; his gauges confirmed the presence of stray voltage. The new parlor had been built too well; the ground and the cement floor were too good. It had grounding rods that went six feet into the ground. Its electrical circuits were so good that these rods picked up the stray voltage from the power lines running along the road that they would come right through the grounding rods into the parlor. The old wooden milking parlor had provided insulation for the cows. In the morning, when everybody in the nearby town of Rosebush was sleeping, there wasn't a lot of power being used, but at five o'clock in the afternoon, when everybody was home and all the appliances were running, a lot of electricity was being generated and some of it ran loose through the ground and into the stainless steel palace.

The Grahams sued the local power company and won a judgment. Then they asked the power company when they were going to fix the problem. "Fix it?" they said. "We're not changing anything." So the problem did not go away. The Grahams eventually sold their entire herd and became an organic farm. They raise turkeys, chickens, and beef, and everything is organic. And they took all that beautiful new equipment out of the state-of-the-art milking parlor and converted it into their own slaughterhouse.

A new barn may be more comfortable to work in than an old wooden barn, but it can take several months before the barn is ready for full operation. There's an illness I've seen at most a half-dozen times in my career called new barn pneumonia, which happens only within the first two months cows are in a new barn. It's a bacterial infection that may be caused by the vapors from fresh cement; the vapors irritate the lungs, and the irritation can cause a buildup of fluid. This buildup allows bacteria to grow, and the cows get sick. The condition is treated with antibiotics and basically letting the barn settle, but if it isn't diagnosed correctly, it can be a serious problem.

Many of the regular farm calls consist of herd management; examinations and vaccinations; pregnancy checks and calving and foaling; treating common conditions like milk fever; castration; and, unfortunately, euthanizing. But even those pretty regular appointments can all of a sudden become emergencies. One morning Ike Swarey called because one of his cows hadn't come up from the pasture. Dr. Kurt went out to the farm in Rosebush, and they found the cow out by the river, lying on her left side and bloated. Those were sure signs of milk fever. She was in really bad shape, and he needed to get calcium in her as fast as possible. Normally you try to roll the cow up on her chest so you can inject her in the neck, but this cow's legs were out and she was too big to move. He decided to put the first bottle of calcium in her mammary vein. Mammary veins are about as big as a thumb, but they tend to bleed. The most important thing when giving an animal calcium is to run it slowly because the heart is very sensitive to the body's calcium level, and if the calcium level rises too quickly, it can kill the animal. It's hard to find the right balance: If the animal is in bad shape, it needs a big dose right away to survive, but if you give it that dose too quickly, it'll die.

Dr. Kurt was trying to go slow, but when he was halfway through the first bottle, that cow took a couple of deep breaths; then everything stopped. She quit breathing and lay there motionless. Dr. Kurt remembers thinking, *Ah crap, I've killed her right in front of the owner.* He ripped out the needle, put his knees together, and on his knees started jumping up and down on the cow's chest. He was doing cow CPR. He jumped on her over and over with his knees. He wasn't giving up. Over and over.

Suddenly that cow gave a big heave and started breathing. Ike never said one word. Dr. Kurt couldn't believe it had worked. He put the needle back into her mammary vein and gave her the rest of the bottle. Then he and Ike rolled her up on her chest and he gave her the second bottle in her neck really slowly. When he finished, they waited a few minutes; then the cow kind of struggled onto her feet. She was pretty wobbly. Those two men walked with her up to the barn. Ike was always quiet; he said what needed to be said, and this time he didn't say a single word about this. Dr. Kurt packed up his tools and left. He had mixed feelings: First he thought he had killed that cow—but he felt really good about saving her life.

The next day Dr. Brenda went out there to check up on the cow. When she got back to the clinic Dr. Kurt asked her if Ike had said anything to her. "He did," she told him. "He wouldn't shut up. He kept going on and on about this vet who kept jumping on the cow's chest. He said he'd never seen anyone do CPR on a cow to save its life." Dr. Kurt was beaming he was so happy. When I heard about it, I thought, *Sure, but I'll bet you wouldn't give her mouth-to-mouth!*

We're called out to farms regularly to perform castrations. On the show they've actually shown several castrations. And every time the Nat Geo Wild crew is filming this operation, as soon as I start someone always yells, "Cut!" And everybody laughs—except the animal; the animal doesn't think it's funny.

It's easy to make jokes about this procedure. We had a segment on the show in which three nice young girls brought in their dog, which had an abscess in its testicles—they were swelled up like a bowling ball. As the narrator was explaining to viewers what was happening, they showed me holding his swollen scrotum, and the narrator said seriously that those girls had "left the animal in Dr. Pol's hands."

When we first opened the practice, there hadn't been a large-animal vet that castrated horses in the area for years, so the word got around that we were here, and that first summer I must have done forty stallions. The reason to castrate an animal is because it makes it easier to handle. It looks a lot more painful than it really is. It doesn't hurt the animal at all because I give them a good anesthetic before I do my work. And once an animal is gelded, it becomes a whole different animal. On the program a woman brought in a nice Arabian stallion she had rescued, but he was mean. "You can't turn your back on him," she told me. Well, when I was done his whole personality was different. Those hormones were gone. "He'll make a good riding horse," I told her, and he'll have a much better and longer life.

The way Charles describes that is simply, "Take the balls out and the brain comes back."

Many horse veterinarians are very brave in my eyes because they do standing castrations. That means they don't lay the horse down; they just put a local anesthetic in the area and castrate the horse standing right there. They grab hold of the scrotum, pull down, and cut. To me, I don't want to put myself in danger if something goes wrong. I have been told that many times people cut their hand when they are hanging on to the testicle and the horse moves a little; that scalpel blade slips and you end up slicing your hand. No, thank you. I'll do it the safe way.

Usually I do the actual operation by myself. The only time

I needed help was when I was castrating a Belgian horse that probably weighed twenty-six hundred pounds. This was a big animal, and honest to gosh it took two vets, Dr. Ashley and me, to do the job. I grabbed hold of the testicles with both hands, braced my feet against this horse's belly, and pulled. Dr. Ashley put the clamps on, cut off the testicles, and stopped the bleeding. We untied the horse to allow it to get up by itself, which I always do. Eventually it got up and walked away perfect.

My horses get two tranquilizers. The first one calms them down; the second makes them lie down on their side. They are out cold; that way if anything goes wrong, I can fix it. In my forty years, out of the thousands of horses I've castrated, I've lost only two. Of course I remember them. The first one was a two-week-old Belgian colt that the owner wanted castrated young because he wanted a nice gelding. I cut off one testicle and that went fine, but when I cut off the second I noticed what looked like a rupture. That's not good. So I closed it up good and tied off the sac. About twelve hours later, the owner called and told me, "You know that sac you tied off? All the guts are falling out." I raced back there, and that colt's intestines were dragging on the ground all around the pen. I immediately put the horse down—once the intestines are on the ground, there's nothing that can be done—and then I looked to see what had happened.

The intestines had come out through the first cut I'd made. I had looked at it, but I hadn't seen any rupture there at all. I should have tied off both. But by that time there was nothing I could do.

The second horse was a four-year-old cryptorchid pony. A

cryptorchid animal is an animal in which one testicle hasn't descended; it's still in the belly. It's inside, it's warm, it produces hormones, but the sperm is dead. As a result the animal is sterile but at the same time very unpredictable because its testosterone is just way too high. Cryptorchid horses can be dangerous because you never know how they are going to react. This wasn't a farm call; the owner brought the pony to the clinic and I did the operation. It was quick and uneventful. I can do the procedure in about twenty minutes, which is pretty fast. I told the owner, "This guy has to stay in the pen by himself. Keep him away from the other horses for a week."

"Okay," he told me.

I warned him again.

"Okay," he told me again.

Four days later he calls and tells me that pony is dead. "Why?" I asked. "What happened?"

He said, "Well, you must have done something wrong."

I went right over there. That horse was in the pen with his mares. The mares were in heat and the pony had tried to jump them and busted his sutures. The intestines had busted through and it killed him.

"It's your fault," the owner told me. "You pay for it."

I explained as nicely as I could that the answer was no. I told him pretty strong that it was his fault. If he had listened to what I told him and left that horse by itself in a pen, it would have been healed up. Instead he brought the horse home and threw it back in with the other horses. I don't get angry too often, but if anybody was the horse's ass, it wasn't that horse. Those were the only two animals I lost after I'd castrated them.

Castration is another small procedure that a lot of farmers now do by themselves, or have their neighbors do for them, to save the money. It's not especially difficult and generally it goes pretty well. But while I was out one day I got a call from Diane in the office asking me where I was. "By Clare," I told her. "What's going on?"

One of our Amish clients had started castrating a stallion and something had gone really wrong: "Its intestines are hanging out."

My cell phone rang; it was that client. "Where are you, Doc?"

"South of Clare and flying low. Get a clean sheet. Whatever happens, keep those intestines off the ground." I just floored it and kept going. When I got there, the horse was standing still and about five gallons of its intestines were resting on a towel being held under it by two men. It was a Clydesdale, a very big horse. This was the first time I'd ever seen anything like this. "This is what we're going to do," I explained. "It's going to get a couple of shots. When I give it the second one we're walking it outside, but you guys hang on to that towel. Now, just go slow." The first shot calmed him down, and after the second shot we walked the horse out slowly. I was hanging on to the tail a little bit. "Watch out now," I warned them, "because it's going to fall."

We let the horse fall on its side with the towel underneath. How nobody got hurt I don't know, but we were all fine. When the horse was out, I started washing its intestines off, disinfected them, and then just tried to push them back in. I couldn't. The testicles come down out of the belly into the scrotum through a narrow ring, and by this time the intestines were swollen and wouldn't fit through that ring back into the belly. I had never dealt with this problem and I didn't have too much time to figure out what to do. I just had to take a chance if I was going to save that horse. I reached inside with my fingers and found the ring, and I cut it. I made a much larger hole, cleaned it up as best I could, and stuffed everything back inside. I put some penicillin straight in the belly because back in college when we did C-sections we'd put penicillin straight in the abdominal cavity and it had worked well. As far as I could figure, a C-section was about the closest thing to this problem that I knew anything about. It had worked beautifully then to prevent infection; maybe it would work here too. I had nothing else.

I sutured everything shut and we let the horse stand up by itself. "I'm not promising anything," I told them. "Usually when the intestines are out, that's it. But keep it on antibiotics and we'll see what happens." That horse never went off its feed; it never had colic; it never showed any sign of distress. Two weeks later they sold it at auction for a good price.

I felt pretty good about that. I figured a combination of experience and luck had allowed me to save that horse, and I felt darn sure I would never have to deal with that problem again. Except that two weeks later the same person called me. "You didn't do it again, did you?" I said. I thought I was making a joke.

"Yeah, I did, Doc." This time it was a four-year-old Belgian. The Amish don't use an anesthetic or a painkiller when doing a castration, so when this farmer made the cut, the horse just started pushing, and pushed its intestines right out through the ring.

"I'm on my way." When I got there I saw that five-gallon

pail of intestines under the horse. If seeing strange things bothers you or slows you down, being a large-animal vet definitely is not the job for you. Between the two of us we managed to get that horse down on its side. Then we rolled it onto its back and cleaned it up, and I very carefully stuffed the intestines back inside. "Don't do it again," I advised the owner. That horse lived too.

I had never even seen one of those before and I'd done two of them in two weeks, and those remain the only two like that I've ever done.

The only animal that ever gave me a problem during a castration was a billy goat. One fall a lady made an appointment to bring her goat in to be castrated. No problem. But at the time of the appointment, this fancy-dressed woman came into the clinic and suddenly everybody started looking around. *What's that awful smell? Is it that lady? It can't be; she's dressed so nice.* She was wearing a very nice dress, but that smell definitely was coming from her. Nanny goats love that smell, it's like perfume to them, but it definitely doesn't work with humans. It even bothered me and I've worked standing in manure. One by one every person in the front of the office got up and walked into the back room like they had a reason to be there. Diane was the last one to go. As she walked away we looked at each other and she smiled knowingly. After all these years she knew exactly what I was thinking: *You're going to leave me too?*

I had to stand there and take care of the client. Well, this lady had a horse and she wanted a companion for that horse, so she went to the market and bought a nice goat. But she didn't know the first thing about goats. Goats are in season in the fall, and this was a billy goat, an especially stinky animal. They just pee and flip it between their front legs. They do that so when they mount a female they leave their scent. Billy goats all want their own offspring. Don't ask me why. So if they find one with their urine scent on her they think, *Okay, I already did this one, I don't have to do it again.* But if they smell urine from another goat they think, *Wait a minute, it's my turn,* and breed that one. So when they are in season, when they're rutting, they can smell real bad. I put my oldest coveralls on and went outside. It wasn't so bad outside. There was a pretty good-size billy goat in her trailer; it had long, curved horns and I couldn't get anybody to come and help me. I put a rope around those horns and tied him as close to the wall as possible. With goats we don't cut the testicles off; instead, we just clamp them. So I grabbed one testicle and put the clamp on it, and oh boy. He started screeching, and wow! He did a complete flip, a beautiful somersault, head over butt. I did my best to hold on. I didn't blame him at all, but at that moment it was every man or goat for himself. I let him get back on his feet and waited until he settled down; then I put the clamp on the other side and got out of there quick. As soon as I got outside I took off my coveralls and went back to work.

Taking off those coveralls didn't do any good. When I got inside everybody told me to go outside again. They weren't as nice to me as they had been to that lady. Turned out that terrible smell had gone right through the coveralls to my regular clothes. I changed my work clothes and threw the dirty clothes in the washer. Inside the clinic that lady was not welcome, but if she happened to run into a nanny goat she definitely would have been more popular.

People ask me, with all the farm calls I've made, is there one that stands out? One that I remember more than any other? And the answer is absolutely yes. No one in my family will ever forget this one. This was on Christmas Day in the early 1990s. Charles was about eight years old and the two girls were teenagers. The whole family was home and Diane was planning a special kind of fondue dinner that we all could do together, when the dang phone rang. Okay, the phone rings, you got to answer it, even on Christmas Day. It was a calving, which meant I had to go take care of it. But the farmer wasn't going to be there to help, so I decided to take my daughter Kathy with me. Charles and my other daughter, Diane Jr., stayed home. I was hoping it wouldn't take too long and we would be back in time to enjoy our family dinner.

It was a nice December day, the ground was covered with snow, and as we drove to the farm we passed lots of farmhouses all lit up and looking very warm and welcoming. When Kathy and I got inside the barn, I examined the cow; that calf inside her was a big one. There was no way it was coming out the normal way. The only chance that calf had of surviving was for me to do a C-section. Honestly, I haven't done too many of them in my career. Most of the time it costs the farmer more than its worth, and usually a calf this big is already dead inside the cow and we cut it up instead of doing a C-section. But when I reached inside, I could feel that this calf was plenty alive; it was moving around and felt healthy. I thought, *This is the only chance we've got.* But it's not an easy operation and I needed a lot more help than I had. I called Diane on the radio and asked her to bring the other kids over. This was going to be the most memorable Christmas they ever had.

We were all in that barn around the cow, which was lying down on her bed of hay comfortably. I gave each of my kids a job to do. Charles and Diane Jr. were each holding on to a part of the uterus. That uterus was real big and much too heavy for any one of them to be able to hold up alone. I carefully cut open the cow's belly, reached in, and took out that calf. It was alive and, once I got it breathing, real curious. The kids were just amazed at this, their eyes couldn't have been bigger, but I reminded them not to let go of anything. I sewed up the cow and she was fine. After she got on her feet I waited until she started cleaning her calf; then we packed up the kids and we went home for dinner.

That was the Christmas farm call none of us have ever forgotten.

SIX

A Life-and-Death Business

No matter what other animals we kept, we always had a Great Dane. And of all those dogs, the most memorable was Maeson. I don't favor one dog more than the others, but Maeson was a remarkable animal. She was my blood-donor dog and she loved to be around the clinic, but she really belonged to Charles. They loved each other.

It didn't start out that way. Charles was sixteen when we got her; somebody didn't want her anymore and gave her to us. That first day she wasn't very friendly to him at all. When he went near her she growled at him and bared her teeth. The next day Charles told her, "Look, if you're going to live here, you and I have to get along. So why don't you go for a ride with me." He had to go to the post office, and he opened the door of the Jeep for her. She hopped in, she looked at him, she must have decided he was okay if he was taking her for a ride, and that was it. After that they were inseparable. She followed him around the house; she went everywhere with him; she slept in his bed with him. He was her person, and that was it.

But what she loved best was to be with him in that Jeep. All he had to do was jangle the car keys and she'd be standing at the door, ready to go. He'd put the top down and take the doors off, and she'd sit in the passenger seat and she wouldn't move. He'd leave her there while he ran his errands, and when he came back she'd be sitting and waiting patiently for him. Okay, she also loved beer and fireworks. You couldn't open a bottle of beer without her being right there ready to share. Once she actually took a bottle in her mouth, gripped it with her teeth, tipped her head back, and drank from the bottle. Honest to goodness. And if fireworks were exploding, she couldn't help trying to grab the burst. And somehow she seemed to know when a person or even another animal needed her help, and whatever help she could give, she would give it with a wagging tail.

When Charles went off to college, she missed him terribly. He couldn't take her with him and she loved being on the farm too much anyway. All of her friends were there. But whenever he'd come back, she instantly became his dog again. The problem with animals is they get old too quick, and they get sick. When Maeson was nine, Charles was home for Christmas vacation. After he went back to California Maeson started to get dopey. When she didn't get better after a few weeks I did a blood test. She had leukemia.

When I told Charles, he asked me to keep her alive until he could get home in March. I did the best I could; I gave her transfusions, I tried different treatments, and she had her good days and bad days but she survived. Leukemia is usually a tough cancer for animals to survive; it's fast acting, but I think she just decided she was going to stay alive until Charles got home.

Finally, he got home. She perked up and they spent a good week together. It looked like she was not sick after all. One day they drove into town and stopped at Wendy's for burgers—there was no reason for her not to eat anything she wanted—but mostly they just hung out together. We had a birthday party for Charles and Diane Jr. that week and she licked ice cream off the plate, but none of us could bear to discipline her at that point. Later that night, as they got ready to go to bed, she decided she wanted to go out. That wasn't too unusual; sometimes she liked to spend a few minutes outside before settling down. It was snowing outside when Charles opened the door to let her out.

This time she didn't come back. She knew it was time, and I guess she felt she had said her good-byes. Charles went out into the storm looking for her, and he found her walking down the driveway, walking away. She made it through the night, but the next day she wouldn't eat or drink, and she wouldn't make eye contact with anybody. At night he brought her to bed with him, but she wouldn't stay there. Instead she lay down in front of the fire in the living room. Charles brought his blanket and pillow in, and that last night he slept there with her.

The next day we all said our good-byes, and then we put her down at home, where she was so deeply loved. I cried too.

There are few places where you have to deal with life and death on a daily basis more than on a farm. We even breed animals and fight for them to live knowing that they are meant to be slaughtered. Saving lives and putting down animals are part of the business: the best part and the hardest part, respectively. I couldn't even begin to estimate the number of animals I've delivered, or euthanized. But I'll tell you, even now, even after doing it for more than four decades, delivering a live animal—it can be a calving, a foaling, a C-section on a dog, it doesn't matter—when they come out alive and take their first breath, the feeling is almost euphoric.

When an animal is born, whether it is born naturally completely healthy or if we help it survive a difficult birth, the first thing it has to do is breathe. Just take that first breath. That's not as simple as it sounds. Sometimes when an animal is born, its nose and mouth—sometimes even its windpipe—is covered or blocked by a layer of mucus, which prevents it from breathing. When you see little bubbles coming out of its nose, that's a very dangerous sign. When a calf comes out the first thing I do, right away, is douse it with a big pail of cold water. I just dump it right over it. Believe me, that gets its attention. I've done it that way my whole career; I've also taught the farmers I've worked with to do it. Most of the time the cold water dissolves that mucus. But if the animal is still having trouble breathing, I pick it up by its hind legs and start swinging it around. It doesn't look so nice, but when I do it, I can see the mucus running out of its nose and mouth. The centrifugal force makes the mucus fly right out of the animal. Then I put it down and hit it hard with a flat hand on the chest. I'm not going to hurt it; you can't break a calf's ribs with your bare hand. But all of that usually gets it breathing. That sounds traumatic—cold water, swing it around, hit it in the ribs—but it works for me to get them going.

We used to do the same thing with puppies—we'd swing them till they started breathing—but unfortunately puppies are slippery, and one time one of my assistants was swinging a pup and it slipped out of her hands and scooted across the floor. It was absolutely fine, although maybe a little bit disoriented: That was some fine hello to the world. Other vets use their own methods to clear the breathing passages. I've seen people hang a calf over a gate, head-down, and just start slapping it. It doesn't matter; whatever works is the right way.

I remember my first delivery in the United States. This was before I had my license, while I was still riding around assisting a vet. We had a lambing and Diane decided to come along with us. That vet reached inside the ewe and came out with a cute little lamb, but it wasn't moving. I went to work on it; I started rubbing it down, reaching into its throat trying to clear the windpipe, just doing anything I could think of. I hadn't yet developed any system. And as I was working, he pulled out a second lamb, and this one he gave to Diane to work on. She went to work on it, although she really didn't know what to do. But all of a sudden I heard the first little throat-clearing cry—coming from Diane's lamb. As Diane has been reminding me ever since then, "Mine survived."

There is no right way or wrong way; when an animal is struggling to breathe, you do whatever you can think of to clear all its air passages. You've only got a very few minutes. I've had people complain about my method. They see me swinging a cute little lamb or puppy and they think I'm torturing that animal. The fact is that sometimes it is absolutely necessary. If an animal is born with its airways clogged with mucus or with part of the afterbirth covering its mouth and we wait too long for its mother to clear it, it may die. That happens with deer all the time, but we don't see it too often because other animals will drag away the remains.

Those first few moments of life are the most beautiful thing in the world. I can never forget the first time I was really aware of it. I was young, very young, and I was with my mother in the kitchen. One of our horses was due soon. My father and my brothers had been working with the horses; they'd unhitched them and turned them out in the pasture. My mother was looking out the window. One of the mares was just grazing; suddenly she lifted her head and lifted her tail, fluid started flying, and her colt came flying out right afterward. My mother took me outside to see it. I couldn't believe how amazing it was. The mare turned around and started licking it; it sort of stumbled to its feet, and that was it. One minute and that colt was born into the world.

At college we had to attend five normal births of horses to graduate. Our problem was that mares give birth so fast that we could never get there fast enough to see one, much less five. By the time we even got notified, it was too late. The professors knew it and the stable hands knew it. So as soon as it looked like it was close, we would call each other and race over to the stable on our bikes. We never, ever got there in time, but the stablehands let us sign the paper that proved we were there. The truth is that I never saw a horse give birth until I was working in Michigan, and even then it was just by accident that I was there when it happened.

I've seen and assisted at several thousand births, and as many times as I've seen it, it still amazes me. Foals are born very fast; calves can take a lot longer. Sometimes the calf's head pops out first and you can see it shaking its head while the rest of its body is still in the birth canal. Then when it finally does come out, the cow gets up and starts working; she licks it off. Then sometimes she'll also give it a little butt with her head: *Come on, wake up, get going.* Calves will sit up pretty quick, shake their heads to clear their nose and throat; then within several minutes they'll try to get up on their feet. It is so funny watching them taking those few off-balance, wobbly first steps. But pretty soon they'll be standing there on all four legs, their whole body shaking while the cow is pushing them to get moving. Within a short time, they will be walking on their own.

When you look at nature, it becomes obvious that it's humans who are born fairly premature. A baby can't do anything for itself. It can't even crawl. About all it can do is suck. If a human was born and no one was there to help, it would just lie there and die. Not animals. Animals somehow get up and manage to find their way to their mother's nipple and start nursing.

It doesn't matter what animal it is; it will figure it out. Even a stud colt, which is pretty much dumber than a rock, will try to find the milk source. It may need some help, but it gets there. Donkeys are supposed to be dumb animals, but within an hour after being born, the little donkey is racing around, bouncing off the walls. When you see this small donkey, whose ears are bigger than the rest of its body, running around its mama, it's the cutest thing you have ever seen. Sows have multiple piglets and every one of those little ones will fight their way to the sow's milk; sometimes they go between her hind legs, sometimes around them, but they will get there.

Two hours after piglets are born they're nice and pink, just lying there grunting and having the best time.

When it comes to giving birth, nature does an amazing job; most of the time we don't have to do anything to help. It's only a very small number of births where a vet's assistance is needed. This just might be the most important part of a large-animal vet's job. I had a professor in college, Professor Vander Kaay, who told us all the time, "A veterinarian is only as good as he is an obstetrician. If you don't get that calf out, you're no good." In school we spent a lot of our time working on malpositioned calves. Calves are supposed to come out head first with the head resting on the front legs. And probably 90 percent of them do. The others are turned around or their legs aren't in the right place. After you've done it often enough, when you reach inside an animal and feel any part of the fetus, you should be able to know instantly what it is—and you'd better know where it is supposed to be.

If a calf or a foal is malpositioned, meaning it's turned around, or the head or a leg is turned back instead of forward, or twisted so it can't come out, it will die. And if it dies and we don't get the remains out of the mother, she will die too. Those remains will become toxic real quick and kill the mother. If the animal inside is still alive when we get there, the first thing we try to do is reposition it. Most of the time medical doctors do not reposition; instead they do a C-section. They cut open the mother's belly and take out the baby, then sew up mama. Usually it's fine. It doesn't work that well in a barn. I don't like doing C-sections; one, because we're not in anything resembling a sterile environment, and two, because it puts way too much stress on an animal. Some large animals won't survive the procedure. So instead, we stick our hands inside the uterus and start manipulating the fetus, trying to put all the parts back where they're supposed to be. After doing it all these years I've learned which parts can bend and how much. For example, while you can move a calf around quite a bit, you can't turn it around completely in the uterus. It's impossible. So when we've got it as straight as it is ever going to be, we pull. And we keep pulling. Repositioning an animal can take a lot of time and a tremendous amount of effort, but when it is successful and you see mama licking that little one, there is such an incredible feeling of satisfaction, I wouldn't begin to know the words to express it. That's really a life we've saved.

I have a client who was the son of my very first Amish client, and I remember that first summer he was trying to get his own farm going. He called me one day in August when it had to be one hundred degrees, easy, asking me to get over there as fast as I possibly could. One of his cows was in trouble. He only had a few livestock, so losing even that one was going to make a significant difference to him. I soaped up my hands and my arms, reached inside, and began feeling around; I closed my eyes and saw with my hands exactly what was going on. The calf was still alive, but its head was twisted underneath its front legs. I knew how to fix that. But every time I tried to put him in position to be born, he would turn his head the other way. "This is a bull calf," I told the farmer. "It's stupid. It doesn't want to come out." Then I went back to work.

That sweat was pouring down my body, I was soaked, but I just kept wiping it away. That calf seemed healthy enough, but just as stubborn as all get-out. Or, in this situation, not get out. It took me quite some time to maneuver that calf into a position to be born; then we hooked up the calf pullers to his front legs and started working; we just pulled him right out. *Welcome to the world, sonny.* He turned out to be a big, healthy bull calf.

I can remember several of the easiest deliveries I've ever assisted. In recent years a lot of people, including Diane and myself, have begun keeping a bunch of chickens around just so we can have fresh eggs. Some people had a chicken that was trying to lay an egg but couldn't do it. They had watched the show, so they called me. I told them, if it's in there and it's big, then you put mineral oil around it and make it smooth and slippery; then see if it comes out. If it's still not coming, just break the egg inside, but make sure you pull out all the shells. Hopefully the next one won't be as big.

Unfortunately, a lot of deliveries aren't so simple and they don't have a happy ending. Nature has a way of weeding out the weak and the sick while letting the strong and healthy live, improving the herd. For example, if an animal's pelvis is too small, that animal has a lot less value because it's going to struggle giving birth. I remember that after pulling a good-size calf from an Angus I told the farmer, "Her pelvis is way too small." A month later he told me the calf was doing fine but that heifer was going to slaughter because her pelvis was way under normal size for the breed, so she was never going to be a good breeding animal.

Sometimes there is nothing that can be done to save the calf or the foal, and then the only thing that matters is to save the life of the mother by getting the remains out of her. That can be real complicated; there is always a reason the animal was not born naturally, and that reason sometimes makes it hard to get it out of the mother. One afternoon Dr. Ashley and I came back from a farm call and I was told that Dr. Brenda and Dr. Wendy had taken a student with them to deliver a colt out of a Percheron mare. They had left more than an hour earlier and nobody had heard from them. A Percheron is a big, strong horse, a draft horse. It shouldn't have taken that long. "Okay," I told Dr. Ashley. "Let's go."

Dr. Brenda was completely frustrated. The mare was down, it had been tranquilized, but the colt was dead and its remains were in a terrible position. Dr. Brenda was lying on the ground trying to move it around, but it was just jammed in there. She was exhausted. Dr. Ashley and I lay down and took over from her. No way one person could have done this. We worked inside the horse together; I had both arms in and Dr. Ashley had one hand in there; we were just trying to bring the body around so we could get it out. I started by cutting off the head, and when I did all the blood came out. The two of us were lying there in it, but we couldn't stop working. The front legs were far back, and working together we managed to bring them around to the front and then were able to pull the remains of the colt out. One person working alone never could have gotten that colt out.

We'll do whatever is necessary to save the mother. If necessary we'll break the dead animal's legs or twist body parts around. It's dead; we're not hurting it. But if that doesn't work, we have to cut it into pieces while it's still inside the animal and get the remains out that way.

Different vets use a variety of tools to do that cutting; I use a tool called the fetotome, which I brought back from the Netherlands; it's essentially a thin wire running through two tubes. You wrap the wire around whatever piece you want to cut, then pull the handles to tighten that wire. It's quick and so easy to use, even Charles can do it. We got called to a farm where they were raising what they called Michigan Texas longhorns, and the first thing they did was warn us that they were not very tame. We could see those long horns for ourselves; those horns were literally about the length of a car. The calf was dead, they told us; they just wanted us to save the cow. They'd been nice enough to catch her and put her in a pen. When I reached inside the uterus, I felt the front legs, then the neck, and then the head, which was way underneath the legs. If they had called me when the calf was still alive, I definitely could have gotten that head around and saved it, and we also would have had more room in the uterus to work; but because the cow had been straining so long, the uterus had contracted, so it was squeezed very tight around the remains. But they hadn't called me in time, so our job was to get the remains out of the uterus quick before they became toxic. Charles has become real good with the fetotome. It took him only about twenty seconds to cut off the head. There was nothing to it. I put my hand on the vertebrae, where we cut the head off so it wouldn't scratch the birth canal. Then we pulled out the rest of the remains by hand. Then the cow was fine and healthy enough to breed again.

That call was a little unusual; most of the time we don't know until we get to a farm whether we can save the calf or the foal. In the summer of 2013, for example, we got a call from a beef farmer who had a cow that was struggling to give birth. The Nat Geo Wild film crew actually got to the farm before I did. One of our cameramen asked the farmer's son, "How tame is this cow?"

"Oh, I can just go right up to her and pet her."

Okay. So that cameramen squatted down a few feet in front of the cow and started shooting. She looked at him and didn't like what she was seeing. So she lowered her head, flipped her ears back, and charged. Knocked him flat on his back. He was very lucky he didn't break his shoulder, although he was sore for a long time. Then the farmer's son pointed out, laughing, "I guess she's not as tame as you thought."

By the time I got there, she was enclosed in a small pen. And she was real unhappy to be in there. Whatever was going on inside her body, she was going berserk, jumping and kicking wildly. I asked the farmer, "How long has she been trying to have a calf?"

"Three days," he admitted. "We couldn't catch her." Suddenly she slammed her whole body into one gate at its corner and almost went right through it. This was a dangerous animal. "Everybody get away!" I yelled. "Get off the ground. Get on your cars. Get on the truck." After forty years of doing this, there's no backing away for me. I felt bad for this animal. Three days is much too long to leave any animal in this condition. Something obviously had gone very wrong. I managed to get two ropes around her and cross-tied her in the gates. I tried to work like that, but it was impossible; she was just kicking and swinging me back and forth. It wasn't safe for anybody to be near her, but especially me, so I tranquilized her. When she had finally quieted, I reached into her uterus and I got one hand on her calf's shoulder blade. But it was already so rotten I could just about cut the skin with my hands. It was decaying inside her. If we had any chance of saving this cow's life, we had to work very quickly. "I'm starting to cut, Charles," I told him. I cut the first piece and yelled to him, "She still breathing?"

"Nope." She had died right there. The toxins had poisoned her and there wasn't anything we could have done to save her. Three days was just too long with a dead calf inside.

Nature allows smaller farm animals to have multiple births because so many of the little ones don't survive, while large animals tend to have single births. Very few large animals have multiple births. Horses, for example, almost never carry twins to term; cows do occasionally. I remember once getting an emergency call from a farmer whose cow had given birth to twins the day before; she wasn't doing very well, he told me. That didn't surprise me much. Most cows can't sustain twins, but as soon as I put my hands inside her uterus, I figured out the problem—that cow actually was having triplets. It was amazing. I pulled the third calf, and the cow was fine. That was just about the only time I've seen triplets being born.

Many years ago I was at a large-animal vet convention and I met a tiny female vet with long red hair. I don't see a difference between men and women in the profession. In my practice everybody gets paid the same and we all do the same work. But this big-time vet came up to her and thought he was being smart. He said to her in a real loud voice, "So you're in the beef practice?" He didn't add, "Little lady," in a condescending voice, but that's what he meant. When she told him she was, he asked, smartly, "Well then, how do you get the calves out?"

That woman did not hesitate. She told him, "That's easy. I just crawl right in there and kick them out. Why, how do you do it?" I laughed so hard that man turned and just glared at me. But it was a silly question; in this business it doesn't make a difference how strong you are; what matters is how smart you are. You have to be smarter than the animals; otherwise, you're done for. The goal is to get the delivery done any way possible.

Not too long after Dr. Brenda came to work at the clinic, she was on call on Memorial Day. We were enjoying a family picnic when the telephone rang. A big Belgian was trying to give birth to a colt; the front legs were out, but not its head. We talked about it and I made a few suggestions and she went back to the farm. A few minutes later she asked me to come and help. The farm was only about ten miles away, and Charles drove there with me. When we got there we saw about a dozen men leaning against the railing watching Dr. Brenda work, as if they were an audience for a comedy show: *The Female Vet Delivers*. I don't know where those people came from on Memorial Day, but they all were just watching and waiting for something to happen. It's one of the facts of a vet's life that somehow, anytime we've got a problem, there's always an audience. In this situation none of them had offered any help; they were just there for the story they would tell later on.

The front legs were hanging out of the mare's butt; they were out so far they actually were hitting me below the knees. I tried to reach inside to grab hold of the head, but it was too big. In moments like this a whole film runs through your mind, reviewing all the different things you can try, all the things you've done in similar circumstances. "Okay, Brenda," I said, "we ain't got no choice. It's coming out this way. Let's get the calf pullers." All the onlookers' eyes almost popped out of their sockets.

We put the chains on just below the elbows. I told her, "When I say go, you pull as hard as you can as fast as you can." When we were all set, I reached in as far as I could and pushed the neck as far back as possible. The neck of a colt is so long that you can bend the head back right against its flank. "Go ahead." She started cranking, the chains tightened, and slowly that colt began moving. I think the mare helped her, pushing hard to get it out. With all of us working together, it finally came sliding out. A second later the afterbirth came flowing out. Then the exhausted mare fell down for a few seconds, but she got right up; she had her responsibility. She took a few steps and looked at her colt and saw that it was dead. Then she started eating.

So when I hear people criticizing the women in this profession I can hardly believe it. When I was going through vet school, we had only five or six girls in our group of three hundred, but they were as tough as beans. They weren't as strong as the men; so what? For a large-animal vet that's not necessarily a bad thing. We don't wrestle a lot of animals. The women generally were smaller than the men, so there were things they could do that most of us couldn't do. Because their arms tend to be slender, they have a lot less trouble reaching inside a small farm animal without causing damage. They can squeeze into smaller places in a barn. I've always had women working for me and I've never seen the difference.

In fact, there are very few times when we just need brute strength, and when we do there are usually people around to help. Gilbert Tinsey and Fred Hazen, who met in college and started farming together, called me when one of their big Brown Swiss was struggling to give birth. Oh, it was a big calf and it was malpositioned. I managed to straighten it out and put my chains around its legs and told them, "Okay, guys, start pulling." That was a fight. "C'mon, guys, you're young," I told them. "Can't you get this calf out? Pull a little harder." They worked up some sweat and it took both of them working to get the calf out. A big calf like that is money in the bank; it's the kind of thing farmers depend on. And then, as I always do, I reached inside the cow and felt around just to make sure that there wasn't another one. Gil and Fred were starting to walk away—they'd been working hard—when I stopped them. "Guys," I told them. "Pick up the chains. There's another one."

We pulled that one out too. The guys told me later that they weighed both calves and estimated, with the fluids that were in the uterus and everything, that cow lost about 270 pounds giving birth. That was too much. That cow never got up again. She didn't eat; she didn't drink. There was nothing we could do to save her. She was just spent. That cost them $1,000 at that time, but at least they got the two calves out of it. That's the cycle of life you see all the time on a farm.

I don't really have much of a preference as to which animals I work with. I like the fact that horses generally deliver quickly. One of my Amish clients called me on a Sunday and told me his horse was struggling to have a colt. "How bad is it?" I asked. "What's going on?"

"Not much," he told me.

"Okay, when she starts to deliver, call me and I'll come right over."

He didn't call me till Tuesday morning. "You better come out here right now. Something's wrong."

This horse was so tall I had to stand on a bale of straw to work on her. When I reached inside, all I could feel were the hocks of the colt. If an animal is still alive, when I grab hold of its leg it will move it. This foal did not move. It was dead. Worse, it was badly positioned, which is why it hadn't come out naturally. Sometimes with a malpositioned horse I can push hard on the hocks, then grab a hoof and pull the leg straight. But this one was so big it wouldn't budge. I was hanging on to the hocks with both of my feet literally off the ground and I couldn't move it. I thought, *Oh my gosh, this is a tough one.* So I got my fetotomy knife and cut off the hind legs underneath the hocks. Then I got my calf puller and put the chain around the hind legs and started pulling. I pulled that animal out piece by piece. It was huge. It was four feet tall at the withers, and when we weighed it, it was 148 pounds. I put antibiotics in the mare's uterus and she seemed fine. In fact, a month later she was pregnant again. That was too much for the owner; he didn't want to go through that again, so he sold the horse.

The smallest farm animals that I've delivered are pygmy goats. Their kids are about the size of my hand. I can easily hold a newborn in one hand. Make a circle with your thumb and forefinger, and that's about the size of the head. I actually can get my whole hand inside many of those small animals—they stretch pretty well—but there's not a lot of room in the uterus for me to work. When I needed to pull a small animal, I generally would put my fingers in the fetus's eye sockets, which allowed me to get a good hold; then I just pulled it out.

When delivering piglets, some vets like to use a special pair of tongs that fit over the piglet's head or a snare, which allows them to grab hold of the piglet and pull, but those never worked well for me. So I made my own pulling tool for pigs; it is a long metal rod with a hook on the end. Piglets are similar to babies; when they're born, their heads are bigger than their bodies. And generally pigs come out headfirst. Using this tool I reach carefully inside and hook them in the bottom jaw, underneath the tongue, and gently pull them out with my hand on top of the head. That hook leaves a tiny hole, but that doesn't cause any problems and heals up in just a few hours. If a piglet was coming out backward I could hook its hind leg and just hang on. I've saved a ton of piglets that way, and I've never hurt one of them. That was my own invention and it worked like a charm.

While seeing a healthy animal take its first steps always fills me with happiness, part of my job also sometimes requires me to put down animals, to euthanize them. Without question that is the hardest thing I have to do, and it's no easier now than it was when I was starting out. There isn't anything about it that's enjoyable. I've never gotten used to it, but I understand that sometimes it's not only necessary; it's the most humane thing to do. I can't stand seeing an animal suffer, and when its quality of life is gone, that animal is suffering. If the animal has a quality of life, I'll do my best to keep it alive. A gentleman from the South carried his big old dog into the clinic one day to see if there was anything we could do to help. That dog couldn't even climb up the four steps out in front. He told me he'd already been to three other vets and they wouldn't treat him: He was too old, they said; let him be. I asked him if they had taken X-rays; they hadn't. When I did I saw that the hips were not good, but otherwise the animal was in good shape. I put the dog on an arthritis joint lubricant and a painkiller. A week later the owner called to tell me the dog was bounding up steps.

Six months later the dog had a stroke and the owner brought him back to us. It was time then, and we put the dog down. "Thank you," he told us. "At least we had another six months together."

I have my own method of administering the euthanasia solution. First I give the animal an anesthetic, and only after it is asleep and pain-free do I give it the second shot. It's a lot easier for people to see an animal simply go to sleep gently than to die suddenly. The counties all around us have adopted this method. I had a call from some people I didn't know over in Clare. Their daughter was a vet who lived in Colorado, and she had a horse that was old and suffering from arthritis, and she hadn't been home to ride it for a long time. They called me because they had heard about my method. The nicest thing you can ever do for people is to euthanize the animal quickly and painlessly. Don't prolong the agony. I went over there and they told me all about the horse. I gave the horse the first shot and it lay down. Then I gave it the second shot in the chest. They had already dug a hole for it. But two days later I got a card from them thanking me for putting down their horse so humanely.

We were taught how administer the euthanasia solution into a vein in school, but I learned by accident that if you put it directly into an artery instead of the vein, it acts much faster. I like that, because putting down an animal is always hard enough without prolonging it. I learned this when a regular client who operates a horse rescue farm brought a pony to the clinic in a trailer. "He's a mean bugger," she told me. When anybody got near him he'd start kicking and biting.

"Where'd you get him?" I asked.

"These people were going to put him down. They didn't want him anymore," she said. In the few weeks he'd been on the farm he'd caused a lot of trouble. He was dangerous to both people and other animals. She wouldn't let kids go anywhere close to him and when he was let loose he went after the other horses, kicking and biting them.

"That's why they didn't want him in the first place," I guessed.

This woman was part of an organization that rescued horses, then tried to find homes for them, but there was nothing that could be done for this pony. They couldn't give him away because they were afraid eventually he would hurt somebody, and they couldn't keep him on their place forever because he was dangerous to the other horses, so they wanted me to put him down. He was in the trailer and he was wild. Nobody could hang on to him. We cross-tied him to hold him, but he was still trying to jump. He was so dangerous that I was going to do just one injection. I wasn't going to risk my own safety for him. I had a good-size needle ready, and as he jumped up I hit him with it in the side of the neck and pushed the plunger. Instantly, that pony dropped dead. Whoa. It was very unusual that it happened so fast. I started thinking about it and I realized, *Wait a second, that wasn't in the vein; it was in the artery.* From that time on I began doing the euthanasia procedure differently; I injected the animal in the artery and it was dead within seconds.

With some small animals I use a different procedure. Those small animals can be real dangerous if they get their teeth or claws into you, and because they're so small you're forced to get close to them to give them the shot. In one of the segments on the show, a client brought in a beautiful iguana with a big tumor on its mouth. Reptiles can make nice pets; not for me, particularly, but for some people. One of my other clients had a pet iguana. She actually would take a bath with it—at least she would until she ended up in the hospital with a serious case of salmonella.

That was fine for her, but this iguana with the tumor was an old guy that had stopped eating, and the owner had decided to put it down. This iguana turned out to be a mean animal. The owner had brought him to the clinic in a cat carrier, and we couldn't get him out. We eventually put some sticks through the bars and he got mad and opened his mouth, and as soon as he did I shot the euthanasia solution mixed with an anesthetic directly into his mouth. It went through the mucous membranes quickly and knocked him out. I'd learned that technique when I had to put down a feral cat.

This was a wild cat that was attacking all the animals around the clinic. It wasn't a sweet, playful house cat; this was a mean, aggressive bastard with sharp claws. If she could get those claws into someone, she could do serious damage. I finally trapped her in a large cage, but I couldn't get close enough to give her a shot. Oh, she was angry. When I walked by the cage, she'd fly right at me and hang on the side, hissing with her mouth wide open. Finally I loaded up a hypodermic and when she leaped at me and opened her mouth, I shot the solution right into it. It took her a minute or two, but eventually she was flat out.

I won't let an animal suffer. Most of the animals I put down are either old or sick; in either case they feel vulnerable and probably wouldn't survive too much longer anyway. One case I will never forget was an eighty-seven-year-old woman and her daughter who brought in their twenty-seven-year-old cat. That cat had terrible kidney problems and its quality of life was completely gone. But after twenty-seven years the bond between that woman and that cat was so strong that I knew what it was going to do to her. I had no choice; I didn't want any of them to suffer another day. I euthanized that animal that day, and I never forgot it.

It's cruel for people to keep an animal alive to make themselves feel better, however good their intentions are meant to be. Clare County Animal Control called me on a very hot summer day when they discovered a woman who was keeping forty horses. She was trying to save these animals, but what she was really doing was torturing them. She had these horses in twelve-square-foot pens made from gates. She had hay but no water; she had to pump the water out of a pond into a tank. There were a few pine trees on the property, so there was no shade. When I got there my mouth just dropped open. She had old racehorses; she had crippled horses, old mares—it was unbelievably sad. One of the horses was blind, and he was alone in a pen. A blind horse can function if he has a buddy he can depend on; he learns how to stay with him. But this guy was alone and afraid; he had no life. The lady was there and I just lost my temper. I don't have much of a temper, but when it goes, I have a hard time controlling it. I said, "What in the world are you trying to do with these animals?"

She said, "Oh, I'm trying to save them so they can live longer."

I got right in her face and I told her, "These animals should not live longer. They have no quality of life. You are not doing these animals any favor." I was so angry. We had some people come up with trailers for the horses that were salvageable, and the police took this woman away. Then one of the animal control officers asked me what we should do, and I told him, "Get the backhoe." We ended up putting seven horses in the ground that day. When she was tried for animal abuse, I ended up writing a letter to the judge; he sentenced her to three months in jail and prohibited her from owning animals ever again.

I've seen that same thing too many times. I had to put a twenty-four-year-old Belgian mare down that had so much arthritis I could see the pain in her eyes. It couldn't be put on painkillers because it got terrible diarrhea. A young girl looked at me and told me proudly, "I saved this horse from slaughter two years ago."

And I looked right back at her and said, "Well, you didn't do it any favors." I know that was a callous thing to say; I know she meant well, but keeping that animal alive in that condition was not what anyone would do for a living thing she cared about.

But that's the kind of thing that happens when people attribute human qualities to animals. They're not human; they're animals. I guarantee that no one cares about animals more than I do. But they are not the same as human beings. Animals can be trained, and most animals have some type of memory, but they cannot reason. There are animals that can use tools; crows will use a stick to punch into a wormhole in a tree, chimpanzees will put tables and chairs on top of each other to climb high enough to reach bananas, but you can't teach an animal to reason or understand why one and one makes two.

I love Disney movies—I love *The Lion King;* I get tears in my eyes every time I hear the music—but the animals are portrayed as human, with human emotions and human desires, and animals are not humans. *Bambi* is a good story, but it attributes human emotions to deer. Deer generally don't know enough to get out of the way of a speeding car, much less process emotions. That's why I have no problem—and I hope God doesn't hold it against me—putting down an animal when its quality of life is gone. Animals know when it's time. They walk away and they don't come back. They want to be alone. They're not afraid; being afraid of death is a concept they don't understand. What is interesting is that when I have to put down an animal, the other animals will stand nearby watching, but they don't express any response beyond curiosity. There's no sense of sympathy or sadness; those are human emotions. Instead, it's *What the heck is that guy doing? How is it going to affect me? And most important, when am I going to get fed?*

Of course it's painful for anyone to watch an animal being

euthanized, especially an animal that he has taken care of and loved. It's painful for me too. We had a wonderful Dane named Neena, and she was deteriorating, but she still liked to roll around and play, and as long as she was happy I did everything possible to keep her alive. She loved sitting out in the sun. When she was having trouble walking because of her arthritis, I would actually pick her up and walk her outside. I did that one day and I came back a half hour later and said to her, "You ready to come back in?" Instead of looking at me as she always had done, she looked away. She wouldn't meet my eyes. It was time and we both knew it. It was hard. There was so much love in this dog. We said good-bye and I put her down. When I gave her that shot and she closed her eyes and put her head down, I could almost see the pain leaving her body. You think that didn't hurt me terribly? But that's what I had to do for that animal.

Believe me, I love my animals. We've had at least a dozen Danes. They're all buried out in the back and I can tell you where each one is. We all get attached to animals—not just little animals, but horses and even cows. Every single animal has its own personality, and people can become real attached to any animal. Farmers have favorite cows, and they also have cows they don't like—and those cows won't like those farmers right back. Even dairy farmers, who look at everything from an economical point of view, sometimes make exceptions for their favorite cows. While some farmers have no problem eating their own cows if something happens to them, I've known farmers who become so attached to a cow that they won't sell it and when it dies or has to be put down, they bury it on the farm. Dairy farmers have to touch their animals twice a day, often for years, and they form a bond, if not a real friendship. A few dairy farms have cow graveyards out back beyond the barn or in a field.

People who grow up on a farm understand that large animals are a product, and at least some animals are raised to be slaughtered. That's just the way life is. Sometimes it's unavoidable. One time I had a calf that was being born with its hind legs forward, and the tail was already out of the cow. Normally in those situations I can push the tail back in and bring the hind legs around so the calf is in the right position to be born. It takes two hands to do it, but it isn't that difficult. But this time I pushed the calf in and I felt the entire uterus completely tear off. It just fell into the belly. The farmer looked at me and asked, "What happened, Doc?"

"I can't believe it," I said, surprised and very disappointed. "The whole uterus tore off and everything is down inside." He asked me what we could do. "Take it to slaughter," I said. "That's the only thing we can do." That decision was made for me. That animal would not have survived, and if the owner got it to the slaughterhouse right away, at least he would salvage the meat. Whether it is unavoidable or by choice, you still have to learn to accept it. That's not so easy sometimes. When Charles was four years old we had a Dane that got prostate cancer, and I had to euthanize him. I did it while the kids were home because I wanted them to learn to deal with the reality of life and death; as a result, Charles still remembers it because it was our first Dane.

But eventually they learned how to accept it. When our kids were growing up, we had them raise sheep for their 4-H project. We bred and raised our own. We had a ram and ewes and every year we took the offspring to the fair, knowing they would be sold for meat. It might sound cruel making children raise an animal knowing it is going to be sold, but it makes them respect the whole circle of life and take nothing for granted. One year Charles practically raised two female sheep by himself; their mother wasn't that interested, so he bottle-fed them. They were very tame and became more like pets than a project. He really bonded with those sheep, and that year it was especially hard for him to bring them to the auction. Fortunately, the people who bought them wanted them for breeding purposes, so they took them home to introduce them to their new boyfriends.

Making the decision to end an animal's life usually isn't difficult. There are times when it's just the right thing to do. I had clients who bred and sold Belgians, beautiful big draft horses. They had a four-month-old colt with great bloodlines that just wasn't walking right. After examining the horse I realized it had serious neurological problems. Its senses hadn't developed completely. I'd seen this only a couple of times before, and I knew there was nothing that could be done to fix it. That horse was stumbling around, falling down, and bumping into things. He was probably more of a danger to himself than to people. I told the owners that the kind thing to do for that animal was to put him down.

While the owners understood and accepted it, their teenage daughter had a more difficult time. She had become pretty close with that horse. I talked with her for a little while and explained the whole situation. Eventually she agreed it was the right thing to do. A few weeks later she called and asked if we were hiring; she had planned to go to nursing school but had decided she wanted to work around animals. We did hire her and she worked in the office for almost seven years. She still comes around to visit with her own child.

A lot of the time we'll euthanize an animal because it isn't going to survive anyway and it would be cruel to prolong its suffering. One of the worst things I've seen in my career started on a Sunday night in the early spring when Dr. Rachel got a call from the state police. They were on a farm and needed help. An Arabian mare had just given birth to a colt and couldn't get up. Dr. Rachel went out there, and when she realized what was going on, she called me right away. We had a bad situation. The mare was so emaciated, it didn't have the strength to get up. The colt had died because the mare had been too weak to push it out. Neighbors had seen that horse struggling and called the police. Dr. Rachel put the mare down. But that was just the beginning.

While she was working on the mare, another two-year-old mare fell down and started floundering around. It was also too weak to get back up on its feet. Dr. Rachel eventually counted twelve horses, and the only food she could find was half of a round bale of hay. These horses were starving to death. I went back with her Monday morning. By then animal control had arrived and intended to take all the horses. It was probably the worst pen I'd ever walked in. There was liquid manure in that barn that went over the tops of my boots. I had to climb on the gates to move around. Two more horses were already down in the muck and couldn't get up, so we had to euthanize those animals. The other horses were running free. It was obvious nobody was caring for these animals. Animal control took them away and there was a big story in the newspapers.

The strongest horses were in a little bit better shape because they had been at the top of the pecking order, and whatever food there was, they got most of it. But none of them had been cared for at all. None of them even had a halter on. Eventually we needed to put them in a trailer. Some of them I had to tranquilize on the fly; as they ran by me, I popped the needle in their rear, and when they had quieted down I could put a rope on them so we could drag them into the trailer. But one of the young mares just refused to go. Tranquilizer or not, she wasn't moving. Finally I got frustrated and pushed her from behind—and when I did she kicked me hard. *Oh yeah?* I thought. *I'm trying to help you. I'll show you.* So I booted her right back, right in her butt. It didn't hurt her, not a bit, but it definitely got her attention. *Oh, you mean me? Oh, okay.* Then she jumped right into that trailer.

We took those horses that had a chance of surviving to a good, clean farm, where we could give them care. There was one gray stallion we thought we could save, but three days later he just laid down and died. About six horses survived. But even most of them had been in that muck so long without having their feet trimmed that the outside wall of the hoof had grown all the way underneath and around. So they weren't walking on the bottoms of their feet, but instead on the sides. It was as if your fingernail had closed completely over the top of your finger. They started trimming their hooves. Every three weeks I had to go the farm, stand behind a gate, and tranquilize them so the farrier could work on their feet.

Eventually I had to testify in court, and that owner went to jail for three months. When he came out he managed to find himself a lawyer, and he sued me and the county for taking his horses. He claimed we had shut down his business. His business? I asked his lawyer, "That's his business? Did you ever ask him how many horses he's sold for a profit?" Within a week they dropped that lawsuit.

I think we ended up euthanizing five horses. We didn't have any choice; they were in such bad condition they could not have survived. But there are other situations when we had to do it because the animals had become dangerous to people. I don't blame the animals; animals aren't born to be vicious, but when they are taught that behavior, it's almost impossible to change it. And then you have to do something about it. I had a good client whose son had brought home two Rottweilers and done nothing to tame them, so they terrorized anything they came into contact with. "We've got to put them down," my client told me. "They're not safe and if they attack somebody I'm going to be in big trouble." These were very big and very dangerous dogs. The male probably weighed as much as 150 pounds, the female maybe one hundred pounds. When I got there they were in a small, rickety pen, and as soon as we got close, they bared their teeth, started snarling, and got ready to attack. I got the tranquilizer ready; as soon as the owner opened the gate, the male just flew at him, and I harpooned the dog with the tranquilizer. Same thing with the female. I have no idea how these dogs got to be this way, but they were dangerous and had to be put down. Eventually they would have hurt somebody.

There are times when we just get lucky, when people are prepared to have an animal put down and we're able to save it. We had a woman drive up to the clinic with her horse in a trailer. She was practically crying as she led him out into our parking lot. "We were riding and the horse fell down on its front knees," she told me. "He couldn't get up for a long time." She'd brought him back to the stable and put him right into the trailer. She expected there was something majorly wrong with his muscles, she told me, and the most important thing was that he didn't suffer. He'd been a good horse and she wanted to be good to him. I checked that horse over and I couldn't find anything wrong with it. No way was I going to put it down in that situation. We took blood and discovered that the horse was low in vitamin E and selenium. I treated the horse and she took it home. That horse had some good years left in him.

I remember another farm call I dreaded. When we got the call I drove out to the barn, thinking, *I'm going to have to put this horse down.* This old man was thirty-three years old and had very bad arthritis, especially in his legs. When I got to the barn, he was lying in a very well-bedded stall. I told him, "Get up, come on, come on," and with only a little bit of effort he got up and looked at me like he was wondering, *Okay, now what do you want me to do?* It turned out I had gotten to the place a little earlier than the scheduled appointment; his owner was a state trooper and a few minutes after I'd gotten there she came speeding down the road to meet me. She had owned this horse since he was foal, she told me, and he was an important member of her family. She'd lived a large part of her life with this animal and now she was dealing with saying good-bye. Not easy for any of us.

We talked about the horse so I would understand their relationship, and as we did I could see she was not ready to give up. Instead of trying to talk her into it, I honored her wishes. After so many years, it's easy to tell when people need a little more time, so I gave her the painkillers and explained how to use them. I knew this wasn't kind to the animal, but sometimes, as in this case, it just felt like it was the right thing to do. I warned her that it wasn't going to be long before he was not going to be able to get up anymore. And when that happened he would start struggling. Then it would be time. But she needed those last few days. I got back in my car and drove to see my next patients, two dogs that had gotten too curious about a porcupine. And the truth is I felt very good about what I'd done.

The case I will never forget was an eleven-year-old black lab that a woman brought in. I took a look at it and thought, *Holy moley, what is that thing hanging off it?* That dog had a fifteen-pound tumor hanging from its back and off to the side. It had started as a small fatty tumor and kept growing and growing and got big in a fairly short time. That dog looked like a hunchback. When you see something like that, people get prepared to say good-bye to the animal. "Is there anything we can do?" she asked.

After examining the dog, I said, "Sure, we can take it off him. That dog is healthy. You can still enjoy him." I cut the skin open and reached in with my two hands and took the tumor out. It was like a big, ugly ball. The skin had been stretched around the tumor, so I cut off a piece of skin probably a foot long and six inches wide, clamped some blood vessels, put a drain and some antiseptic in there, and sewed the dog up. The drain came out four days later, the stitches came out two weeks later, and that dog was running with that lady again. You can't imagine how good something like that makes me feel.

I've seen the whole cycle of life countless times. People ask me if I can identify any of the animals I've delivered, and the answer is there have just been too many. If an animal had unique markings at birth I might remember it, but generally, no, I can't. And as far as I know, I've never had to put down an animal I helped bring into this world. I sure hope I never do.

SEVEN

Never Turn Your Back
on an Angus Cow

One day more than twenty years ago, my friend Ike Swarey was hauling a wagonload of manure. One of the four horses pulling the wagon was being trained, and it was still a little skittish. Somehow the manure splattered and that horse lay down and didn't want to get up. Ike smacked it so it stood up, but one of its back legs got caught in a rope. Ike tapped that back leg to make the horse pick it up; instead, that horse kicked him right in the middle of his face with its heavy metal shoe.

How Ike had bent over so far I don't know, but there was nothing anybody could do for him. By the time they got him to the hospital he was dead.

It's not only the animals that get seriously hurt or even killed working on a farm or a ranch. Being a large-animal vet is a dangerous job. I've never been afraid of an animal, but I've always been respectful of their capabilities. While I've never known an animal that set out to hurt a person without a cause, I have seen people get hurt. I've been hurt myself. Animals are bigger and dumber and stronger than they can possibly understand. In any physical confrontation between a human being and a large animal, that animal is going to win. If you put an animal in a position where it feels vulnerable, it will defend itself any way it can: It'll kick or butt or bite, it'll try to trample you or hook you with a horn or scratch you with a claw, and if you happen to be in the wrong place at the wrong time, there isn't much you can do about it. A lot of times when we're treating sick animals, they don't feel like being pushed or prodded; they don't want anybody forcing open their mouth or sticking them with a needle. So they react. Every animal has its way of defending and protecting itself. Pigs will try to run over you and then chew your arm or a hand. Goats will sharpen their horns so the tips are like daggers and try to catch you with that knifelike point. Animals don't want to hurt you; they want routine; they want the same things done the same way every day. So anytime there is a change, they become alert and anxious and get ready to defend themselves. Horses will run away, and cows will attack, especially if a calf is nearby. People don't think of cows as aggressive animals, but I guarantee nobody makes that mistake more than once.

Sometimes the animal doesn't even have to feel threatened; it can push you or run you over without even being aware that you're there. Those accidents happen. On the show one time we were moving some cows around in a small fenced-in area.

Next thing I knew, poor Charles was trapped between two cows. That's not a sensible place to be, and we had to move those cows pretty quickly to make sure he didn't get hurt. In the practice we've all been bitten by dogs, scratched by cats, and pecked by birds. We've been chased, knocked down, and run over by cows and horses and pigs. But mostly we've been kicked. Believe me, if a large-animal vet says he or she has never got kicked, that person doesn't work. Everybody gets kicked—everybody. The first time I got kicked I was only four years old. We had a nice young colt in the pasture and I wanted to pet it. I walked up to the colt and reached out at it—and it kicked me on the inside of my thighs. I was wearing shorts and it left me with two black-and-blue hoofprints. I started bawling and ran back home. I told my mother what had happened, and she turned me over on her knee and gave me a spanking. That colt didn't know me, she said, he was protecting himself from a stranger. That's what animals do, she told me, and it was a lesson I never forgot.

I have been kicked too many times to remember them all. The worst was when I was doing pregnancy tests for a very good client. He forgot to warn me that one of those cows liked to kick people. I chased that cow into the barn and was walking behind her. I wasn't even touching her, but the next thing I know she lets fly with her hind leg and gets me square in the pubic area. Oh my gosh. It hurt; it hurt bad. I couldn't get up; I was squatting in the holding area, moving gingerly from one foot to the other, waiting for that wave of red-hot pain to subside. Meanwhile, nobody knew what to do. I heard my client whispering to his wife, "Should we go help him?"

"You go ahead," she told him.

"I'm okay," I said, but I said it in a wheezy, high-pitched voice and without a lot of conviction. It took me about five minutes before I could stand mostly straight up. As soon as I could, I went over to that cow and kicked her in the butt as hard as I could. The pain in my foot took the other pain away!

She turned her head and looked at me, probably thinking, *Are you talking to me?* In response, she tried to kick me again. This time I grabbed her tail and cranked it around a few times; and then it suddenly occurred to me that I was having a fight with a cow. "Forget it," the farmer told me. "We're shipping her out because she kicks us all the time too, when we're milking her."

I was black-and-blue in that area for a week, and I definitely walked a little funny. Well, maybe not so funny to me. Like every other large-animal vet I know, I've been kicked all over my body; I've been battered, bruised, and bloodied, and both of my knees have been bent almost all the way back. Horses will warn you before they try to kick you because they have to shift their weight to the other foot, but cows can kick at any time without a warning. As long as you're standing to the side of the animal, though, it's harder for it to get you.

I get bloodied all the time; the closer you get to an animal, the safer it is; if you're close to an animal, you can feel it moving so you know what its going to do, making it much less likely you'll get in its way. Being close also makes it hard for the animal to kick out at you or get up any momentum, but it also means that you're continually catching your hand or your foot on things and getting cut. Usually those cuts are minor— put a Band-Aid on them and forget about them. The only time I went to a doctor for a cut was when I sliced off the tip of my finger when I was trying to trim a cow's hoof. I was holding it, and just as I moved the knife down, she moved up. The hoof slipped out of my hand and I sliced into the tip of my finger. The blood started squirting out. I looked at the farmer and said, "Well, I always wanted to finger-paint." I put a bandage over it and finished the job. That bleeding wouldn't stop, though, so I went to the doctor's office. "I can suture it," he told me, "but it probably won't hold." He put four sutures in there to hold that fingertip in place, but eventually it just dried out and fell off. I still have feeling in the finger, but the top of that finger is pretty flat. But this is a profession where you're constantly getting little cuts and bruises that you just have to ignore. I've got little scars everywhere, but the worst-looking scar came from a very minor injury. I was doing pregnancy checks and a cow backed up, and my arm moved over a partition and I scratched my arm on a metal burr. It barely even bled. I took off the plastic glove I was wearing and cleaned the scratch good, and pretty much forgot about it, but when it healed up it looked like I'd been in a knife fight.

I have a small painting hanging in my house that one of my clients did for me; it's painted on barn wood and it shows a rancher standing outside a pen, watching a very angry bull tied to a post with a thin rope. The vet is holding a large syringe and obviously getting ready to give that bull a shot while the rancher is saying to him, "Hey, Doc, I just had a sobering thought. That rope only cost three dollars."

Well, I know that feeling. We try to be careful, but there is only so much we can do to protect ourselves and still do our job. I can't even remember all the times I've been hurt. One of my clients was a nice young couple trying to make a living on a small farm, but they just didn't have enough money to take good care of their few cows. They hadn't dehorned their cows—either they couldn't afford it or they didn't know how—but for me the result was the same: Those cows had sharp horns. I went out there on a Saturday evening to do a calving and successfully pulled a big healthy calf from a heifer. That big cow was down in the little dirty pen and I needed to get her up. I carried what is called a Hot-Shot, an electric stimulus sort of similar to a Taser. I hit that cow with it, and it got up—it got up real quick and charged right at me. I started backing out of that pen, but suddenly I felt two hands on my back; the woman who had been helping me wasn't fast enough to get out of the way. I was stuck there for a few seconds—too long. When that cow swung her head, I wasn't completely out of the way, and her horn caught me right in the middle of my palm. It ripped open a big, deep hole. I used paper towels to try to stop the bleeding.

It was after eleven o'clock at night when I got home. Everybody was sleeping. I went into the clinic, cleaned the gash, and washed it and sewed it up by myself. One-hand stitches are generally pretty loose, so a day or two later we took out the stitches and Dr. Brenda redid it nice and tight. The only evidence is a half-moon scar in the middle of my hand.

Another time I was examining a cow that was coming down with milk fever but was still on its feet. I put a rope around her neck and wrapped it twice around a beam, as I often do. The problem was that this was a round beam. I was standing in a manure patch, holding on to the other end, when the cow decided to walk away. Pound for pound, cows are much stronger than horses, and when she started walking there was no way I could hold on to that rope. I let go, and because I had no footing I couldn't move quickly enough. That rope whipped around the post and snapped back and hit me right in the forehead. I was lucky it didn't hit me an inch lower and rip out my eye, but it opened a long thin wound in my forehead, which started bleeding, and there was nothing we could do to stop it. The blood was dripping down and I was pushing paper towels against it, and finally I got it to stop. "You all right?" the farmer asked.

"Of course," I told him, although I was pretty angry at that cow. I grabbed the rope again and tied it really tight this time and treated her. I went back to the clinic and Dr. Ashley closed the wound with several stitches.

Usually on every farm there is one cow you have to be extra careful around; otherwise, she'll kick the daylights out of you. Angus cows, for example, are the dickens. They're mean. One thing I know for sure: You should never turn your back on an Angus cow. But there also is the other type of cow, the friendly cow that comes right up to you and practically demands you scratch her head. Those nice cows are the ones you have to be extra careful about: Back in Harbor Beach my colleague went to treat a Brown Swiss with milk fever. Brown Swiss are big, nice cows. He was bending over and examining this cow when another cow came up right behind him and nudged him; she wanted to be petted. Without looking, he reached behind him and swatted the cow's face. *Oh yeah?* That cow put her head down and literally butted him up in the air and over the bars of the stall.

We spend a lot of time working in awkward positions or trying to hold big animals, so it isn't unusual to strain or pull a muscle or a tendon. I was giving pills to a cow one morning and she tried to butt me; as she swung her head, I was trying to hold it, and then she suddenly turned the other way and I started slipping. That was it. I could feel the triceps in my left arm ripping. My arm was hanging there, completely useless. I couldn't pick it up. It took it about a month to heal and I had to do all my pregnancy checks with my right hand.

I've had to have only one surgery. I was doing pregnancy checks at Fox Dairy in 2006 when a big old cow came running into the parlor straight at me. I put out my hand to stop her. My arm was rigid in front of me, my elbow was locked— and she ran straight into it; my hand popped back and pushed my rotator cuff out of place. Oh my, that one hurt. Felt like my shoulder just got yanked back. She wasn't trying to hurt me; she was just being pushy. It didn't matter; the damage was done. My arm just fell right down and I couldn't lift it. I was almost finished with the pregnancy checks and I didn't want to have to come back, so I supported my left arm with my right hand and just pushed it into the remaining cows to do the checks. When I pulled my arm out I had to catch it; otherwise, it just fell. At first I figured it was like so many other injuries I'd had, that if I just gave it a few days I'd be fine. I went back to the clinic and tried to work, but my arm was just lying useless in my lap. As much as I didn't want to, I knew I had to have it examined.

The MRI showed I had damaged my rotator cuff. The doctor wanted to wait until the inflammation went down before deciding what to do. I struggled with it for two weeks. The pain went away pretty quick, but I didn't get much strength back. In the meantime, I ended up treating a prolapse, meaning the cow's uterus is outside and has to be pushed back inside. It was a big, big pile of bloody mess. We pulled the cow's hind legs back and I just started pushing with both hands. How I got the uterus back in I'll never know, because I didn't have any strength in that shoulder.

When the two weeks were up, the doctor told me to hold my hands out in front of me. When he pushed down on my left hand, it didn't offer much resistance. "Okay" he said, "let's do the surgery."

I spent six weeks with my arm in a sling. Diane and I had moved into a new house at the time, and I was helping get settled. I never thought I'd miss sticking my arm in a cow's butt, but I couldn't wait to get back to work. It reminded me how much I love what I do. Sometimes when you do your job every day you forget how much you enjoy it, so this was a good reminder.

The one animal I never take my eyes off is a bull. Bulls can't be trusted, simple as that. When I'm working with a herd and there's a bull in that herd, I'm starting with three strikes against me: I'm a stranger, I work with his ladies, and most of the time I smell like blood. As far as a bull is concerned, I'm just a moving target. I'm not scared of them, but I watch them because I know what they can do. You're a bull. Fine; you stay on your side and I'll stay over here on my side. Way, way over here.

I always tell people who work with animals that the most important thing to do for their own safety is to always let the animal know where they are; conversely, when there is a bull in the yard, I always want to know where it is. I've never been in a situation where I feared for my life, but I have been helped over gates by bulls many times. We had an Amish farmer who was moving, so all his cattle had to be tested for tuberculosis. I had a young female college student helping me at the time. We tested the cows and had to examine the bull. He was in the pen with a long chain on his nose ring, so I grabbed hold of the chain and wrapped it tight around a post and then handed the end to this student. I hopped into the pen and injected the bull with the serum, and just as I got done the student helper yelled, "I can't hold him." The bull pulled the chain out of her hand. I didn't hesitate a second: I took one, two big jumps, and then I took a six-foot jump and went over that fence. It was about the closest call of my whole career; that bull helped me a little: He pressed his head against my boot and pushed it against the fence as I went over it, and that boot came right off my foot as I jumped for safety.

Bulls are serious about hurting you. They're nasty sons of guns. They don't want anybody encroaching on their territory. A bull's job is to protect his ladies, and that's what he's going to do. A bull will kill you by knocking you down, kneeling over the top of you on his knees, and crushing you with his head. A bull will crush every bone in your body. There was a farmer outside Grand Rapids whose herd was being tested for TB, and he went out in the pasture to get his bull. When the farmer didn't come back, his people went looking for him and found his body. The bull knew this guy—this was the person who fed him every day—but the bull must have felt threatened and attacked him. This was one of those rare cases when the animal did bite the hand that fed it.

Back in Harbor Beach one time, I was on a farm treating a down cow with milk fever. I was walking toward the cow carrying a bucket filled with calcium in warm water. I took a few steps and heard *Rrrrrrrr . . .* and I thought, *Oh my gosh, here comes the bull.* Actually, I thought a lot of four-letter words.

I did not know there was a bull in the herd, and he'd caught me out in the middle of the pen. The only thing between us was the down cow. I thought, *Okay, to get me, you've got to come over that cow.* We had started to play ring-around-the-Elsie when the farmer, who was there watching with his four-teen-year-old son, shouted to me, "Oh, he's just a young bull. He's just loud." Sure, but I noticed he was shouting it to me from outside the pen.

"You get that bull," I told him. "You get that bull out of here right now or I'm leaving." Truthfully, right at that moment, as long as that cow was between me and this bull, I wasn't going anywhere. "Get the bull out of here and shut the door."

I have to give him credit: He hopped into the pen and chased that bull away. He put the bull on the other side of the barn and shut the door. It was like a garage door or a store security door, made of metal and about eight feet high and twelve feet wide, and it rolled closed. *Okay,* I thought. *Okay, now I can take care of that cow.* And just as I finished, that bull came through the door. He knocked it right off its rollers with his head and pushed it up. I got out of that pen real quick. The next morning the farmer called back to tell us the cow hadn't gotten up yet. Another vet in the office was going to go out there, and I warned him, "Don't go in the pen until somebody is there with a pitchfork."

When he came back, he told me, "Somebody's going to get hurt with that bull." Several weeks later we read in the paper that the bull had gone after the farmer's son. The son got his leg broken and suffered a bunch of cracked ribs, but he was lucky, he was still alive.

There was only one bull that I ever liked. I had a husband and wife who did dairying, and they had a four-year-old Holstein bull that was a pet. A Jersey bull is meaner than a junkyard dog, but the Holstein bulls can be okay. When you walked into their barn, this bull just came right up to you. He never bellowed at anybody and was never threatening. But before he let you go to work with the cows, he insisted that you scratch his head. He was firm about that: *You want to work with my ladies, you better scratch my head.* It turned out that he wasn't a very good bull. When we did pregnancy tests, none of the cows were pregnant. He was just too big and friendly and he couldn't care less, so they had to buy a younger bull to get the cows pregnant. But it was very hard for them to sell him because he had become such a nice pet.

One thing you do get used to is getting smacked in the face or the back by tails. Animals use their tails to swat at things that annoy them—vets, for example. We had a farmer who also was a songwriter and a poet, and he wrote in a poem one time that he always wondered how the doggone cow can have eyes in its tail and know exactly where your face is! When a cow starts swishing her tail really fast, she's telling you to watch out: Whatever you're doing, she doesn't like it. A cow tail hurts more than a horse tail when it hits you because it has a lot less hair covering it. A tail can sting you for a few seconds, but the only real damage it can do is if it catches you in the eye. On our farm in the Netherlands my father cut the hair off the cows' tails, because if the tail dragged on the floor it would become caked with manure, which gets hard and hurts when you get hit with it. A cow always wants to know where you are; again, when you're standing close to an animal, its tail usually will hit you in the back of your head. Sometimes, though, you'll turn your head at just the wrong time, and *swoosh!* It always ticks me off when I get hit with a wet tail. *Darn, she got me again.*

At one point farmers used to dock, or cut, cows' tails because they believed it kept them cleaner. That proved to be of no value, so they don't do it anymore. Animals don't need their tails to survive. There are dogs and cats that are born without a tail, and other dogs' tails are cut off. Our dog Maeson did fine when she lost her tail in an accident with a car door.

Probably the most common injury vets face is being bitten by a dog. I don't get bit much anymore, but I did have one associate who, for some reason, dogs loved to bite. Maybe they talk about it—*Did you bite him yet? Go ahead, he doesn't mind.* It seems like every time I turn around he's at the sink flushing it with lots of cold water and an antiseptic. We get a lot of big dogs in the clinic. In fact, of all the different animals we treat in the clinic, the ones I like dealing with the least are unsocialized dogs. They're scared and they don't trust too many people, and so they try to protect themselves. Unsocialized animals are the hardest patients for us to treat in the clinic. Sometimes they try to make a break for it, but when they see they can't get away, they start snapping at anyone who comes close to them. What I usually do is try to look them right in the eyes, get their attention. If you're looking directly into an animal's eyes, it rarely will attack you. Rarely, not never. Then you have to be firm with an animal. The pecking order with animals is pretty short; it's you or it's them. Let them know that you're the master and most of the time they won't challenge for that position. One lady brought in a mutt for examination. She was sitting in our waiting room and the dog was lying underneath her chair. When I walked into the room, the dog didn't even say hello. He just lunged at me, trying to bite me. Well, that's not nice. The lady said, "I'm sorry, he's kind of mean."

"Let me have his leash, please." When she handed me the leash, I told the dog, "You come with me." The dog resisted; he wasn't going anywhere. So I held up the leash in the air until the dog was completely off the ground, and I carried him through the clinic, like a fish on a hook, into the examination room. When I finally put him down, I told him, "You sit." He growled. Okay, so I picked him up again and he swung around a few times. I let him down and told him again to sit. He sat. You can't let an animal boss you. Once that pecking order is established, everybody is happier.

At that time we had a student intern from Michigan State working in the clinic, and he didn't like what I did at all. He told me he'd never before seen a vet pick up an animal on a leash like that. I listened to what he said, and when he was finished, I offered him the leash. "Okay, here he is. You get bit."

You have to let an animal know you're the boss. When clients bring a cat into the clinic in a carrying cage, I'm usually the guy they ask to take it out of the cage. I don't mind; for some reason cats don't scratch me very often. Cats are confident creatures; they believe they're in charge, so you have to show them you're not afraid of them. If they think of you at least as an equal, they won't bother you. There was one cat that we kept in the office that treated all of us as his equal. His name was Midnight, and, obviously, he was a black cat. He was a neutered male that somebody brought to the clinic and never came back to pick up. I think they expected us to find a home for him. Usually that's not possible. If we kept all the cats and dogs people want to get rid of, we would be running a zoo instead of an office. But for some reason this cat stayed. And slowly he gained control of the office. When people came into the clinic he hopped up on the counter and watched them. Midnight wasn't afraid of anything. Sometimes a dog would bark and Midnight would just look at it from his perch on the counter as if to tell the dog, *Don't waste your bark—you can't get me.*

Midnight eventually got all of us well trained. When he was ready to eat, he would walk over to the electric can opener and press down on the lever with his paw. As soon as we heard the sound of that motor, somebody would get up and open a can of cat food for him. He didn't have much patience, though. After pressing down on the lever, he would turn around to see who was responding to it, and if nobody was moving fast enough, he would press it again, and continue pressing it until he was fed.

Actually, it isn't just the physical injuries vets have to careful about; there are also diseases that can be passed from animals to humans. When you're working in the type of generally unsanitary conditions we face every day, it isn't unusual for infectious diseases to spread and take hold. When you're standing in manure or reaching inside an animal, you definitely are exposing yourself to a lot of potentially serious problems. When I was starting out, I knew a lot less about protecting myself and took a lot fewer precautions. While I haven't caught a bad case of any of these diseases, like everybody else, I use all the safeguards I can. We all do.

The sister of one of our dairy farm clients got all these little red bumps on her chest and hands that itched terribly. Her doctor told her it was an allergy and prescribed cortisone, but that didn't help at all. In fact, the cortisone actually aggravated it. Finally she came to us. Dr. Brenda and I both recognized it right away. "That's mange," Dr. Brenda said.

I scraped a little bit off her hand and examined it under the microscope. I found the eggs of the scabies mite. "That's what it is," I told her. She went back to her doctor, and this time he gave her the right medicine. Within a short time she was fine.

Humans can get mange from pigs or dogs. One time we had a pregnant lady with a potbelly pig come into the clinic. Dr. Eric examined the pig and told her it had mange, pointing out the spots. "Oh," she said to him, plopping her belly on the table and lifting up her shirt, "so is this mange too?" He turned bright red and practically ran out of the room. Fungal infections, bacterial infections, mange, salmonella, like that woman with the pet iguana got—these conditions can be transmitted from animals to humans, but most of them aren't very serious and can be treated pretty easily.

But there are some diseases that can be dangerous. For example, brucellosis, or Malta fever, is a serious bacterial infection that can be spread through raw milk or meat and sometimes is carried in secretions or even the afterbirth of aborted fetuses. Before we started wearing plastic gloves, it was reasonably common among vets. In cows it will cause abortions; in humans it can cause very high recurrent fevers and muscle pain, and can last for years. We had to be especially careful about poking ourselves with used vaccination needles, which could be contaminated with the bacteria that cause the fever. A live vaccine was created, though, and between inoculating calves and doing herd checks, we've basically eradicated the disease in Michigan. We don't even test for it anymore.

Swine flu also can occasionally be transmitted from pigs to humans, but usually only to people whose immune systems are already weak—the elderly or very young, for example. Pig flu can be very dangerous, but that's just part of the problem. Pigs have so many communicable diseases that the normal small pig farm has just about disappeared. The big concerns have taken over that business. And those farms are bio-secure. Anybody who works in the barn or with the breeding sows— the pigs that give birth to piglets—has to take a shower before going in and after coming out. It's like going into a high-tech lab. We still have pigs going to the fair, but they almost never go back home. The pigs and the fat steers and the sheep don't go home from the fair—they are sold there; the pigs go to slaughter. But because people are showing animals, there are washing stations by every barn and people are urged to use them, because people from the city in particular haven't built up the kind of immunity to animal diseases, especially those carried by pigs, that farmers have. I've never had a problem because I'm around them all the time and I'm careful.

I've been working at the fair for more than thirty years. I make sure the animals that come to the show are healthy, but because of what I do, I won't be a judge. People make enemies that way. This is a serious competition, and I don't ever want anyone thinking I favored the son or daughter of a client over another person. So I just check everybody's animals' health. On a Sunday afternoon in the summer of 2012 I had just gotten done checking all the goats when someone came looking for me. "There's a problem," he said. "You'd better come look at this pig."

That's never a good thing to hear. One sick pig can infect all the others. I followed the young man into another barn, and what I saw there wasn't good. This was a single pig that had been raised by a young man. As I examined it, he told me how much he needed the money he was going to get from selling this animal. I wasn't sure that would be possible. The pig was not doing well. It was a very hot day and he had brought the pig to the fair in an open trailer with the hot sun beating down on the animal. When I checked out the animal, his heart rate was over 150, his temperature was very high, and he was very stressed. "Can you help him?" that young man asked.

"I can try," I told him. The pig did not look good. I gave it some drugs that lasted for a very short period of time. Then I told the superintendent of pigs, "You get here Monday morning, six A.M., and make sure this pig is still alive. Otherwise get it out of here before people come and see a dead pig." We kept treating that pig and it kept getting better. Monday night it was up and eating, and on Tuesday it went into the show ring. By Thursday, when it got sold, it was completely healthy. I had been extra careful about this animal because I didn't want to take the chance that pig might infect other animals or, more dangerously, humans. But it worked out very well.

We've also been fighting TB it seems like forever, but there are still four types of TB bacteria that have survived: avian, marine, bovine, and human, and then there are varieties in between them. We don't see much rabies in the practice, but we know the potential for it is always there; we're always looking out for it, especially among animals that people let loose.

The little things that definitely are communicable from animals to people that we can never eliminate is fleas, lice, and ticks. Especially fleas. There is no way of ever getting rid of them completely. For animals in very extreme cases, fleas can be deadly. I've actually seen a calf become anemic and die from fleabites. They're more of an irritation than a real danger to humans. They don't like to stay on humans, but before they leave, they bite. There are some good products on the market now, but nothing works perfectly. There are dogs and cats that are just flea incubators, and no matter what you do to those animals, you can't get rid of them. When Dr. Sandra first moved here, she found a nice apartment by the lake. It had been cleaned, it had been fumigated, and it had been empty for at least a couple of months. But when she came to work, she told me that she was allergic to something in that place. She showed me some red bumps, and I told her, "That's not allergies; those are fleabites."

She didn't believe me. She went to a doctor, who told her they were caused by some allergy and put her on cortisone cream and spray. It didn't work at all. I told her again, "It's not working because they're fleabites."

That wasn't possible, she told me. That apartment had been empty for a long time. Fleas couldn't be living there for so long. But eventually she realized I was right. So she had the apartment fumigated again—and the fleas came back again. You can kill all the fleas, but the next spring they'll be back. The larvae get into the carpet or the furniture or the curtains and seems it can live forever. Finally I told her, "You know what you should do? Get a dog. That dog will act as a magnet for fleas when he's in the house. Then you treat the dog with flea products. That'll get rid of them." That's the best remedy you can find. So that's what she did, and it cleared up that problem. Maybe the dog didn't like it so much, but with the flea treatments he was fine.

Ticks you've just got to be careful about. Fleas can jump; ticks sense heat underneath them and drop onto whatever that warm thing is. As long as you look for the ticks and pull them off before they attack, they generally don't cause real problems. All of those little bugs are part of the job we have to deal with.

We get calls at the clinic all the time asking us how to deal with potentially dangerous animals. A lot of these calls involve a neighbor's dog. Diane usually speaks to these people. Sometimes they're hysterical and the first thing she has to do is calm them down. She's real good at that. One woman called up, and at first Diane couldn't understand her because she was crying; but slowly Diane figured out this woman wanted to know if I could tell the difference between bat guano, or bat manure, and mouse droppings. She thought she had a bat in her house, she told Diane, and she believed it had gotten into her bedroom, where it had found her underwear and been attracted to it. She was pretty sure this bat was still hiding somewhere in her bedroom, and since she was having her period she was really afraid the bat was going to come after her and bite her. That's why she was too scared to go to bed at night. She was calling because she had found a little piece of feces that she thought had probably been left by this bat and had put it on top of her washing machine so she wouldn't lose it before showing it to me.

Diane takes every call seriously.

Unfortunately, the woman continued, her boyfriend was having someone over, so he cleaned up the place and threw the feces away. She had searched all over for it, but she couldn't find it.

Diane spoke with her calmly, asking her questions, explaining things, and offering some suggestions. It seemed like every time she had this woman calmed down, she suddenly would ask, "But what if it comes after me?" and start crying again. Diane finally convinced her to ask her father, who lived only a few blocks away, to come over and see if he could find the bat. They were on the phone for more than forty-five minutes. The woman promised she would call back if they couldn't get rid of the bat. The fact that we never heard from her again made Diane very happy—whether they got that bat or not.

Animals can be dangerous. Animals can kill people. There are a lot of dangerous animals out there—and I have seen them while consulting with the different law enforcement agencies. In rural areas vets are often asked to work with different public agencies. I have been working with various public agencies in the area for decades. Whenever there's a problem that involves animals, I get called: "Doc, can you come down and help us out?"

We had a case in 2013 in which an infant was left alone in the living room by his mother for a few minutes. He was in one of those bouncy chairs, so she thought he would be safe. But when the mother came back, she found the child lying out on the balcony. She rushed him to a Grand Rapids hospital; fortunately, his wounds weren't too serious. There was a pit bull in the house and the police suspected that this dog actually dragged the child out of the bouncy chair, brought it out to the balcony to its nest, and mauled it.

When the baby's parents saw what had happened, they panicked. They put the dog in a cage and drove it about fifteen miles out of town, then dumped it by the side of the road. When the hospital reported the baby's injuries, the police went out and found the dog and brought it to the dog pound. Because the dog had not been vaccinated, it was put in quarantine. Two days later it came down with parvo, a highly contagious virus. The pound wouldn't treat the virus because the dog was in quarantine; instead, the dog was euthanized. Well, if the dog had attacked that baby, it would have been euthanized anyway, but as I discovered, that wasn't what happened.

Everybody knows that pit bulls have a reputation for being very dangerous. I've treated a lot of them, and it may be true that they have more brawn than brain, but they are not bad dogs. It's the people who don't take care of them. I've learned how to deal with pit bulls: When a new client brings a dog to the clinic, I never just approach it. I give it a little time to smell me, to get used to me. I always talk to the owner while letting my hands hang at my sides. Then I'll go down on one knee so I can talk to the dog at eye level. And when I do finally reach for the dog, I do it slowly and give the dog a chance to sniff my hand. I've never had a problem with an overly aggressive pit bull.

There have been many cases in which pit bulls did attack people, so at first this looked like it was going to be a pretty simple case. The police brought the dog remains to me as well as pictures of the wounds on the child and asked me to confirm their belief that the dog had attacked this baby. They wanted me to make an imprint of the dog's jaw so it could be compared to the bite marks on the child. But as soon as I looked at the dog and the photographs, I knew there was something wrong.

The dog was a pit bull cross; there was a little bit of a boxer in there, so he had a tremendous underbite. His bottom jaw was almost two inches longer than it should have been. "Those aren't teeth marks," I told the police. "Those are claw marks." Then I told them what I thought probably happened. "This baby was crying, *I want my mommy,* and the pit bull wanted to help him. I know that's not what people believe, but pit bulls love humans. They can be wonderful dogs. In the right situation, a pit bull will give up its life to protect a human. So I'm guessing this dog heard the baby crying and wanted to take care of it. They do that by touching. The dog's claws had barely scratched the skin. The wounds weren't very deep at all." And the wounds certainly couldn't be matched to the dog's teeth marks. If that dog had been attacking the baby, he would've grabbed hold of an arm or a leg. And once it had grabbed hold, it would not have let go. Those dogs were bred to grab bulls by the nose, so if it had wanted to hurt that baby, it would have. The fact that the child was found perfectly safe with the dog nearby told me everything I needed to know. As far as I was concerned—and I explained this to the police—that dog was exercising its own motherly instinct; it was trying to soothe a crying baby, and because of that, the dog died. If that infant's parents hadn't left it alone, none of this would have happened. In this situation I found myself being the advocate for the animal, not that it did any good.

The police also asked me to conduct an autopsy on the dog; they wanted me to remove the brain so it could be tested for rabies. All those tests came back negative. Finally they wanted me to cut off the dog's head and feet and preserve them in the event this case went to trial. Instead, we saved the whole dog. That whole case was a tragedy for everybody.

I was also brought into a case by a pathologist out of Grand Rapids. A two-year-old girl had died, and the officers who had gone to her house had been stunned. People might have called it a pigsty, but pigs are clean animals; they keep the places they eat and sleep clean. The police officers said this little girl's house was overrun by dogs and cats, and nobody had bothered to clean up their stool. The cops said they could scrape the manure right off the carpet and the kids were crawling through it.

This wasn't the fault of any animal, but a child had died. The pathologist had found spots on the child's liver that he thought might be worms that had been caused by exposure to the fecal matter. Then he sent us a sample of the stool they'd scraped off the floor to see if we could confirm the presence of worms. I looked at the sample under a microscope, and it was just loaded with worms' eggs.

A few weeks later the pathologist sent me pictures of the liver—with a note explaining that he hadn't found any worms at all in it. Instead he'd found a lot of little white spots that he couldn't identify. He couldn't confirm the cause of the child's death and asked me to help.

When I looked at the liver sample, I knew exactly what had happened. I knew because I had seen the same thing years earlier when I'd done some autopsies on pigs. At that time we were struggling to keep worms out of pigs. We didn't have the drugs we now have, so it was a real problem. What would happen was that roundworm larvae would crawl through the pig's body, right into the liver. The larvae would die there and the result would be scar tissue. I told the pathologist, "You will not find worms in those white spots. That's scar tissue; it's where the larvae died. But those white spots mean the liver is infected." That little girl's liver was filled with white spots, and that's why she died.

Sometimes it's just too easy to blame animals for the actions of humans. Honestly, there have been many times in my career when instead of protecting people from animals, I found myself protecting animals from people. I was in the clinic one morning when an officer from the Department of Natural Resources showed up with about a dozen cages in a trailer. Inside each cage was a pretty unhappy-looking raccoon. Raccoons can be a nuisance, but generally if you leave them alone, they'll leave you alone. I had never seen anything like this. I asked him, "Now, what in the world are you doing with these things?"

"We found a guy who was trapping live raccoons," he said. "He was selling them in Kentucky."

Selling raccoons in Kentucky? That sounded a bit like a sorry joke. Unless something very strange had been going on,

I knew that there was no shortage of raccoons in Kentucky. "Why would anybody want to buy a raccoon?" I asked.

"Those Kentucky hunters will shoot anything that comes into their yard," he explained. "But they all have dogs that want to hunt raccoon, and there's not enough there for them. So he was selling them to these hunters, who would turn them loose, then hunt them with their dogs." While it was legal to shoot raccoons in Michigan, it was not legal to trap them and sell them, because they belong to the state of Michigan.

So now the state of Michigan was the proud owner of a truckload of raccoons. "What are you going to do with them?" I asked.

He didn't exactly know. "That's why I'm here. How do they look to you?"

They looked like healthy and pretty angry raccoons to me. "Well, they all look mean," I told him. "But they all look healthy enough that if you set 'em loose they'll be fine."

He nodded. "I think that's what I'll do, then."

"Don't get bit," I cautioned him.

I enjoy hunting, but this wasn't hunting; this was just cruelty to those animals. I guess that shouldn't surprise me anymore, but it does still amaze me that people can be so cruel to animals. We had a cat named Tripod for several years, and he was named that because he had only three legs. Someone had found him and brought him in. He had a broken leg that couldn't be saved, so we amputated it. The people who brought him in couldn't afford to keep him, so we ended up taking him. We used to let our cats out at night if they wanted to go. One night not too long after Charles had started driving, he was on his way to pick up a pizza when he saw Tripod crossing the road—and then saw another car swerve to purposely hit the cat. He couldn't believe that anyone could be that cruel. Well, that's one place where animals seem to have more sense than people. I've never known an animal to hurt another animal for absolutely no reason. Animals might be protecting themselves or their family, they might be hungry, or they might be territorial, but just to hurt another living thing? No, that doesn't happen in nature. So I don't think it's correct for someone to refer to an awful person as an "animal."

Many years ago, we rescued a beautiful metallic black Great Dane. She was a nice dog; while she wasn't exactly timid, she was docile. She attached herself to Diane, who referred to her as "my black shadow." Wherever Diane went, this dog was right there behind her. It was the funniest thing; when Diane was vacuuming, she'd come into the room and that dog would be a step behind her.

On Thanksgiving Day we went to Diane's mother's place. We left the dog at home in the garage with an open door leading out to the fenced-in backyard, so she could get outside if she needed to. By the time we got home it was dark. We couldn't find her; she wasn't in the garage or the backyard. That was real strange; there was no reason she would have left the backyard. So we got in the car and drove around looking for her. We were concerned, but there was nothing we could do that night.

I got up early the next morning to look for her. I found her lying by our mailbox next to the road. Someone had shot her with a high-powered rifle. We never had a clue why she was out there or why someone would have done that to such a sweet animal. It was deer season, but a black dog that size couldn't possibly have been mistaken for a deer. I didn't understand that at all. Every year in the clinic we see animals hurt in hunting accidents, but those are accidents. This had to be intentional—had to be.

I've rarely seen an animal try to hurt a person for no reason, but I have seen the evidence of what people will do to animals. Having spent my life among animals, I have a lot of respect for them. Back in the Netherlands after the war, people didn't have much, so in the summertime in particular they came out to the farm to try to get their strength back. My mother cooked for them and we let him see the animals. It seemed like it was good for them. The horses we had, we broke to ride. And these city kids came out there and wanted to ride a horse. We didn't have saddles, so they rode bareback. I don't think I was more than seven or eight years old when these teenagers showed up. We put one of them on a horse and he started riding. He didn't know what he was doing, but once the horse settled in, it start trotting slowly. That teenager couldn't hold on, so he slipped off the horse and fell underneath its four legs. That horse stopped dead in its tracks. It didn't move. That boy crawled out from underneath and as soon as he was clear that horse took off like a battleship. But it had been so careful not to step on the boy. Even at that young age I remember being aware of that, even if I didn't quite understand it. I've always loved horses, and it's possible my love for them began that day.

I still see that type of behavior pretty often not far from the clinic. In 2004 Jodi and Ty Stuber founded the nonprofit HopeWell Ranch in Weidman, and I became their vet. What they do there is have horses work with people of all ages and disabilities, but especially young people with physical and learning disabilities, especially autism. They have close to twenty horses as well as different small animals, and we take care of them all; I cut their rabbits' teeth and I take care of their horses. Seeing those horses working with those kids is amazing. In particular, I remember a case with a boy who hardly was talking. They brought him out next to a horse and told him to go ahead and pet the horse. He was pretty tentative at first—a big horse can be mighty imposing for a small boy—but he got up the courage and began petting it. And then in response, that horse bent its head way down and tucked that child underneath its head and between its front legs. It was as if it was protecting him. It was an unbelievable thing to see. Horses make great therapy animals; when you see a child who can't walk or has difficulty walking on his or her own riding on a big horse, moving freely and easily in any direction he or she wants, just like any other kid, even if it's for only a few minutes, it makes your heart burst.

Animals can even be taught to get along with other types of animals. We see that all the time. For a time we kept a few sheep at home. We had a ram we named Herman—Herman the ram. Rams are supposed to be pretty mean—that's probably why they're called rams—but Herman was as nice an animal as you could want to meet. When he saw people coming, he would run up to them and bang them gently with his head, demanding that they scratch his head. Well, I don't know exactly what happened between Herman and the sheep, but he just didn't want to live with his ladies anymore. So he started hanging out in the stable with the horses and eventually moved in with them. The horses didn't seem to mind at all. And every night when I called the horses to get fed, they came galloping into the barn. We threw down hay for them, and then Herman came trotting in. He did develop a special friendship with one horse and he spent most of his time in that horse's stall. When we finally decided to get rid of the sheep, we couldn't get rid of Herman, so he lived out his life happily with the horses.

Elsie the cow also decided that she preferred to live with the horses. Elsie and the horses weren't as friendly as Herman and the horses were, but there was mutual respect. There were never any problems between them. Then we got a goat. Usually goats and horses get along pretty well, but the horses didn't like this goat at all, and the goat was scared of the horses. But Elsie and the goat became friends. Sometimes the horses tried to gang up on the goat, and that goat ran from them and hid in the safest place it knew—under Elsie. The goat literally stood under the cow and just looked at the horses, and because it was Elsie, the horses left the goat alone.

We have had all types of pets and never had a problem that I can remember with any of them. For me a pet is an animal you can talk to that will respond. At any time, we'll have horses, lots of dogs and cats, some birds and fish and chickens, and sometimes a goat or a sheep. Right now we have five pet peacocks. When people find out we have five peacocks, they're usually surprised, and eventually they ask me why. "Because they're so smart," I tell them. When they ask for an example, I tell them that they're smart enough to get me to take care of them!

The fact is I really love those birds; I love their colors and I love the sounds they make. We've kept peacocks for at least twenty-five years. They're tropical birds, so they have to live in the barn. I feed them corn and minerals, oats, and a lot of dog food. Peacocks love dog food—don't ask! But in springtime a male peacock will pick a spot, and that's it—that's his spot. It stands there with its tail open in a half circle and screeches, and that sound travels for miles. That's its mating call; it means, *Hey ladies, here I am. Don't I have a beautiful tail?*

The female answers that call and they mate; then the female goes off and lays the eggs and takes care of them. The male just stays there, spreads his feathers, and looks good. The peacock's call does sound a little like a person calling for help, so we have had people respond to it, calling to ask if someone at the house is in trouble. We always thank them for responding but explain that the call isn't meant for them. Sometimes when a male is on its spot I walk behind it and quick grab one feather. The bird instantly drops its feathers, turns, and looks at me, as if to ask, *Now, what did you do that for? Can't you see I'm busy looking for girls?* As soon as I leave, its feathers go back up again.

I've never had any problem with those birds. When I drive up to the house in my car, they stand there waiting patiently for me. When I put out their food, they come right up to me; like any animal I've ever known—except those bulls, which might be why they're called bullheaded—they don't bite the hand that feeds them.

The one thing I know is that whatever those birds get from me, I get more from them. When I look around and see my animals, there is a feeling of satisfaction I get that is impossible to describe. I have been so lucky to have been able to spend my life around animals—both my personal life and my professional life. In December 2013 I was asked by Central Michigan University to be one of the speakers at its commencement address. I thought for a long time about what I wanted to tell those young people. I was supposed to speak for ten minutes, and Diane was worried about that, although honestly she knows me enough not to be worried that I wouldn't speak for less than that.

I have learned a lot of lessons doing my job that might be valuable to other people. For example, there are times in life that you're just going to have to stand in a hole filled with manure to get the job done, and when that happens you do it and then you just wash it off and take satisfaction that you did a good job. I thought that maybe I should tell them about the feeling I still get every single time I help bring a calf or a lamb or any type of life into the world, or when I give an animal the treatment it needs; that feeling that, in my small way, I've helped a living creature. But finally when I stood up in front of almost twenty-five hundred people and looked down to see Diane sitting there with her eyes on her watch, I told them that the most important advice I could give them was "Never give up on your dreams. If there are molehills in the way, walk over them. And if your job is like a hobby, then you'll never work a day in your life—and they'll still pay you for it too."

EIGHT

TV or Not TV?

Welcome to Weidman

When Charles first approached me with the idea of doing a reality television show, I certainly didn't take him very seriously. Charles has always had a very good imagination. When he was in third grade, his class had a substitute teacher. Charles was not making it easy for her, and she finally said to him, "Charles, do you want me to call your parents?"

And he looked right at her and told her, "You can't. They died in a fire." The teacher started crying. Then when she found out that Charles had made it up, we were invited to meet with her. Through the years we met a lot of Charles's teachers and principals that way. He never did anything to hurt people, but he was always in the middle of some problem. Charles once described himself as a tornado just ripping through life. When Diane and I insisted we raise sheep to learn the importance of work, we decided we would raise only black sheep. When our kids first started bringing them to the fair, they were the only members of 4-H with black sheep. The judges didn't like them and asked them to bring white sheep.

If somebody told Charles there was something he couldn't do, well, that's exactly what he wanted to do. I can't imagine where he got that from. Charles wanted someone to tell him the difference between black sheep and white sheep. "A sheep is a sheep," he said. Charles finally wore the judges down; he kept bringing his black sheep, and after a while nobody said anything to him anymore. That was Charles; he always liked being the one who stood out. Growing up, he made it clear that he had absolutely no interest in being a vet, no way; instead he wanted to be in the entertainment business. He had started making movies when he was eight years old. After graduating from college in Miami he moved to Los Angeles and started working in the type of jobs young people trying to break into that industry do. Being honest, it never occurred to me—and it probably didn't occur to him for a long time—that there was any part of my world that other people would find entertaining.

Apparently he told his colleague out there, Jon Schroder, and his boss at Nickelodeon, Patrick Garney, crazy stories about his childhood and his family, especially me. I don't know exactly what stories he told them: delivering cows in a blizzard; dressing up as a woman—a woman with a pretty thick mustache—for the community fund-raiser; or the time a policeman stopped me going . . . much too fast in my fancy Plymouth Prowler—but only because he wanted to see that unique car. But the three of them came up with the concept of doing a reality show about the practice. It was left to Charles to try to talk me into participating.

Charles and I have always had a very good, but sometimes loud, relationship. Neither one of us has ever been afraid to express his opinion. I remember one time we were having a discussion and it got louder and louder. Finally Diane got up to leave and said, "You guys go fight somewhere else."

"We're not fighting," I told her. "We're debating."

"Well, you're awfully loud about it."

I agreed, "We're debating loudly. We have to scream to get our point across."

You always help your kids in any way you can, but at first I didn't think this was such a great idea. Or, to be honest, at second or third either. Charles said, "Dad, we should make a reality show about you." I told him it seemed to me that there were enough reality shows on TV. "I know," he agreed, "but they're not real. We want to do a real reality show."

Charles also made the point that overall the entertainment industry hasn't been especially supportive of the family farmer in recent years, and this would give us the chance to show how hard farmers work and how well they treat their animals. He reminded me of the thing I've been saying his whole life: If you don't treat animals well, they won't treat you well.

Charles didn't exactly dare me to do it, but he made it clear it was sort of a challenge. Basically, I thought, *Why not? It'll never get off the ground.* And no matter what happened, for me this was a good opportunity to spend some time with my son, whom Diane and I didn't get to see as often as we liked. So in the summer of 2010 Charles came out to Michigan with three other people to film what is called a "sizzle reel." It's a brief, four- or five-minute film used to sell a show.

They filmed for about seven days and ended with twenty-seven hours of tape. It was nothing special, just me doing my job and a little bit at home. During that time we went on a call to a small dairy farm and discovered a small calf that had broken its leg. The farmer couldn't afford to pay for reconstructive surgery and he didn't want to pay for me to put a cast on the leg. He didn't believe that the leg could ever support the full weight of a dairy cow, so he asked me to put the calf down. But with the farmer's okay I used a long piece of PVC pipe as a splint and duct-taped it around the calf's leg. I went back a couple of weeks later and that little calf was hobbling around just fine. It was still limping, but it definitely was going to live. The farmer didn't allow the crew to film any of that, but it made a real impression on them, and those people who still work on the show talk about it occasionally.

One afternoon they filmed me with my horses; one of them, the only one left that we'd brought from the Netherlands, was real friendly. She comes right up to me and I can handle her without a halter. She never fights me, whatever I want to do. I happen to love the smell of horses, and I know that horses greet each other by blowing into each other's nostrils. So while they were filming she came up to greet me and I put my head against her muzzle. In the photograph it looked like I was kissing this horse. I had no problem with that.

The truth is, I have never had any problem making fun of myself. That never bothered me. But please, don't ever call a large-animal vet a ham. That's bad for business. Diane was a member of an organization called the Jaycettes, the female version of the Junior Chamber of Commerce. One time they had to put on a play for a district meeting and didn't have enough volunteers. Diane told me a friend of ours would dress as a woman and be in it if I would, and that man's wife told him the same thing about me. I agreed—but he backed out. I stuck big balloons under a tight sweater; I wore nylons and put on a blond wig and a short skirt. I can tell you, no man with a mustache who puts balloons under a sweater and pretends to be a woman is going to have any problem kissing a horse.

Charles and Jon began taking this sizzle reel around to the different cable networks trying to sell the show. As I'd predicted, there wasn't a lot of interest in a show about a seventy-year-old vet kissing horses and getting very familiar with cows. They got turned down by a lot of places. One cable network executive explained to them, "We want people to stay tuned to our programming. This is a channel changer." Other networks were nicer, telling them nobody in the world would be interested in this show. Finally they went to a new channel, Nat Geo Wild, which was going to be all about animals. "He's kind of a funky guy," they said. "And he kisses horses. Maybe we should give it a try."

Charles and Jon came back to Weidman with a ten-person crew and shot four pilot episodes in four weeks. Even then I wasn't taking the whole thing very seriously. My attitude was *Just enjoy this while it's going on. It's a little bit different and it isn't going to last very long.* While some of the people on the crew had been around animals, most of them hadn't, so I did have some fun with them. The thing that caught their attention right away was how easily, and how often, I stuck my hand up a cow's butt. That wasn't exactly something people in the entertainment business see too often; in fact, one day I had a lot of fun with them. I reached deep inside and pulled out a big wad of manure and smelled it. I could hear their *Oooohhhhhh* moans, so I smiled into the camera and told them, "That smells like money to me."

Then we were invited to be at the Television Critics Association, which is a bunch of journalists and bloggers who preview all the new shows and write about them. I was on the stage with a man who hunts big cats in the wild to put radio collars on them, a man in search of the world's sixty deadliest animals, and an Australian who is a crocodile relocator. The relocator catches wild water buffalo in his spare time. When I was up there with him, I was thinking, *What the heck am I doing here with these guys?*

Then all of our shows went on the air. They ran *The Incredible Dr. Pol*—I had nothing to do with that name, by the way, though one time I did ask Diane if she wanted to call me the Incredible Dr. Pol. She didn't. And people watched it. So they ran it again. Then they had a marathon and the audience continued growing bigger and bigger. And eventually the show became Nat Geo Wild's most popular program.

The success of the show pretty much surprised everybody. Instead of the original three people, all of a sudden there were twenty-five people working full-time on the show. I made one rule right at the beginning, and we haven't changed it: The animals come first. I told the crew that I wasn't going to change the way I did my job and it was up to them to keep up with me. "Nature doesn't wait for film crews," I said, "so I'm not going to either." The film crews had a lot to learn about life, and death, on the farm. One time we got a call to go to Dave Livermore's alpaca ranch, because one of his birds was about to have a *cría*—that's the Spanish word for a baby alpaca. When it's born it's called a creation. The crew wanted to film the birth, so they actually camped out there for twenty-four hours just waiting. I was laughing. "You guys can wait forever," I told them. "It isn't going to happen."

"Oh yeah," they told me, "it is."

"Have fun," I said, and when the *cría* wasn't born, they packed up their cameras.

I was on call a week later on a Saturday afternoon when Dave Livermore called me again and told me the *cría*'s head and one leg were out, but the rest wasn't coming. "Is it alive?" I asked him. It was alive. "I'm on my way." Normally the crew doesn't follow me on the weekend, but I called Charles and told him the alpaca was giving birth. Then I got in the car and flew low.

I was there in less than five minutes. I got there before the film crew. That *cría* was too valuable for Dave to wait for some cameras. I pushed the head back in as much as I could and managed to turn it enough to get the other leg out. I pulled the *cría* out alive and kicking. It took me five minutes and I was already cleaning up when Charles and Jon Schroder showed up and saw that little creation being introduced to the world.

It took some time, but we finally figured out the best way to film the show. There are three four-person camera crews: One is supposed to stay with me, the second one is supposed to hopscotch ahead and get to my next appointment to get the lights and cameras set up, and the third crew is with Dr.

Brenda or in the clinic. Probably the hardest thing for the first crew to do is just keep up with me. So I did make a compromise for them; I've slowed down a bit when I drive—but sometimes they still can't keep up. And sometimes they get lost; they get very, very lost.

Also, I go where I'm needed and sometimes that means I don't follow the schedule. The crew will be set up and waiting for me, thinking they got me this time, when we get an emergency farm call. The weather doesn't help them too much either: At least twice we've had to pull their cars out of snowbanks.

When we first started filming the show, the crew had a lot to learn about working in this part of Michigan. But I was impressed right away by their talent and dedication. The first time I worked with cameraman Mark Myers, for example, was a bitterly cold day in winter. I'm used to that weather and wear the proper clothing. The crew was filming an interview outdoors with a client, the wind was howling, and the temperature was dropping. Mark was holding on to a metal rod at the end of the camera; he was losing feeling in his fingers, but he didn't say a word until the interview was completed. Then he went back to the car and put on some hand warmers, but it was a little too late; he never got the feeling back in the end of his pinky. When something like that happened—and believe me, that was not the only time—I began to realize they were serious about this show.

At the beginning, there was some question about how our clients would feel about being filmed, especially our Amish clients. There wasn't much I could do to help there, although most of these people knew me and trusted me. But there have been cases that were filmed that the clients did not want shown for personal reasons. At the beginning of the second season, a client brought in this friendly little basset hound. The owner had left it on a metal chain, which had somehow gotten wrapped around the dog's leg and cut off the circulation. We had to amputate the leg to save that dog's life, but the client refused permission to film it. I didn't blame him. It was an accident, but there were some people who might have blamed him.

Ironically, because the channel isn't carried by our cable network, only those clients with satellite television get to see the show when it is initially broadcast. One time we hosted a kind of marathon viewing for our neighbors and we had videotapes of some of the shows running upstairs and downstairs, but other than that, people in our area generally have to wait until the show is available on the Internet. Because Charles is a producer, he gets unedited versions and sometimes shows them to Diane and me, but often the show gets edited even further after that. We had a friend who brought her dog in and agreed to be filmed. We always tell our clients we have nothing to do with the editing and have no power to decide what's in or what's out. The editors are the people who take the mountain of tape the camera operators shoot and turn it into one entertaining hour. Diane and I are as surprised as anyone else when we see what makes it on the air. The only difference is that when we finally get to see the show, we also know what didn't make it. When we watched the show on Charles's computer, this woman and her dog were in it, so Diane told her she was in the show. Unfortunately, when it was broadcast, though they did show the woman walking up to the clinic with her dog, the whole case was cut out. We felt terrible about that, and since that time we always tell people who ask that we haven't seen the edited version of the show.

I don't really know how other shows work, but for the most part we've kept our crew pretty much together, and we've all gotten to know one another, and respect one another, and in many cases become friends. There have been times when I've had to have them help me. I was on a farm call one time with Charles and field producer Mike Stankevich. I was trying to pull a calf that had decided it wasn't interested in being born. It was fighting me pretty good and I needed people on the calf pullers while I maneuvered it around inside. I had Charles on one end and Mike on the other end, and I was screaming instructions at them. I was not going to lose this calf or its mother. Finally I had them pulling pretty good, and that calf said, *Okay, I'll be born now,* and it came practically shooting out. The second it stopped fighting, Charles and Mike went flying backward and hit the ground. That calf came out alive and ready to start kicking. And Charles and Mike didn't get one frame of film.

Of course I'm going to use crew members if they're there. In March 2014 a dairy farm had a cow struggling to give birth. When I got there I discovered that cow had a twisted uterus and the only way to save it was to get it untwisted and get that calf out of there. The best chance we had to save this cow was for me to grab hold of the calf in the uterus while the cow was rolled, which could untwist it. The client didn't want this filmed, but the crew had come along with me anyway. That was perfect; I needed them to roll the cow. We began rolling that cow back and forth, back and forth. I wasn't about to give up. We rolled it again and again. Finally, on our fifth try, we got the uterus straightened out—and as we did, the tail slipped out of Mike Stankevich's hands and whacked me right in the head. I was able to go in there and pull out the calf, which unfortunately was dead—but we had saved the cow.

We've also had to teach some of the crew members how to be safe around animals. A lot of them grew up with Disney animals, and I don't think any character ever got stomped or had an eye poked in a Disney cartoon. One thing about our camera crew—they always want to get closer; they always want to get the best possible shot. We have had people get knocked over and stepped on—even Charles, who knows better but sort of forgot about it trying to get the best possible story.

I think what has been the hardest thing for the members of the crew to deal with is the fact that in this "real reality" show, the cases don't always have a happy ending. What they probably weren't prepared for, coming from Hollywood, was the reality of dealing with life and death every day, sometimes several times a day. I've had several members of our crew tell me how tough it is for them, at least at first, to see me euthanize an animal. Jon Schroder, who created the show with Charles, told me that sometimes he'd wake up in the morning praying he wouldn't have to witness euthanasia that day. I rarely cry, but I still feel it; a lot of crew members have cried, and occasionally when we're dealing with an old animal they still do. In several instances I've had to put down horses around thirty years old that the owners have had most of their lives. It breaks your heart to see that. While I would never say I'm used to it, I am able to separate my job from my emotions—

and I honestly believe I'm doing a favor for these animals. But for the crew this is all new, and sometimes I see the tears coming down their faces while they're running the camera. Normally there is always a lot of chattering going on—we've always got a lot to talk about—but after I've had to put down a beloved horse or a dog or a cat or almost any kind of pet, the silence can get very, very loud. But as Jon has said, "It's never enjoyable, but it is something you get used to after a while, and you even accept the fact that it's the most humane thing to do for the animal."

Diane and I, and just about everybody who works at the practice, have bonded with the crew. It really has become a nice situation for all of us, and most of the time it's like being with friends. A couple of the crew members even moved their families here while they were shooting. And we've also become involved with their animals. When we first starting shooting the show, Jon had a fifteen-year-old pit bull named Hazel who was very sick. He was told there wasn't too much that could be done for the dog. He drove from Los Angeles to Michigan with that dog, and we were able to keep it alive with a good quality of life for almost another year.

We had another dog, a mixed-breed collie that had been run over by a car just before Thanksgiving in 2013. The county brought it to the clinic and we were able to save its life. Its leg was broken, so we put it in a cast. We had no idea who owned this dog or why it was running free. We waited a couple of weeks and nobody claimed it; in the meantime, two different people on the crew had become attached to it, and both of them said they might want to adopt it. But when some people in town showed interest, they were given preference.

Most of the crew went home for the holiday, and while they were gone I had to amputate the dog's broken leg. The people in town decided they didn't want it anymore and a member of the crew adopted it—and naturally he named it Skippy.

But maybe the real test of the crew's commitment was doing a pregnancy check. This is something we do practically every day, but for people who haven't done it, the thought of putting an arm all the way inside a cow—especially a cow filled with manure—is probably a lot more difficult than the reality of it. Even though Charles had grown up inside the business, he had never done it, for example. So one day after I'd done some pregnancy checks, I asked the crew if they wanted to try it. Not everybody wanted to do it, but several people did. Some of the people had excuses—one of our producers told me, "I don't want to hurt the cow!" "Oh," I said to him, "don't worry about it. You won't. She won't even know you're visiting!" I showed them how to do it and explained what they should expect to feel. I know the thing that surprised everyone was how much room there is inside a cow and how hot it is. Believe me, it's hot in there. We spent about an hour doing it, and months later we were still talking about it.

I don't think it is an especially good way for people to bond, but in our situation it worked very well. Charles was one of the first to go, and he went right ahead and stuck his arm up the cow's butt. Then he smiled as if he'd found something; he hadn't. I remember after producer Pete Berg, pulled his manure-covered arm out, he said, "High five!" And we raised our hands way up in the air and slapped hard—and manure splattered all over the place.

Maybe that would be a good way for some of these Wall Street firms to bring their people together.

Diane and I have been surprised by so many of the things that have happened because of the show, but honestly nothing has been more enjoyable than watching Charles become an important part of it. Initially that wasn't any part of the plan. Charles was the creator and a producer; it wasn't even determined if he'd be on the show. But in small ways at first his role as the comic relief grew and became more important. That's Charles on the screen; the camera brings out that part of his personality. Charles has spent his whole life trying to make people happy, often at his own expense. Diane has warned me, for example, not to mention that video he made in college in which he dressed up as a woman wearing red bikini underpants. Dressed as a woman? Like father like son!

Charles would be the first one to admit that he's always been a bit clumsy, so it doesn't surprise any of us to see him get himself in tough situations. There are people who believe that some of those situations are planned or scripted. Nope— maybe he pushes things just a little, but there has never been any attempt to create a problem. When we started filming the show, they told me, "Be normal; don't try to do anything special; try to forget the camera is there." Well, you never forget that it's there—there's a whole bunch of people following me around—but what happens is that eventually you take it for granted. Only once was there even a suggestion that maybe Charles and I should get into it a little, and I said no. I make fun of Charles, Charles makes fun of me, sometimes we laugh at each other, but we don't fight and we never did. I think what becomes evident is the love we have for each other, even when he's messing up. Again. But we did come very close this one time.

Diane and I had gone to the Netherlands and left the kids in charge. There could have been a very good subtitle for this one: "Every Parent's Nightmare." Oh my gosh, everything went wrong, and when they called us and happened to mention that somehow the gates had been left open and all the horses had got loose, believe me I was very thankful there was an ocean between us.

People ask me, "Did that really happen?" Better they should ask Diane, who was with me when I heard about it.

But what the show has done is brought Charles and me much closer together as adults. I think for the first time we both realize how alike we are. And for the first time we really appreciate each other. Charles used to take every opportunity to not be with me—he never wanted to go out on farm calls; he wanted to be home watching TV or playing movies. As far as he was concerned, riding with me was a punishment, and sometimes he would just sit there and sulk.

Charles and I have talked about how this show has changed our relationship, and the way he described it is, "When you're young, you can't wait to get out of the house. You can't wait to get away to magical places like Los Angeles. My dreams led me out there, but a piece of me always stayed home. It always missed the small-town atmosphere. I still get bored sometimes, but I'm thankful that I've been able to come home and spend a lot of time here."

What also has been really surprising and enjoyable is the fact that all of us are recognized by people who have seen the show. The show is broadcast in twenty-six countries. At first it was just in Mount Pleasant that people would stop us; Diane and I would go into a store and somebody we didn't know would mention to us that they had seen the show and enjoyed it. I think most of our neighbors were pleased that the show was doing a very fair job representing the values of our area and, more important, presenting the small farmer in a positive way. Honestly, that would have been enough for me; I think everyone wants to have the respect of his neighbors. Now we get messages and e-mails from all over the world, from Indonesia, South Africa, Thailand—whoever thought people in Thailand would be interested in cows in Weidman, Michigan? I even heard from my high school math teacher in the Netherlands, who wrote that he remembered me. Honestly, I wasn't sure if that was good or bad. Dr. Sandra got a wedding proposal from someone who watches the show in Ecuador, who thought he would be a very good match for her. But she was already engaged, so she turned him down.

In the fall of 2013 Diane and I went for vacation to a small resort in Montego Bay, Jamaica. Within an hour after we got there, a man came up to me and asked, "Aren't you that veterinarian?"

"I am," I said.

"You're Dr. Pol, right?"

Next thing, another person was showing all of us the Chinese version of our show on his cell phone—and there I was, speaking Mandarin. I never even knew there was a translation for "golly" in Mandarin.

More and more, Diane and I, and also Charles and Dr. Brenda and Dr. Sandra and everyone in the office, have gotten recognized. People just want to shake our hands or ask for an autograph. There have been so many moments that I never could have dreamed would have happened. It's not like I'm a Real Housewife of Mount Pleasant. We're just a rural vet clinic. Several people have actually put meeting us on their bucket list. In 2013 we got a call from the companion of a seventy-eight-year-old Dutch woman who was dying of lung cancer. They lived several hours away, but the companion wanted to surprise her friend with this visit. She waited until the woman was strong enough to make the trip; then started driving, without telling her friend where they were going. As soon as they saw the sign for Weidman, the woman knew, though. The two of them sat on our couch for more than an hour, meeting everybody: Charles and Dr. Brenda, all the people in the office. We spoke mostly in Dutch. She was on oxygen, but there was such a brightness in her eyes. Being able to bring happiness to another person that easily is an unforgettable experience. It reminds me of the impact the show has on people, young people as well as adults. We get so many letters from young people who write to tell us that they never miss the show and when they are older they want to work with animals like we do.

Diane and I are both very happy that this has happened to us later in life. It's a lot of fun and it's certainly ego boosting when people tell me how much they enjoy watching me do my job, but by now we're very well grounded. Our values are pretty strong. Years ago we learned what things make a difference in our lives, and those things aren't going to change at all.

Not only do people recognize us; they often ask us questions about their animals. We literally get calls from people all over the country asking our advice. Legally, I'm not allowed to diagnose animals over the phone, and I wouldn't do it anyway; but what I will do is make some basic suggestions as well as recommend good local vets. Diane almost always speaks to those people and generally gives them commonsense advice. "My dog's got diarrhea—what should I do about it?" "My cat swallowed some chocolate—is that going to hurt him?" There are people who just want someone to talk to, and Diane just can't help talking to them. When they meet Charles, they ask him the same types of questions and Charles has a pretty good answer for most of them: "I'm not a vet, so I'm not qualified to answer that, but that sounds like it could be serious and you should take the animal to a vet." Actually, when we started filming the show, the crew depended on Charles's ability to explain in laymen's terms exactly what was going on. I think it surprised him, and I know it surprised me, to find out how much knowledge he had picked up through the years.

Naturally the vets on the show are the people who get most of the questions, and if we can help, we do. But every animal is different and we would never want to take the risk of diagnosing an animal we haven't examined personally. Similar symptoms can have very different causes, and without seeing and touching an animal, it's often impossible to make the correct diagnosis—and in some cases the wrong diagnosis could lead to terrible results.

There are people who have learned about us by watching the show and have made long drives with their animals to see us. Not too long after the show went on the air, I got a call from a young man who had an eighteen-year-old Australian shepherd, a nice little dog. He had been working in the field and caught the dog chewing on a porcupine. Naturally the dog got countless quills in his mouth. His local vet wanted to do blood work and other tests, estimating the bill at $700. "I don't have that kind of money," he told that vet. "I'm gonna have to shoot my dog." The vet apologized but told him there was nothing he could do. That young man had watched the show and called to see if we could help him. Well, I certainly didn't want him to shoot his dog. "It'd be nice if you could afford to do the blood work," I told him. "There's things we can't do without it." I told him I would use a reversible anesthetic but he would have to sign a paper that he understood and accepted the risks.

He was happy to sign the paper, he said. It was about five o'clock and he was almost fifty miles away. He walked through the door no more than forty-five minutes later. "How come you didn't get a ticket?" I asked him.

"I know the back roads."

I examined the dog and he seemed to be pretty healthy, but dogs that old don't necessarily tolerate anesthetic so well. We gave him a reversible anesthetic that would not last too long and started pulling quills. And pulling more quills. The dog survived the procedure without any problems, and within thirty minutes the two of them walked out the door. But only one of them was wagging his tail.

Not everyone likes the show. There have been some complaints about the way I conduct my practice. To be honest, not everyone in the profession likes me. That's okay; I'm not so crazy about some of the things I hear about other people. Some of these people don't understand the reality of a small practice like ours. They complain that the standard of care is not up to their standards, that we don't have the fancy equipment some of the animal hospitals have, and not everything we do is perfectly sterile. That's nice for them, and for their patients who can afford to pay for that level of care. But after doing this for more than four decades, I can tell you from experience what is the best way to help an animal and its owner. Animals are a lot more resilient than people, and we don't have all the antibiotic-resistant bacteria in the animal world that you find in the human world. In my practice I always believe I'm treating both the animal and the owner of the animal. I will do everything that the owner wants me to do for the animal, but I can't do more than what the client wants me to do. And, who knows, just like in any other profession, there are people who aren't particularly happy to see someone else be successful. I think probably the best way of judging what we do at Pol Veterinary Services is to look at the fact that we've had so many of our clients for so many years and they keep asking us to come back.

The area in which we live, the way we practice medicine, and the business itself have changed drastically since Diane and I opened up in our garage. It's been very sad to watch the old family farms that once took up every foot along the dirt roads disappear, to be replaced most of the time by corporate farms. That's an important part of America that has faded away and isn't coming back. But that corporate influence is present in the small-animal clinics too, as large chains are buying up small practices and forming groups—and for them, profits are the only goal that seems to matter. In addition, a lot of the drugs and supplies that once could be bought only from vets can now be bought in the giant pet stores or purchased online for considerably less money. While that is great for the client, it isn't so good for the vet. In Harbor Beach a pretty high percentage of profits came from selling drugs; that's not true anymore. Rather than selling products, we really are selling our services.

On the other hand, I've always felt the measure of a human being is how he or she treats other people—and animals. After all these years, it is clear that what animals want is to be treated decently, with some degree of respect, and when you do that, they will treat you well. Most animals, by nature, willingly will give whatever they have, from their strength to their loyalty, as long as they are not abused. And it is gratifying to me to be able to say that it is my experience that so many young people—our future—seem to understand this and take care of their animals with compassion, good sense, and respect.

I'm not really a collector of stuff, but for many years I have collected old veterinary books, and sometimes I just like to browse through them to see how vets treated animals as many as 150 years ago. It never ceases to amaze me how much those early vets could do with such simple tools. And when I do look at these books, there is one thing that seems to come through clearly to me: how much these men have in common with me and almost all the other vets I know. We may not always get along so well, we may not always agree on the best way to treat an animal—but the compassion seems to be just as intense today as it was much more than a century ago. This is a profession that people just don't go into unless they care about animals. It's not a profession you go into to make your fortune; that isn't going to happen. It's not a profession you go into to earn the gratitude of your patients; believe me, I've had cows kick at me the next time I saw them after saving their lives. And it's not a profession anybody goes into because of the prestige or the comfort; believe me, I've spent a lot more time lying in the mud with my shirt off on freezing-cold or sweltering-hot days with my hand inside an animal than I have in the air-conditioned clinic. So the question is, Why do people become vets?

I became a vet because it was the only thing I ever wanted to do. Obviously, no animal has ever paid me one penny for the work I've done. In fact, the animals I treat may know my scent, but they sure don't know my name. What they have given me, though, is the most incredible satisfaction imaginable. And I am still thankful for that every single day.

In our wildest dreams, Diane and I could never have anticipated that we would one day have our own successful television show, write a bestselling book, have people come from all over the country to visit our little practice, and be recognized wherever we go in the world. But with all the wonderful things that have happened to us since Nat Geo Wild began broadcasting *The Incredible Dr. Pol*, we have to admit there is one thing that gives us the most satisfaction: Our son Charles has a regular job.

Every parent knows exactly what I mean. What makes all of the wonderful things that have happened to us even more enjoyable is the fact that our success is all Charles's doing. It was his vision. He was the one who believed his father was strange enough that other people would find him entertaining. I decided to take that as a compliment. I don't kid myself (and if I did there are a lot of people who would remind me): The reason our show has been so successful isn't because of my good looks, my clever jokes, or my sophisticated demeanor. It's because the whole audience and I share one very important bond: We love and care about animals and want them to be as healthy and pain-free as possible. I can be a little gruff, I speak funny, and sometimes I'm probably a little too blunt—

that's why people describe me as a "real character"—but I've learned that what comes through to people about me, more than anything else, is the compassion that I have for my patients. That means both my two-legged and four-legged patients.

Among the many things that Diane and I are grateful for is the fact that all this attention and this media popularity came later in our lives, long after we'd figured out those difficult questions: Who are we and what do we want to be? It hasn't changed much in our lives—except for the fact that when I make a barn call there are often two or three cars behind me filled with crew members. I can say with 100 percent honesty that the only difference this attention has made in our lives is that it has enabled us to meet a lot more nice people than we otherwise might have.

While very little has changed for us in Michigan, when we do leave home we often meet fans of the show and people who have enjoyed this book. What might be a little surprising is that a lot of times it is young people who recognize me first and tell their parents. One thing though: I was warned that people were going to ask me, "Are you Dr. Pol?" That hasn't happened that much; instead, they point a finger at me, smile, and say, "You're Doctor Pol!" I guess there aren't that many other people they could mistake me for.

When we do stop to talk, our conversations almost always begin with "What happened to that dog . . . ?" or cat or horse or even cow. I don't think most people ever believed they would care about the health of a cow, or would be affected when an animal they see on television or read about has to be put down.

After we discuss the show or the book, almost inevitably these people want to tell me about their own animals and ask me questions about them or their own vets. Maybe other TV stars get shown photographs of cute babies or pretty girls; people love to show me the photographs of their pets. I don't mind that at all; I've spent my whole life caring for animals and loving my own animals. I'm no different than the people who enjoy the show or the book; I don't think there are too many things that make me happier than one of my horses or dogs happily wagging its tail or nuzzling me or brushing up against me. That's their way of saying, "You're all right, I like your scent!"

People ask me why their dog is gnawing at his leg or why their cat likes to be under the covers; and sometimes they talk about their pet's condition and ask me if their vet is doing a good job. While I explain that I wouldn't diagnose any animal without personally examining it, I often tell them there are a few things about living or working with an animal that can be applied anywhere. The first is that animals are pretty darn smart; they can tell who cares about their safety and their health. The most important treatment anyone can provide for their pet—or equally in my business, their farm animal—is simply to let them know that you care about them. For a farmer that means doing things like keeping their barn clean and making sure their stock is fed and gets proper care; for most of us it means making sure our pets are fed, treated well, and have shelter on the coldest nights. An animal will let you know when it trusts you. Scared, wary animals don't make productive farm animals and they won't be good pets.

When they ask me about their vets I tell them how many

wonderful, dedicated men and women there are in this profession. Just as with farmers who depend on vets to help them maintain their business, it's important they find a vet they can trust, who is concerned for both his two-legged and four-legged patients.

We also continue to have visitors coming into the double-wide or sending me books that they would like autographed. That's also a nice difference for me, as until recently the only place people wanted my signature was on all the monthly checks.

Appearing on television, writing a bestselling book, and working with our son has been very rewarding for Diane and me. We have appreciated every single moment of this experience. And every once in a while I kind of pause and wonder why it has happened. And the answer, I think, goes back to the values that our family has always lived by; we believe in working to the best of our ability, being fair and honest, never forgetting how important it is to laugh at ourselves—and Charles—sometimes, and finally, treating all of the creatures on this earth with dignity, respect, and love.

ACKNOWLEDGMENTS

DR. POL

I would like to acknowledge those who shaped my life so that this book could become a reality.

My parents, Harm and Klaasje Pol, who taught me that animals should be an integral part in everybody's life, but became especially so in my life.

My brothers and sisters who helped raise me and especially my brother Jan and my sister Hennie, who reminded me about events and remembered things about my youth that I had forgotten.

Dr. Van der Eyck, who introduced me to veterinary medicine, and Dr. Drysdale, who introduced me to veterinary medicine in the United States.

Dr. Hentschl and Dr. Arbaugh, who helped me in my first job.

All my associates through the years who helped build this practice to what it is now.

My wife, Diane, who has stood by me throughout all these crazy years and kept the whole family together, despite all the interruptions that happened all the time.

ACKNOWLEDGMENTS

Our children, Diane Jr., Kathy, and Charles, who are successful in their own businesses and are still a big part in our lives!

All our clients throughout the forty-plus years who let me treat their animals and trusted me that I would do my best for them.

And a big thanks to the clients in these last years for their patience to make this show and book a reality.

Also thanks to David Fisher, who organized all my memories and put them on paper.

DAVID FISHER

I would like to acknowledge my longtime colleague, Bill Shinker, for his vision in seeing what this book could be; our editor, Brooke Carey, for her extraordinary persistence and guidance under tremendous pressure; and editorial assistant Leslie Hansen for her continued calm and encouragement for helping make make this book a reality.

I am grateful to Charles Pol for . . . well, for everything he has done, which includes . . . everything. It is completely accurate to say that this book would never have happened without him.

I am fortunate enough to have the services of Casson Masters' Scribecorps. Every nonfiction writer needs a transcription service that can be depended upon completely and is there to do that little extra that makes a writer's life easier, and that is Scribecorps.

It is the pets of my life that helped make me appreciate the truly incredible Jan and Diane Pol, both the cats and the dogs, but it was Belle who sat with me as I wrote every single word.

In every book I write I acknowledge the assistance of my wife, Laura Stevens, and that is appropriate. Her loving support is the foundation of every page. I am a truly lucky man to have found her.